THE NEW ENGLAND COMPANY 1649–1776

THE NEW ENGLAND COMPANY 1649-1776

MISSIONARY SOCIETY TO THE AMERICAN INDIANS

WILLIAM KELLAWAY

GREENWOOD PRESS, PUBLISHERS
WESTPORT, CONNECTICUT

Library of Congress Cataloging in Publication Data

Kellaway, William.
The New England Company, 1649-1776.

Reprint of the ed. published by Longmans, London.
"List of manuscript sources": p.
Includes index.
1. Indians of North America--Missions. 2. Society for Propagation of the Gospel in New England. I. Title.
E98.M6K28 1975 266'.5'90974 74-33895
ISBN 0-8371-7995-5

Originally published in 1961 by Longmans, Green and Co., Ltd., London

Reprinted with the permission of Longman Group Limited

Reprinted in 1975 by Greenwood Press,
a division of Williamhouse-Regency Inc.

Library of Congress Catalog Card Number 74-33895

ISBN 0-8371-7995-5

Printed in the United States of America

CONTENTS

ABBREVIATIONS

Acts	*Acts of the Commissioners of the United Colonies*, ed. David Pulsifer. 2 vol. (Records of the Colony of New Plymouth in New England, IX & X; Boston, 1859).
C.S.M.	*Publications of the Colonial Society of Massachusetts* (Boston, Mass., from 1895).
C.S.P. Col.	*Calendar of State Papers, Colonial series, America and West Indies* (from 1860).
Conn. H.S.	*Collections of the Connecticut Historical Society*. 24 vol. (Hartford, 1860–1932).
D.A.B.	*Dictionary of American Biography*. 21 vol. (1928–37).
M.H.S.	Massachusetts Historical Society.
Ms.	Unless otherwise stated, Ms. followed by a number refers to a unit in the New England Company's archives deposited at the Guildhall Library, London.
N.E.H.G.R.	*New England Historical and Genealogical Register* (Boston, Mass., from 1847).
P.C.C.	Prerogative Court of Canterbury.
P.R.O.	Public Record Office, London.
Sibley	J. L. Sibley and C. K. Shipton, *Biographical Sketches of Graduates of Harvard University* (Cambridge, Mass., from 1873).
S.P.G.	Society for the Propagation of the Gospel in Foreign Parts.
S.S.P.C.K.	Society in Scotland for Propagating Christian Knowledge.
Univ. of Va.	University of Virginia, Alderman Library.

PREFACE

This is not an official history of the New England Company and any views expressed in it are my own. However, I am deeply indebted to the Company's Court for permission to make use of its records. Although they are far from complete, these records provide the most important source for my book; indeed it would have been impossible to write it without them.

The American colonial period saw numerous attempts to convert the Indians of New England, most of which were supported by the New England Company; but a number were not and these, for the most part, fall outside the scope of this study. It has not even been possible to mention every missionary in the Company's employ, especially those working during the middle decades of the eighteenth century, a period for which the records are especially uneven. Where no record of payment to a particular missionary occurs, I have generally assumed that he was not employed by the Company.

In quoting from manuscript sources, I have tried to retain the spelling and capitalization of the original, but have usually extended contractions. I am indebted to the following institutions for permission to quote from records in their custody: the Alderman Library, University of Virginia, the Massachusetts Historical Society, Dr. Williams's Library, the Royal Society and the Society for the Propagation of the Gospel in Foreign Parts.

I have received encouragement from many people, from my former colleagues at Guildhall Library, and above all from Dr. A. E. J. Hollaender. Dr. Michael G. Hall drew my attention to the Company's Letter book in the Alderman Library of the University of Virginia. Dr. Stephen T. Riley kindly supplied microfilms of manuscripts in the Library of the Massachusetts Historical Society. Professor Carl Bridenbaugh read my typescript and made a number of useful suggestions. A. H. Woolrych offered invaluable criticism of the first chapter, and A. G. Watson and Mrs. P. M. Jacobs helped me with the proofs. To all these people my thanks are due.

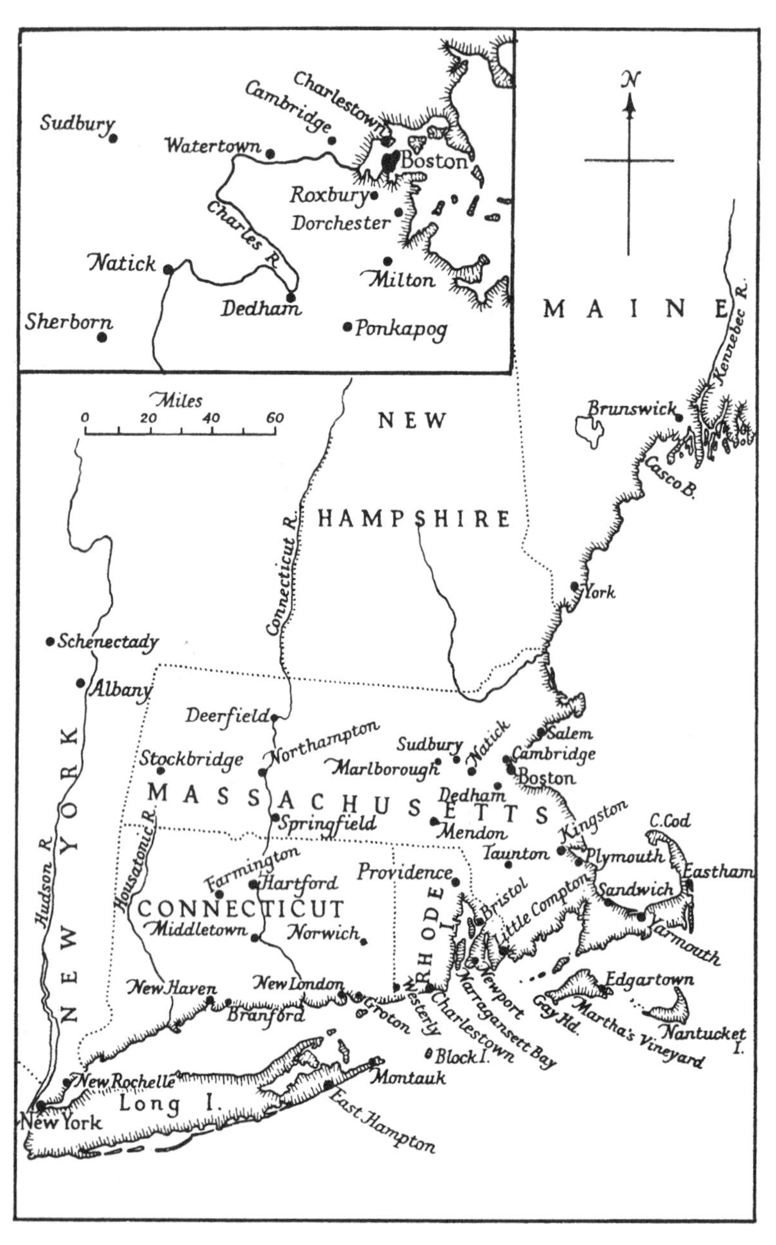

New England with an inset of Boston and its environs

1

Introduction

THE New England Company is the oldest English Protestant missionary society. It was founded in 1649 by the Long Parliament, and had as its aim the conversion of the Indians in New England. For more than one hundred and twenty years, indeed until the American War of Independence, this small English body financed missionaries there; since then, it has continued its work in Canada. For its first fifty years it was alone in the field and even during the eighteenth century other missionary societies only partially concerned themselves with the Indians. The Company's function was a simple one: it collected and invested funds, the interest from which was sent annually to commissioners in New England, who paid the missionaries' salaries. The following chapters deal in turn with the Company in England and the Commissioners and missionaries in America, for the New England Company offers in fact a remarkable early instance of Anglo-American co-operation.

The project of converting the Indians was current in England long before the founding of the New England Company. Ever since English seamen first set foot on the North American shore the clergy at home had preached and written of it, and it had figured regularly in the arguments of the early advocates of colonization. The enlargement of Christ's kingdom and the enrichment of England persuaded by turns, and no vision of empire appealed more to that age than this of Englishmen carrying the banners of the Protestant religion to the New World and placing there a check upon both Spanish and Catholic aggrandizement.[1] Richard Hakluyt warned his fellow countrymen that the conversion of the heathen was an imperative duty whose neglect would

[1] L. B. Wright, *Religion and Empire. The Alliance between Piety and Commerce in English Expansion, 1558–1625* (Chapel Hill, 1943).

bring about the collapse of colonial enterprises, as was happening in the Spanish colonies where it had been but a hollow papist pretence. He also pointed out that true Protestant converts would be an irrefutable answer to the empty boasts made by the Spanish and Portuguese. And when Englishmen read, in Bartolomé de las Casas, of the cruelties inflicted by the Spanish upon the natives of the West Indies, it became almost a matter of common humanity to rescue them from the Spanish yoke and bring them to the true knowledge of the Gospel.

The conversion of the heathen also found a significant place in any discussion concerning the rights of Englishmen to lands in North America. It was very early acknowledged that the right to settle on the Indians' land must rest either on their consent or on conquest; but in pointing out that only by settling among them could they be made Christian the case was raised to a moral plane. The more extreme claim that God had expressly reserved for English use the land of North America was widely advanced in England by the beginning of the seventeenth century; its corollary — that the Indians had no right to the land — engendered in the minds of some a moral objection to colonization. To this objection the conversion of the Indians provided a ready and convenient answer. As one writer put it, the colonists had no intention of supplanting the natives, but — 'Our intrusion into their possessions shall tend to their great good. . . . First in regard of God the Creator, and of Jesus Christ their Redeemer, if they will beleeve in him: And secondly, in respect of earthly blessings, whereof they have now no comfortable use.'[1]

What made the conversion of the Indians particularly attractive was the 'litle persuasion [that] will serve to effect this matter.'[2] It was thought that plantations of well-governed soldiery and artisans would provide such an example of good behaviour that the Indians, already athirst for the Gospel, would be readily won. Hakluyt maintained that, when one or two colonies had been established, the settlers would be able to learn the language and ways of the natives — 'and so with discrecion and myldenes distill into their purged myndes the swete and lively liquor of

[1] Robert Johnson, *Nova Britannia* (1609), sig. C1.

[2] Sir Walter Raleigh (?), *Of the Voyage for Guiana* (Hakluyt Society, III, 1848), 147.

the gospel.'[1] This view of the amiable and easily converted native persisted in the writings of colonial propagandists long after there was ample evidence to the contrary.

Such evidence came from Virginia in increasing abundance during the first three decades of the seventeenth century. The earliest settlers found themselves confronted with problems of survival which left little or no room for evangelizing the Indians. While the General Assembly, convened at Jamestown in Virginia in 1619, had found time to enact laws for the conversion of the Indian, it placed more emphasis upon protecting the English from him. The general attitude of the colonists towards him bore little resemblance to the godly concern for his soul enjoined by the clergy from their pulpits. The American Indian was quite unlike any other race that the settlers had seen. To their eyes he was primitive in the extreme, leading a nomadic existence completely outside the experience of Western Europeans. Even at the end of the seventeenth century, Cotton Mather described the Indians as 'the veriest *Ruines of Mankind*, which are to be found any where upon the Face of the Earth.'[2] In the colonists' opinion the Indian was a wild and savage creature to be feared — from whose pillage house and home must be protected. George Thorpe, writing to Sir Edwin Sandys from Virginia in 1621, had no doubt that God was displeased with the colonists' neglect of the Indians: 'yeat is there scarce any man amongest vs that doth soe much as affoorde them a good thought in his hart and most men with theire mouthes giue them nothinge but maledictions and bitter execrations.'[3] Even greater maledictions were heaped upon the Indians after the massacre of 1622. And while it was easy enough for John Robinson to write from Leyden, 'Oh! how happy a thing had it been, if you had converted some, before you had killed any,'[4] in Virginia such a sentiment lacked reality.

But gradually the course of events in Virginia did convince many in

[1] *The original writings and correspondence of the two Richard Hakluyts* (Hakluyt Society, *2nd series*, LXXVII, 1935, vol. ii), 215.

[2] Cotton Mather, *Magnalia Christi Americana* (1702), III, 191.

[3] S. M. Kingsbury, ed., *The Records of the Virginia Company* (Washington, D.C., 1933), III, 446.

[4] William Bradford, *History of Plymouth Plantation*, I (M.H.S., 1912), 367.

England that conversion was by no means the simple matter it had seemed. Writing in 1635, Joseph Mede considered that there was 'little hope of the general Conversion of those Natives in any considerable part of that Continent; yet I suppose it may be a work pleasing to Almighty God and our Blessed Saviour, to *affront* the Devil with the sound of the Gospel and Cross of Christ in those places where he had thought to have reigned securely and out of the dinne thereof.'[1] It was to protest against a growing disillusionment that seventy-six English and Scottish ministers subscribed *A Petition of W*[*illiam*] *C*[*astell*] *Exhibited to the High Court of Parliamen* [sic] *now assembled, for the propagating of the Gospel in America, and the West Indies: and for the setling of our Plantations there* (1641). This petition pointed out that, although the work was regarded as pious and charitable, it had never been undertaken 'in pitty to mens soules, but in hope to possesse the land of those Infidels, or of gaine by Commerce.' This was true of all nations, the petition continued: the Spaniards boasted of many conversions but in fact their monstrous cruelty only made the Indians hate the name of Christ. The English had failed to make any converts — in New England because there were not many natives to convert and in Virginia because the colony lacked able ministers. And the petition concluded that the English colonists 'themselves are become exceeding rude, more likely to turne Heathen, then to turne others to the Christian faith.'[2]

Although the petition was not without bias, it was true that no attempts to convert the Indians were made in New England until the mid-1640s, and this despite the avowedly religious motives of its settlers. Such a task had indeed been written into the Massachusetts charter as the colony's principal aim and Matthew Cradock, the first Governor of the Massachusetts Bay Company, did not fail to emphasize the fact in writing to New England. But in New England itself a far more important matter was on hand, for in both Plymouth and Massachusetts the primary concern was to establish a temporal and ecclesiastical form of government which could be held up to the old world as a model. To such a purpose the conversion of the Indian had to take second place — indeed scarcely that; for the fact is that neither the theology nor the

[1] Joseph Mede, *Works* (1672), 800.
[2] *Op. cit.*, 6, 10.

polity of New England was evangelical in character or readily adaptable to his temporal and spiritual needs.[1]

Most Puritans believed that the establishment of God's kingdom upon earth might actually come about in their lifetimes. The Indians would ultimately be saved, but opinion was divided upon when this would happen: some saw them as one of the lost tribes of Israel who would be gathered in before the overthrow of Antichrist — which was, of course, the more optimistic view. Others, drawing upon Revelation 15 for support, held that their general conversion must wait until after the Jews had been converted and Antichrist destroyed. John Cotton, one of the most prominent exponents of this basically pessimistic position, tied himself in knots in an attempt to reconcile it with the earliest missionary efforts in New England. 'Yet, neverthelesse', he conceded, 'that hindreth not, but that some sprinklings, & gleanings of them may be brought home to Christ, as now and then some Proselytes were brought into the fellowship of the Church of *Israel*.'[2] The dour Presbyterian Robert Baylie, who did battle with Cotton on this, as upon many other questions, regarded it 'both a groundlesse and exceeding unseasonable fancie, too apt, if not guarded against, to discourage and cool the most laudable fit of zeal, that God has lately wakened in the brests of many gracious brethren.'[3]

Although significant of the attitude of many New England ministers, the arguments of John Cotton did not constitute in themselves the greatest hindrance to the Indians' conversion. Far greater was the very nature of the New England Way; it was, in fact, basically antipathetic to evangelical endeavour. In orthodox New England the church covenant formed the basis of a society essentially static in character, a society in which the distinction between the elect and the unregenerate (which

[1] Puritanism in New England has been the subject of a number of works by Perry Miller; of particular value are *The New England Mind: the seventeenth century* (Cambridge, Mass., 1954) and the chapter entitled 'The Marrow of Puritan Divinity' in his *Errand into the Wilderness* (Cambridge, Mass., 1956). I am also greatly indebted to Miss Joan E. M. Bellord for permission to make use of her most interesting unpublished M.A. thesis: 'Puritan ideas of colonisation, 1620–1660' (London University, Nov. 1950).

[2] J. Cotton, *The Way of Congregational Churches cleared* (1648), I, 78.

[3] R. Baylie, *The Disswasive . . . Vindicated* (1655), 42.

latter category included the Indians) was the most deeply entrenched division. The saints called to themselves a pastor who tended to their needs but whose obligations to those outside the covenant were extremely nebulous.

The Presbyterians, who anyway roundly denounced the Church covenant and prophesied the destruction of any society which 'unchurched' the majority, seized greedily upon New England's failure to provide a ministry for the unregenerate as ground for attack. 'What have they to do with those that are without?' wrote Robert Baylie of New England's ministers. 'Their pastors preach not for conversion, their relation is to their Flock, who are Church-members, converted already to their hand by the labours of other men.'[1] New England theologians did what they could to defend themselves but the fact remained that for all practical purposes ministers contented themselves with tending the elect. There was, of course, one notable exception — John Eliot; his concern with the unregenerate Indians was used as the only available example with which to refute the Presbyterian attacks upon New England's ministry.

Nor, in the New England Way, could the unregenerate look to the Synod for succour, for its purpose was purely advisory. Each church remained an independent and autonomous body., thus making it impossible for the Synod to provide any kind of centralized machinery for missionary work. The Synod's helplessness was completed by its inability to ordain missionaries. Orthodox opinion in the Synod would certainly have agreed with John Cotton when he wrote: 'to looke for another new Ministry . . . to attend conversion of soules onely, is to looke for a blessing which the Lord hath not promised: and besides himselfe hath ordained sufficient ordinary means for that end.'[2]

But the greatest obstacle to the rapid conversion of the Indians was the nature of conversion itself. Both Congregationalist and Presbyterian agreed that conversion was not simply a matter of instruction and assent, but a profound spiritual experience to which there was no short cut. Sanctity, for the Puritan, depended upon the concept of re-

[1] R. Baylie, *A Dissuasive from the Errours of the Time* (1645), 60.

[2] J. Cotton, *The Bloudy Tenent, washed . . .* (1647), *A Reply to Mr. Williams*, 127.

generacy which lay at the centre of his theology, and the full experience of regeneration involved not only an understanding of the doctrine of the Fall but a highly sophisticated conception of the way in which divine grace operated. Puritanism was no religion for the illiterate; men were brought to the truth by reason and, in reaching the truth, logic, metaphysics and history played their part. Of course intellect alone was not enough; man could not become regenerate without the gradual working of God's grace which insinuated itself into the souls of those ready to receive it. None but the heretical Mrs. Hutchinson and her followers held openly that God's choice might fall upon the unprepared.

According to William Perkins, whose works were widely read in New England, man could enter upon the labour of regeneration as soon as he felt any desire to be saved. Roger Williams was for once expressing a widely acceptable view when he excused himself from converting the Indians on the grounds 'that Gods way is first to turne a soule from it's Idolls, both of heart, worship and conversation, before it is capable of worship, to the true and living God.'[1] The Puritans believed that God's grace was nearly always given through the established means provided by Him and that these means were the sermon and the sacraments. According to Thomas Hooker, the voice of Christ was made known first through the Bible and then through the Bible as interpreted by the preacher. John Cotton considered that 'the ordinary way of Conversion . . . is by hearing the word';[2] it was through hearing the word that most of the saints first received their call and it was through repeatedly hearing sermons that they remained regenerate.

The conversion of the Indian was thus a matter of the utmost difficulty and the barrier of language made hopes of their regeneration even more remote. As Roger Williams pointed out with some relish, the Indian language was so difficult that none had yet attained sufficient proficiency in it 'to open the *Mysteries* of *Christ Jesus* in any proprietie of their *speech* or *Language*, without which *proprietie* it cannot be imagined that *Christ Jesus* sent forth his first *Apostles* or *Messengers*, and without which no people in the World are long willing to heare of difficult and

[1] R. Williams, *A Key into the Language of America* (1643), 129.

[2] J. Cotton, *The Bloudy Tenent, washed* . . . (1647), *A Reply to Mr. Williams*, 126.

heavenly matters.'[1] On the other hand, few if any of the Indians were sufficiently familiar with the English language to set forth upon the hazardous road to regeneration.

It was clear to all Puritan writers that if anything at all was to be done about converting the Indians they must first be civilized. Only out-and-out critics like Thomas Lechford maintained that they could be converted first and civilized afterwards. The idea of the heathen receiving the Grace of God while still in the savage state was inconceivable to the Puritan mind. Above all the Indian must be made to give up his nomadic existence and live 'in some warrantable calling' which would, in itself, be an important step towards his conversion. It was quickly seen that civilizing the Indian would cost money and that the only hope of obtaining funds for this purpose would be to appeal to the generous in England.

John White, in his *Planters Plea* (1630), had suggested a common stock of £10,000 which would suffice 'to support the weight of generall charges.' As for collecting such a sum, it should be easy: 'what were it for a Marchant or a Gentleman of reasonable estate, to disburse twentie-fiue or fifty pound, for the propagating of the *Gospell*, who casts away in one yeare much more upon superfluities in apparell, dyet, buildings, &c.'[2] In 1631 Richard Saltonstall suggested that either 'the generall state' or 'some large harted men' should contribute to 'the educating of our poore Indians.'[3]

Money had been collected specifically for the Indians of Virginia in 1620 and earlier, but no such attempt was made on behalf of those of New England until more than twenty years later. In 1641 the General Court of Massachusetts sent Thomas Weld, minister of Roxbury, Hugh Peter, minister of Salem, and William Hibbins, a prominent Boston merchant, to England. The objects of the mission[4] were to explain to the colony's creditors why payments were slow in forthcoming, 'to

[1] R. Williams, *The Bloody Tenent yet More Bloody* (1652), 219.

[2] *Op. cit.*, 82–83.

[3] M.H.S. *Proceedings, 2nd series*, VIII (1894), 209.

[4] The mission is fully treated by R. P. Stearns, 'The Weld-Peter Mission to England', *C.S.M.*, XXXII, 188–246, and in the same author's *The Strenuous Puritan, Hugh Peter, 1598–1660* (Urbana, 1954), 157–183.

make use of any opportunity God should offer for the good of the country here' and to further the work of reformation of the churches in England. No doubt assistance for the conversion of the Indians was another, if minor, object of the mission. But John Winthrop was careful to point out that the colony's agents should not 'seek supply of our wants in any dishonorable way, as by begging or the like.'[1]

William Hibbins returned to New England in 1642 taking with him about £500 for the colony and Hugh Peter soon became involved in English affairs; thus most of the work and, in particular, the book-keeping, was left to Thomas Weld. However, in 1642, Weld and Peter together set to work to collect considerable sums of money for charitable purposes. Although it smacked somewhat of 'begging or the like', a collection was taken up in London parishes, with full Parliamentary authority for the transportation of poor children to New England. In this way nearly £680 was raised and personal gifts brought the total to almost £875.[2] In the following year few gifts were forthcoming. In order to stimulate the generous, a small pamphlet was published entitled:

> *New Englands first fruits; in respect.*
>
> *First of the* { *Conversion of some* / *Conviction of divers,* / *Preparation of sundry* } *of the Indians.*
>
> 2. *Of the progresse of Learning, in the Colledge at Cambridge, in Massacusets Bay. With Divers other speciall Matters concerning that Countrey* . . . (1643).

This tract, as the title suggests, was divided into three parts.[3] The first, which has been attributed to John Eliot, recounts sundry conversions which, on examination, appear singularly unimpressive. But the Indians' ardent desire for the Gospel was emphasized and no pains were wasted in pointing out that the English were welcomed by the Indians and that relations between English and Indian were excellent; the English had entered upon their land without violence and without

[1] J. K. Hosmer, ed., *Winthrop's Journal* (New York, 1908), II, 31.

[2] *C.S.M.*, XXXII, 215.

[3] S. E. Morison, *The Founding of Harvard College* (Cambridge, Mass., 1935), 304–5, deals with the authorship of this tract.

taking one acre by force and the English had used them 'fairly and courteously'. Thus all was ready for the Indians' conversion; only preachers were lacking, and the author prayed God that some ministers might now master the Indian language and begin their work. The second part of *New Englands first fruits* dealt with Harvard College and was designed to show that, unlike the projected University in Virginia, it really existed. The third section sang the praises of Massachusetts, hoping to dispel the disparaging accounts of the colony which had become current in England.

New Englands first fruits made little impression upon potential benefactors. It did, however, produce Harvard's first scholarship fund — £100, the gift of Lady Ann Mowlson, and a further £200 or so for the College and for the advancement of learning. Even less was received on the Indians' behalf: an annuity of £20 was the gift of Lady Mary Armine, a well-known philanthropist and wife of Sir William Armine, M.P. for Lincolnshire.[1] Two other gifts amounted to only £12.10s.[2]

After 1643, Peter and Weld collected little more for Massachusetts and in October 1645 their appointment was terminated. The General Court of Massachusetts did not see fit to appoint another agent until the following year. This time their choice — and it could hardly have been bettered — fell upon Edward Winslow. His 'Integritie abilities and diligence', in William Steele's phrase, 'as allso his great Enterest and aquaintance with the members of Parlement and other Gentlemen of quallitie' made him well suited for the post.[3]

Though Winslow's main assignment on leaving New England was to answer the charges made by Gorton and others, the colony's defence drafted in December 1646 by the General Court referred to the good work being done among the Indians by John Eliot. Eliot had only begun his work in October 1646, but the Court was anxious that Englishmen, in general, should know that the principal end of its charter had not

[1] Lady Armine's interest in the Indians may have been aroused by William Wood's *New Englands Prospect* (1634), which was dedicated to her husband and the second part of which dealt with the Indians.

[2] Bodleian, Ms. Rawlinson C934, f. 19; *C.S.M.*, XIV, 125.

[3] *Acts*, I, 163; *D.A.B.*, XX, 393–394.

been forgotten and that Presbyterians in particular should see that their attacks upon the New England Way were without foundation. In fact, Presbyterian criticism did much to remind New Englanders of their duty to convert the Indians. The question had been raised by the General Court in 1644; in that year it was ordered that shire courts should be responsible for civilizing the Indians and for supervising their religious instruction. In October 1645, the Court had asked ministers to consider what should be done to civilize and christianize the Indians.[1] They, no doubt, recommended that further efforts should be made to raise funds in England and the appointment of Winslow provided a good opportunity for this. So in November 1646 the General Court was anticipating the arrival of funds when it authorized the purchase of some land for the Indians. In addition the ministers probably advocated more extensive propaganda in England on the Indians' behalf, along the lines of *New Englands first fruits.*

In fact, an anonymous tract did appear in London, in 1647, under the title *The Day-breaking if not the Sun-rising of the Gospel with the Indians in New-England.* Both John Wilson, a minister in Boston, and Thomas Shepard, one of the most distinguished preachers in New England, have been considered as authors of this tract, but there is no conclusive evidence in either case. At all events, Winslow was probably responsible for seeing the work through the press and, as the last events recorded in it coincide with the date of his departure from Boston, he may well have brought the manuscript with him to London. The tract recounts four meetings with the Indians in 1646. The meetings are of considerable interest as they were the first occasions on which John Eliot preached to the Indians in their own language, although the author of the tract does not mention Eliot by name. The tract contained a careful apologia for the slowness with which New England ministers had set about the work of conversion: 'if wee would force them to baptisme (as the Spaniards do . . .) or if wee would hire them to it by giving them coates and shirts, to allure them to it (as some others have done) wee could have gathered many hundreds, yea thousands it may bee by this time, into the name of Churches; but wee have not learnt as yet that art

[1] N. B. Shurtleff, ed., *Records of the Governor and Company of the Massachusetts Bay* (Boston, Mass., 1853), III, 96–97; II, 84, 134, 166; III, 85.

of coyning Christians, or putting Christs name and Image upon copper mettle.'[1] The writer described the Indians' longings for the Gospels. He thought it an encouraging sign that some of them would be prepared to send their children into English homes in order that they might grow up in the ways of Christ. But this, as he pointed out, however desirable, would be very costly in food and clothing. Therefore assistance from England would be welcome and those who sent gifts should send them direct to the President of the College at Cambridge to avoid possible miscarriage.

Early in March 1647/8 this tract was followed by another, this time under the name of Thomas Shepard, entitled *The Clear Sun-shine of the Gospel breaking forth upon the Indians in New-England*. It, too, was prepared for the press by Winslow who also succeeded in persuading a number of ministers to write and subscribe their names to two dedicatory epistles. The first of these was addressed to Parliament and asked for assistance in very general terms. The second epistle, dedicated to 'the Godly and well-affected of this Kingdome', made much more specific demands. Schools, clothing and food were needed for Indian children, and implements and tools were needed for their parents, so that they could be kept from that idleness which was their besetting sin. Merchants in particular were exhorted to take the Gospel, at their own expense, to the heathen with whom they traded. But all should pray for and contribute towards the work of conversion, the burden being too great for the shoulders of the colonists. Both these epistles were signed by twelve English ministers including Edmund Calamy and Stephen Marshall, the support of Presbyterian leaders being particularly welcome. The tract itself related something of John Eliot's labours and included a letter from him written at Thomas Shepard's request.

The Clear Sun-shine of the Gospel and the advocacy of Winslow were successful in bringing the matter to the attention of Parliament. On 13 March 1647/8 the question was raised and the House of Commons ordered that 'the consideration of affording some encouragement and charity to the inhabitants now in New-England for the promoting piety and learning in that plantation' should be resumed the following week. On 17 March the House referred the matter to the Committee

[1] *The Day-breaking if not the Sun-rising*, 15.

for Foreign Plantations and ordered the preparation of a bill.[1] Winslow, as New England's agent, as the main promoter of the scheme and as a man well versed in colonial affairs, was able to influence the Committee for Foreign Plantations and consequently to play an important part in drafting the bill. Furthermore, the support of the Earl of Warwick greatly enhanced his influence over the Committee. When, in May 1648, Warwick was unable to attend the Committee, he wrote to Lord Denbigh commending Winslow, who 'hath some business with the committee for fforraigne plantac'ons that have long attended dispatch. They doe all concerne severall societies of our owne countreymen there, who may justly challenge very much respect, and one of them hath a more speciall relation to the advancement of religion amongst the native Indians.'[2]

The draft of the bill was prepared by August, and on the 21st of that month the House arranged for its first reading to take place four days later. However, there was a postponement and it was not read for the first time until 30 August. Although the House ordered its second reading on 6 September, this was postponed until 27 September, again until 3 November and then each week until 4 December, when it was finally thrown out on the grounds that it gave insufficient powers to the feoffees.[3]

But Winslow did not let the matter rest; another bill was framed and on 20 April 1649 the House ordered that it should be read the next day, although as usual when the day came the House found no time for its reading.[4] It was two years since *The Day-breaking* and more than a year since *The Clear Sun-shine of the Gospel* appeared when Winslow published, in about May 1649, a tract entitled *The Glorious Progress of the Gospel, amongst the Indians in New England. Manifested by three Letters, under the Hand of that famous Instrument of the Lord Mr. John Eliot. And another from Thomas Mayhew jun.* Winslow dedicated the tract to Parlia-

[1] L. F. Stock, ed., *Proceedings and Debates of the British Parliaments respecting North America* (Washington, D.C., 1924), I, 203–204.

[2] Historical Manuscripts Commission, *4th Report, Appendix* (1874), 274.

[3] L. F. Stock, ed., *Proceedings*, I, 205–207. Edward Winslow, *The Glorious Progress*, sig. A2b.

[4] L. F. Stock, ed., *Proceedings*, I, 209.

ment and the Council of State. In this dedication he respectfully reminded Parliament of the attempt that had been made to frame an act and of its subsequent rejection, adding with no less respect that a new and corrected draft was ready for the attention of the House. The letters he chose to publish — Eliot's and Mayhew's letters — related something of their work amongst the Indians and indicated their many needs: medicines, tools, clothing. An appendix, with less tact than the dedication, exhorted members of Parliament to 'rather steal from your sleep an houre, then suffer that good Ordinance to lye asleep so long.' Ministers were to pray for, and to stir up interest in, the work and 'Masters of money' were urged to part with their gold with the promise: 'If you give any thing *yearly*, remember Christ will be your *Pensioner*. If you give any thing into *banke* Christ will keep account thereof, and reward it.'[1]

No sooner was the tract published than things began to move again in Parliament. On 13 June 1649 'an act for the promoting and propagating the Gospel of Jesus Christ in New-England' had its first and second readings in the House and on being put to the question was referred to a special committee which was ordered to meet at two o'clock on that day in the Exchequer-Chamber and to amend the bill. John Gurdon and Nathaniel Bacon, in particular, were entrusted with the matter. The committee took some time to draft the amendments and to report on them; although ordered to report on 26 June, 10 July and 17 July each time with the caution 'nothing to intervene', something did intervene until 18 July when Gurdon finally reported amendments to the bill.

One of these was intended to alter basically the character of the bill, in order to include within its terms the struggling College at Cambridge. As amended the funds collected would be 'for the maintaining of the universities of Cambridge in New-England, and other schools and nurseries of learning there, and for the preaching and propagating of the Gospel among the natives.'[2] This was not the first time that collections for the Indians had been coupled with collections for the College: *New Englands first fruits* had placed them side by side while *The Day-breaking if not the Sun-rising* had recommended that contributions for the Indian work should be sent to the President of the College. But the amend-

[1] E. Winslow, *The Glorious Progress*, 27. [2] L. F. Stock, ed., *Proceedings*, I, 209.

ment was rejected; the money collected was to be used to encourage 'the preaching and propagating of the Gospel of Jesus Christ amongst the natives, and also for maintaining of schools and nurseries of learning, for the better educating of the children of the natives.'[1] Thus the fostering of Harvard was excluded from the terms of the bill, except in so far as Indian students, or possibly those training to become missionaries, were concerned.

The final reading of the bill was ordered for 23 July and then postponed until 27 July, when it received its third reading and was ordered to be printed. It was entitled 'An Act for the promoting and propagating the Gospel of Jesus Christ in New England.'[2] The preamble, based largely upon the tracts of Shepard and Winslow, referred to 'the testimonial of divers faithful and godly Ministers, and others in New-England', from which it was known that 'some godly English of this Nation' were preaching to the Indians in the Indian language. As a result of this work the Indians were becoming civilized, forsaking their own Gods and calling upon the name of the Lord, sending their children to English schools, putting away all wives but one, and praying to God morning and evening in their families. The preamble thanked God for this beginning but added that the work could not be carried on without encouragement. It pointed out that the English in New England, although willing, were unable to supply this encouragement, having exhausted their resources in founding towns and colonies in the wilderness. For this reason, the preamble continued, it was incumbent upon England to further the work.

The act then provided for the establishment in England of a corporation of sixteen persons: a president, a treasurer, and fourteen assistants, to be called by the name of 'The President and Society for propagation of the Gospel in New-England.' It was granted the usual powers of corporate bodies — to purchase or acquire without licence in mortmain, lands, tenements or hereditaments in England and Wales not exceeding the yearly value of £2,000. It could sue or be sued, plead or be impleaded, make a common seal and by-laws. Under the act the Com-

[1] *Ibid.*, 209.

[2] C. H. Firth and R. S. Rait, eds., *Acts and Ordinances of the Interregnum, 1642–1660* (1911), II, 197–200.

missioners of the United Colonies of New England, or such as they should appoint, were empowered to receive and disburse the money sent across the Atlantic by the Society. Finally it enacted that a collection should be taken up in all the parishes of England and Wales to further the work.

The safe passage of the act, at a moment when the Long Parliament had little time and less inclination to discuss the conversion of New England's savages, must stand as a monument not only to Winslow's persistence and powers of persuasion but also to those who, if only for a moment, abandoned their sectarian quarrels in order to promote a common Christian cause.

2

The Society, 1649–1660

THE members of the Society for Propagation of the Gospel in New England were predominantly prosperous London merchants. Thirty of them have been identified: sixteen were named in the act of 1649 and fourteen were elected subsequently to fill vacancies. Of those named in the act only Winslow and Herbert Pelham seem to have crossed the Atlantic.[1] Winslow, of course, had done so on a number of occasions since his first voyage in the *Mayflower*. Pelham had gone to Massachusetts in 1635, had taken part in the settlement of Sudbury and had served both on the Court of Assistants and as a Commissioner of the United Colonies; but when he returned to England he settled in the country and was not as active in the Society's affairs as his connection with the colony might have warranted. Of those members elected after 1649 probably only Edward Hopkins and Thomas Bell had been to New England. Hopkins, who had been Governor of Connecticut and one of the Commissioners of the United Colonies, returned to England in 1652, whereupon the Society immediately used his name to lend support to its accounts of what was being done for the Indians. At about the same time Thomas Bell returned home from Roxbury where he had been living for some years. It was there that he became personally acquainted with John Eliot, Roxbury's pastor, and with his work amongst the Indians. Indeed, Bell had been responsible for conveying Lady Armine's annuity to Eliot and was probably the only member of

[1] According to Thomas Hutchinson, Robert Tomson, Richard Lloyd (i.e. Floyd) and Richard Hutchinson had also crossed the Atlantic: *The History of the Colony and Province of Massachusetts-Bay* (Cambridge, Mass., 1936), I, 140–1; but see James Savage, *A Genealogical Dictionary of the First Settlers of New England* (Boston, Mass., 1860–2). 4 vol.

the Society who knew at first hand something about Eliot's labours. His business as a merchant of Tower Street, London, left him time to serve the Society and occasionally to correspond with Roxbury's pastor.

Some members, who had probably never even visited the American colonies, had nevertheless strong ties with them. Edward Parks owned property in New England and had a son living there; Richard Hutchinson bought the Boston house of John Winthrop senior in 1649 and from time to time speculated in real estate; Robert Houghton, a brewer and merchant of Southwark, had a married sister living at Charlestown, and James Shirley had long been involved in American colonial trade.

But members were usually chosen not for their New England connections but for their wealth and influence. Wealth, in particular, was an important qualification for membership and it was always hoped that members might make free with their personal fortunes on the Indians' behalf. Thus Erasmus Smyth had seemed an obvious choice because he was known not only for his wealth but also for his philanthropy. Others, like Henry Ashurst, Thomas Babington, George Clarke and Joshua Woolnough, were making fortunes in commerce, while Richard Hutchinson and William Molines were prominent amongst those who combined trade with extremely lucrative government employment. It was said that Hutchinson lost property worth ten thousand pounds in the Great Fire of London, which is some indication of his wealth. He, like Edward Hopkins, was a Commissioner for the Navy before he replaced Sir Henry Vane as its Treasurer. Winslow and Molines were Commissioners for Compounding with Delinquents; Thomas Ayres and Babington were Commissioners for the High Court of Justice; Major William Puckle, Hutchinson's son-in-law, was a Commissioner for the Security of the Protector, and so on. But it was on the commission for 'ejecting Scandalous, Ignorant and Insufficient Ministers and Schoolmasters' that no fewer than ten members of the Society served.

The Society's membership was, of course, entirely Puritan and predominantly Independent. But Presbyterians were not unrepresented; a few members, notably George Clarke of Hackney, Robert Houghton and Richard Floyd, were ruling elders of the classes forming the London Presbyterian Province and represented these classes at meetings of the

Provincial Assembly. Winslow, no doubt, had surmised that a Presbyterian element in the Society's membership might lessen the likelihood of criticism and heighten the inclination of Presbyterians to support the Society.

Although nearly all the members were merchants or engaged in trade of some sort, there were exceptions; Edmond Wilson was a physician. He had been admitted to Emmanuel College, Cambridge, that stronghold of Puritanism, in 1631 and just over ten years later had obtained his doctor's degree at Padua. He practised in London with success, becoming a fellow of the Royal College of Physicians and a Harveian orator. His interest in the Society probably stemmed from his friendship with Winslow who, in his will, had appointed him, with Richard Floyd and James Shirley, overseer to his personal estate in England.

The most eminent of the Society's original members and its first President was William Steele. He had been called to the bar in 1637, had quickly won himself distinction and by 1649 was appointed Recorder of London. Only illness prevented him from taking part in the trial of Charles I, but this did not prejudice his career during the decade which followed. In 1652 he served on a committee for the reform of the law; he was an M.P. for London in 1654 and in the same year became sergeant-at-law. In the following year he was appointed Chief Baron of the Exchequer and in 1656 Lord Chief Justice of Ireland. According to Ludlow he was 'generally esteemed to be a Man of great Prudence and uncorrupted Integrity.'[1] As the Society's first President, however, it must be admitted that he was a disappointment, although he was re-elected annually until the Restoration. Important letters were signed by him until he became Lord Chief Justice of Ireland; thereafter he was kept informed of the Society's affairs but played no further part in them himself.

Many of the President's duties were in fact performed by the Treasurer, Richard Floyd, who until his death in 1659 was the Society's most active member. By modern standards, some of his activities as Treasurer might be questioned. For example, at the end of each year a consider-

[1] Edmund Ludlow, *Memoirs*... (1721), II, 741.

able sum of money rested in his hands. The Society did provide a large iron box with three different keys to hold this money, but it was apparently never used. He divided the money amongst several members, to be held until required. At times he was too high-handed even by contemporary standards; on 19 November 1656 the Society ordered that he should not lend money without its consent, and added the rider that, even when he lent with consent, any loss would be his responsibility. In practice, the Society was too careful to lend very often; in June 1655 it did lend Earl Rivers £600 for twelve months upon a mortgage, but until just before the Restoration, when sound investment in property became difficult, it preferred to avoid making loans of any kind. When Richard Floyd died in September 1659 the Society discharged his executors, Daniel Blundell, his son-in-law, and Francis Warner, who subsequently became a member, on payment of £1,000. This was a little more than half of the cash shown in the accounts as being in the Treasurer's hands. The remaining £950 was found to be in the hands of several members, where the Society was prepared to let it rest for the time being.[1]

The position of Treasurer, left vacant by Floyd's death, was filled in October 1659 by Henry Ashurst. Third son of Henry Ashurst of Ashurst, Lancashire, he had been sent to London at the age of fifteen to serve his apprenticeship. A draper by trade, he had set up business in 1640 with a certain Mr. Row and when, about three years later, Row became a major in the army under the Earl of Essex, Ashurst had the business to himself. According to Richard Baxter, he managed it 'with ease and calmness of mind, and was not by it diverted from duties of Religion.' A staunch Puritan, he had come under the influence of his friend Simeon Ash and was, in Baxter's phrase: '*a meer Scripture Christian*; of the *Primitive Spirit* and strein.'[2] Simeon Ash, who was a supporter of the Society, may well have introduced Ashurst to it. In any case, he would certainly have mentioned the conversion of the Indians to him in their many long discussions together. As it turned out the Society had made an ideal choice of Treasurer, and in Ashurst it found

[1] Minutes (M.H.S. Ms.), 22 Oct. 1659; Accounts, 1653–64 (M.H.S. Ms.); Loose accounts, 1659 (Ms. 7945).

[2] Richard Baxter, *Faithful Souls shall be with Christ*... (1681), 38, 39, 41.

an able and industrious servant who, for more than twenty years, was to work for the Indians' conversion.

Although sixteen members were named in the act of 1649, only about half of these took any active part in the Society's work. But the act enabled the Society to function with a very small Court. For normal business the Treasurer and four members formed a quorum and for election days and matters of great importance the quorum was fixed at nine. In practice these numbers were seldom exceeded and although elections were a mere formality, it was often hard to induce a sufficient number of members to attend. On 4 September 1656 a bare nine members were present on election day, and it was ordered that in future a fine of two shillings and six pence should be paid by any member who failed to attend Court on election days. The order was never put into practice, presumably because it would have been tactless if not impossible to levy a fine upon the annually absent President. Ordinary Courts were held two or three times a month, usually at Coopers' Hall. The Hall was lent to the Society rent-free, the good will of the Coopers' Company being assured with an occasional gift of venison.

The Society's most important task, when it began to meet in 1649, was to collect money.[1] Collections for charitable purposes were, at this time, generally restricted to a specified period, but on this occasion no such limitation was imposed and the Society busied itself with its collection for the Indians for more than ten years. It was laid down in the act that 'for the more speedy and better effecting' of the collection, ministers should read the act itself in the presence of their congregations 'upon the next Lords-day after the same shall be delivered unto them, and . . . exhort the people to a chearful and liberal contribution.' The minister and churchwardens, or overseers of the poor, 'together with such other well-affected persons as God shall stir up to be active in such an undertaking' were authorized after the reading 'to go with all convenient speed from house to house, to every of the Inhabitants of the said Parishes and places respectively' to collect the money. A schedule of donations was to be made and a duplicate of this schedule, together

[1] The account of the Society's efforts to collect money, which follows, is based upon my article in *Bulletin of the John Rylands Library*, **39**, 444–62. I am indebted to the editor of that journal for permission to make use of it.

with the money, was to be handed to the Treasurer of the county. The names of the county treasurers, 'persons of quality' appointed by the Society under its Common Seal, were to be sent to each parish with a copy of the act.[1]

The Society needed many copies of the act for distribution and it had these printed in folio by Edward Husband, 'Printer to the Parliament of England'.[2] Although the preamble made a spirited appeal to contributors, from the beginning the Society saw the need for publicity. Nobody parts with money easily: in the seventeenth century as in the twentieth, a good cause had to advertise itself; and so it was that the Society's first concern was with advertisement. A certain amount of publicity material was already at hand — the Indian tracts, in particular Thomas Shepard's *Clear Sun-shine of the Gospel* (1648) and Edward Winslow's *Glorious Progress of the Gospel amongst the Indians in New England* (1649). But during the following ten years six more tracts were issued, each assuring the reader of the worthiness of the work and of its progress. In 1651 Henry Whitfield published *The Light appearing more and more towards the perfect Day* and in the following year *Strength out of Weaknesse; or a Glorious Manifestation of the further Progresse of the Gospel among the Indians.* The latter was the first Indian tract actually published by the Society. It seems to have been printed in considerable numbers, perhaps more than were needed; there are at least four different issues of it and a re-issue with a new title page: *The Banners of Grace and Love displayed in the farther Conversion of the Indians in New-England* (1657). The Society's misjudgment of the number of copies to be printed did not occur again, and the embarrassing sheets of *Strength out of Weaknesse* must have been a constant reminder that there was not an unlimited demand for Indian tracts. On at least one later occasion, when 3,000 copies of a tract had been ordered, the Court changed its mind and reduced the number to 1,500.

The second tract published by the Society, *Tears of Repentance: or a further Narrative of the Progress of the Gospel amongst the Indians* (1653), was compiled jointly by Eliot and Thomas Mayhew junior. The subsequent tracts of 1655, 1659 and 1660 were again largely the products of

[1] C. H. Firth and R. S. Rait, eds., *Acts and Ordinances*, II, 197–200.

[2] A copy of this issue of the act is filed with Ms. 7963.

Eliot's pen, and the similarity of their titles reflects the similarity of their contents. They were called: *A Late and Further Manifestation of the Progress of the Gospel* (1655); *A further Accompt of the Progresse of the Gospel amongst the Indians in New-England and Of the means used effectually to advance the same* (1659); and *A further Account of the progress of the Gospel Amongst the Indians in New-England being a Relation of the Confessions made by several Indians* (1660). The last of these Indian tracts published in London was also by Eliot and appeared after an interval of eleven years. It was entitled: *A brief narrative of the progress of the Gospel amongst the Indians in New-England, in the year 1670* (1671).

The Indian tracts are often referred to as the 'Eliot tracts', and with some justification. Although Eliot's name appears as author on only a few of their title pages, copies of his letters to the Society or to friends in England form a substantial part of them. If his name did not always appear prominently on their title pages, it was at least partly to prevent the rumour that he was the only labourer in the field.

Because the tracts consisted so largely of scraps — letters from Eliot, Mayhew, William Leveritch and others, describing the work; John Endicott describing visits to Natick; Thomas Allen witnessing the existence of the work, not to mention a maze of dedications — the business of putting them into shape for publication was a considerable undertaking. The Society usually gave the work to a distinguished London minister who penned a dedicatory epistle and saw the manuscript through the press. The story of how the 1659 tract was prepared is typical: the Court first reviewed the material at hand and decided to include, amongst other things, an abbreviated manuscript by Thomas Mayhew senior. An editor had then to be found and the choice lay between Edmund Calamy and Dr. Edward Reynolds. The Court decided in favour of Reynolds; the Treasurer approached him and reported that he was prepared to do the job. Indeed, the report added: 'his heart is in the work.' But the Society did not let the matter rest there, and sent a directive to Reynolds telling him that the Bible was to be printed in the Indian language and that he should mention this fact in his epistle. Several weeks later the Court decided that the abbreviated manuscript of Thomas Mayhew senior should not be included after all and that Reynolds should be notified. The question of what title should be given to the tract was also considered, but finally it was decided that the matter should be referred to Reynolds. It was ordered at the same time that he should be sent a copy of *A Late and Further Manifestation of the Progress of the Gospel* (1655) which may partly explain his striking lack of originality in calling the tract: *A further Accompt of the Progresse of the Gospel* (1659).[1]

The Society's anxious supervision of detail extended beyond the editing, to the printing of the tracts. The Court was constantly on the look-out for the cheapest printer. In 1660 Major Puckle, a member of the Society, obtained two estimates for printing, one from Mary Simmons and another from John Maycock. Maycock gave a lower estimate per sheet and got the job. As it turned out, the Society had been over-zealous and was outwitted, as Maycock used larger type and thicker leads, consequently needing more sheets to complete the work than Mary Simmons would have done.[2]

Although not published by the Society, Thomas Thorowgood's *Iewes in America* (1650) did something to advertise its work. Thorowgood, like Eliot and many others interested in the conversion of the Indians, was passionately devoted to the theory that the Indians were descended from the Lost Tribes of Israel whose wanderings had ended in North America. The theory was far from receiving universal consent and it even brought forth an answer: Sir Hamon L'Estrange's *Americans no Iewes, or Improbabilities that the Americans are of that race* (1652). In 1658 Thorowgood submitted to the Society for publication a manuscript containing his second thoughts on the subject. In June the Society declined to print it, but left it 'unto himself to doe what seemeth good unto him.' In October the Court decided that the manuscript might be worth printing after all and wrote to Thorowgood asking him to return it for further consideration. However, it was once more considered unsuitable as promotion literature. This decision was financially a wise one, for Thorowgood had every intention of seeing his work in print. When he heard that the Society had declined to accept his manuscript he promptly requested that it be handed to Henry Brome, who finally printed the work in 1660.[3] It was entitled: *Jews in America, or Probabili-*

[1] Minutes (M.H.S. Ms.), 6, 26 Feb., 19 March 1658/9.
[2] *C.S.M.*, XXVI (1927), 85–86.
[3] Minutes (M.H.S. Ms.), 19 June, 4 Oct 1658, 14 Jan. 1658/9.

ties, that those Indians are Judaical, made more probable by some Additionals to the former Conjectures. From the Society's point of view, the publication was a useful one. Like the earlier tract of 1650 it spoke highly of the Society's work and any publicity of this sort was grist to the mill.

Further incidental publicity was given by the translation into English of Casparus Sibelius' *Of the Conversion of Five Thousand and Nine Hundred East-Indians* (1650). To this was added an account of 'the Gospels good Successe also amongst the West-Indians, in New-England' which mainly consisted of quotations and extracts from the Indian tracts. Perhaps the most interesting feature of the tract is an extract from a letter written by John Eliot to Hugh Peter and dated 12 October 1649. In it he suggests that instead of collecting money for the Indians it would be easier to collect goods—in particular tools and clothing—for them. He wisely remarks that such goods '*any man can better spare out of his Shop, then halfe so much money to buy them.*'[1]

This letter was also published in *A Perfect Diurnall* for 1–8 April 1650.[2] Nor was this the only occasion on which the conversion of the Indians featured in the newspapers of the day. An unsigned letter headed 'From *Natick* in *New-England* 4 July 1651,' appeared in *Mercurius Politicus* of 18–25 September 1651.[3] It was almost certainly an abridged letter from Eliot, although it was not principally devoted to the Indians. In fact, so uninformative was it that Winslow hastened to send another of Eliot's letters to the editor with the covering note: 'I pray you Mr. Needham in a short preamble declare that the letter you printed the last weeke being so far short of the proceedings in this worke of God in New England is the cause of publishing this. . . .'[4] Marchamont Needham, however, apparently had no wish to devote further space to the Indians in *Mercurius Politicus.* But Winslow had his way, for Eliot's letter of 28 April 1651 to the Society, dealing almost exclusively with the Indians, was published in *Severall Proceedings in Parliament* 25 September–2 October 1651, with a note by Winslow explaining that the letter published

[1] *Op. cit.*, 38.
[2] No. 17, pp. 171–2.
[3] No. 68, pp. 1091–2.
[4] Bodleian, Ms. Rawlinson C934, f. 10.

previously: 'though honest and true, was far short of the work of grace amongst them.'[1]

Apart from the Indian tracts several broadsides or printed letters were published under the Society's auspices and sent out to ministers together with copies of the act. These were purely exhortations to the ministers to further the collection. As early as 1649 the Society printed a letter from the University of Oxford and another from Cambridge.[2] Each was printed on a single small folio leaf; the former was addressed 'To our Reverend Brethren the Ministers of the Gospel in England and Wales' and dated 22 October 1649. It was signed 'in the name and by the Authority of the Delegates of the University of *Oxford* by *Ed: Reynolds* Vicecan: Oxon.' The Cambridge letter was addressed: 'To our Reverend and deare Brethren the Ministers of England and Wales' and dated 24 October 1649; it bears twelve signatures.[3] Both letters were written at the Society's request and, as each made a number of the same points in strikingly similar words, it seems likely that the Society gave the Universities clear instructions as to what they should say. For example, the Cambridge letter ran: '... wee are earnestly sollicited to put our helping hands to a work so purely Christian (as their Letter to us stiles it) and not at all engaged in the unhappy differences of these times.' The Oxford letter ran: 'This Worke is represented to us, and wee doe in the like manner recommend it to you as a worke purely Christian, not at all relating to, or ingaged in the unhappy differences of these sad and discomposed times.'

The Oxford letter reminded its readers of 'how many precious Ministers, and zealous Christians have been by the cruelty and superstition (which some mistooke for piety) of former times forced out of this Land' who went to New England to enjoy liberty of conscience and to propagate the Gospel. It continued: 'wee are assured that God hath, beyond all expectation, crowned their faithfull endeavours for the pro-

[1] No. 105, pp. 1616–20. This letter was also printed in Henry Whitfield, *Strength out of Weaknesse*, 1–5.

[2] The only copies found are at Worcester College, Oxford.

[3]

Ant: Tuckney, *Procan.*	John Arrowsmyth	William Spurstowe
Richard Love	Benjamen Whichcot	La: Seaman
Richard Minshull	Thomas Young	William Dell
Thomas Hill	Samuel Bolton	Rich: Vines.

pagation of the Gospel there, with glorious successe. They who were wilde and barbarous, are now civill and sociable.' The project should be supported, the letter continued, because colonies were worthy enterprises and schools and universities should be encouraged there. 'Finally, wee are obleiged in point of Charity to take compassion on the deluded Indians, and our Christian Brethren in New-England, who have exhausted their Estates in this service, and are not able to carry on the worke to perfection, without some voluntary and liberall Contributions.'

The Cambridge letter laid a similar emphasis upon the value of education but made its appeal a wider one: 'Surely as men, wee are all concerned in the welfare of mankinde; as Christians in the prosperity of the Church; as Ministers in the conversion of soules; as Academicks in the advancement of learning; as Englishmen in seeking the good of those Plantations, the flourishing whereof, would be no small accession to the splendor and glory of this Nation.' It also made the appeal which from the days of Elizabeth had been a commonplace and a popular one: 'Jesuites at this day refuse not to compasse Sea and land, for spreading of Popery: shall Christianity, shall Protestantisme finde fewer Zelots set on worke for their propagation? God forbid.' It finally urged that 'the highest use that money can be put unto, is the furtherance of Religion, and the best way of gaining by it, is to lend it upon usury to the Lord.'

In 1649 the Society approached the Provincial Assembly of London, presumably in order to obtain a letter from that body similar to those from Oxford and Cambridge. On 27 December 1649 the Assembly ordered that the proposal should be referred to the Grand Committee and on 21 January 1649/50 the Assembly ordered more specifically 'that it shall be referred to ye Grand Committee to consider whether there shall bee a letter drawn up for the promoting the Businesse of New England and that ye Report be given in in writing to ye Province.'[1] However, as the matter was not mentioned again in the Assembly's Record Book and as no such letter appears to have survived, it is probable that the Grand Committee refused to take any action.

The Society was more successful — indeed, most fortunate — when,

[1] Sion College, London Provincial Assembly Record Book, 1648–1660, f. 102–3.

about three years after the letters from the Universities were penned, it secured the support of Cromwell. It seems that he signed a letter in the latter part of 1652 or early in 1653, supporting the Society's work and encouraging contributions for the Indians' conversion. The Commissioners of the United Colonies, answering a letter from Edward Winslow dated 2 May 1653, wrote: 'Wee are glad to heare of the Religious care which the Right honorable the Lord Generall Evidences in soe promoteing the service of Christ in publishing the Gospell amongst these poore heathens whoe have soe long sate in darknes.'[1] A more specific reference was made in a letter, dated 2 August 1653, from Sir Richard Onslow, County Treasurer for Surrey, acknowledging 'the printed letters signed by my Lord Generall' which he had read at Quarter Sessions and then 'caused every high Constable to take a proportionable number of them to disperse to the severall parishes.'[2]

The Society did not neglect to seek the support of municipal corporations. For example, Edward Winslow requested the Court of Aldermen in London to foster the cause. The Court recommended it 'to every Minister within this Cittie and Liberties therof.'[3] The Court also ordered a precept to be drawn up and issued 'in the name of the Lord Maior to the Aldermen Deputy and Common Councellmen of the . . . severall Wards, to further the Contribution for advance of the Gospell in New England with their best Assistance.' It is not known how much was collected in the wards but the President wrote to the Deputies in each ward, thanking them for their pains in furthering the collection and asking them to forward the money collected to the Treasurer.[4] Similar action was taken with other towns: the Society's Court enquired the name of the Mayor of Chichester so that 'a letter might bee sent unto him and ye Aldermen.'[5] In fact the Society was tireless in writing letters to the

[1] *Acts*, II, 105.

[2] Bodleian, Ms. Rawlinson C934, f. 67. Eliot's and Mayhew's *Tears of Repentance* was dedicated to Cromwell. This dedication, dated 26 March 1653 referred to '*that liberal and Exemplary Contribution to this Glorious Work lately promoted by Your Lordship, and Your Officers with the Army*.'

[3] Corporation of London, Records Office, Repertory, **60**, f. 238.

[4] *Ibid.*, **61**, ff. 75–76. A copy of the President's letter is contained in Bodleian, Ms. Rawlinson C934, f. 3.

[5] Minutes (M.H.S. Ms.), 28 May 1659.

county treasurers and in writing letters of thanks for contributions.

Above all, of course, the ministers themselves had to be briefed, for it was upon them that the ultimate success or failure of the collection rested, as the Society fully realized: it spared no pains in briefing them. The clergy's attitude to the collection varied enormously, but the response of Henry Newcome, minister of Gawsworth, Cheshire, in 1652/3, is so delightful that it is worth quoting in full.[1]

> There came now orders for a collection for the Indians. A large narrative came with it, and letters, well penned, from both the universities. I was taken with the design; and receiving but the papers on Saturday morning, turned off my ordinary subject and preached two sermons purposely, about Feb. 27th, on 1 Chr. xxix. 3. And the Lord did humble me mightily after evening sermon when I called up the people to subscribe, and they did it so slenderly and acted in it as if I had not said one word about it. But afterwards the Lord moved upon some of them to help me; and I went up and down from house to house, and making every servant and child that had anything to give, I raised it to a pretty sum for that little place, seven pounds odd money.

But the story did not always turn out so happily. Richard Bigge, minister of Winterbourne Dauntsey, wrote to William Cooke, treasurer for the county of Wiltshire on 21 May 1653:[2]

> My service I have accordinge to ye order sent me, publikly in ye Church in the parish of Winterborne Dantsy read your bookes and papers. Sir, of my selfe I am not able any way to promote soe religiouse a worke having but thirty shilling yearely settled on me for my cure. I went with both ye Churchwardens & desyred gratuityes at every mans house; But could force noe man nor persuade any man or woeman to be soe charitable as to give one peny. Thus with my love to you & your wife having I hope discharged my duty I rest
>
> Yours in all Christian
> Love and Service
> Rich. Bigge.

The size of the contributions made by individuals is difficult to estimate but, from the few returns which have survived, average

[1] *The Autobiography of Henry Newcome* (Chetham Society, 1852, 1st series, XXVI), 43.

[2] Bodleian, Ms. Rawlinson C934, f. 72.

contributions seem to have been very small. For example, of the fifty contributors to the sum of £2. 4s. 6d. collected in Winterslow, Wiltshire, thirty-five gave sums of less than sixpence. In Walberton, Sussex, twenty-one people contributed a total of 13s. 7d. At Plaitford, Wiltshire, eight people gave 3s. 5d. between them, Samuel Tarrant, curate, heading the list with sixpence. At Salehurst, Sussex, £1. 6s. 2d. was collected from door to door and 'more in the after noone in ye body of ye Church uppon second motion July 16, 1654 ye sume of 01^{li} 06^{s} 06^{d}.'[1]

Although many parishes contributed comparatively small amounts, the total gradually became impressive. By 1653 it had already reached over £4,500. Of this total the army had contributed about £511, London £961, Somerset was foremost of the counties with a contribution of almost £436, while personal gifts sent direct to the Treasurer amounted to about £861.[2] But the project, like all projects for the collection of money, was fraught with difficulties; opposition was encountered in the city and in the country. Earlier attempts had been made to collect money for the Indians and these were an embarrassment to the Society — in particular the efforts of Weld and Peter.

In 1649 Edward Winslow wrote to Weld, telling him that 'divers Ministers (who used to meet at Sion Colledge)' were slow in furthering the collection of funds 'because they *were unsatisfied in monies they had formerly Collected for transporting children to New England* and never knew how it was disposed, and some went further, in blaming those that had been agents in that worke.'[3] Weld replied to this letter on 2 January 1649/50 and, at about the same time, must have written a tract entitled: 'Innocency cleared conteining a just defence of Mr Weld & Mr Peters. . . . To silence the malitious, to satisfie the sober & to remove the obstruction of ye contribution for propagateing the Gospell to ye Natives in New England. Written by Tho: Weld &.'[4] In spite of liberal Biblical quotation, an explanation of his actions as agent, and a restatement of his accounts, 'Innocency cleared' did not achieve its pur-

[1] *Ibid.*, ff. 52, 54, 59, 61.

[2] Ledger, 1650–60. Printed by G. P. Winship, *The New England Company of 1649 and John Eliot . . .* (Boston, Mass., Prince Society, 1920), lxviii.

[3] Bodleian, Ms. Rawlinson C934, ff. 26–7.

[4] Presumably it was intended to add Hugh Peter's name as joint author.

pose: the Society did not even consider it worth printing. Weld concluded the tract with these words: '(This stone of offence being now rowled away) there may be no obstruction, either in good peoples contributeing or in godly ministers exciting their people to contribute freely to this glorious worke.'[1] However, 'this Old Objection', as Weld called it, continued to hinder the collections. The basic problem remained the same — Weld was unable to show what had become of the money after it had left his hands.

Some time during 1647 he had sent his accounts to the General Court of Massachusetts for auditing, and in the same year Ezekiel Rogers wrote to John Winthrop begging him to see that the Court attend to the matter quickly.[2] Nothing, however, was done until the Society wrote, in April 1651, asking for an audited copy of Weld's accounts, which was in due course supplied by the General Court of Massachusetts. The Society also asked the Commissioners of the United Colonies to account for the disbursal of 'those ancient gifts'. The Commissioners replied in September 1651 explaining that the money had been spent in 'foundation worke' and that to supply an account was now impossible because many of those responsible were either dead or gone away.[3] Consequently, the Society had to carry out its work in the face of 'this Old Objection' and without any opportunity of producing an answer to satisfy its critics.

Apart from the legacy of Weld's and Peter's efforts, the Society had to cope with the insinuations and criticisms of those opposed to New England and opposed to any such collection. It was often argued that there was a greater need to foster education at home than abroad, as Winslow put it: 'our levelers, they will have nothing to doe to promote humaine learning, there is to much of it allreddy.' No 'worke of God mett with more opposition', the Society complained, while 'the malitious prophane carelesse and envious tongues and pens of too many' in New England did nothing to make matters easier.[4]

To all its critics the Society would only answer in the most general

[1] *Ibid.*, f. 30. *Innocency cleared* was printed in *N.E.H.G.R.*, XXXVI (1882), 64–70.

[2] M.H.S. *Collections, 3rd series*, I, 26.

[3] *Acts*, I, 193, 195.

[4] *Acts*, I, 197; II, 431.

terms. Henry Whitfield, in the dedication of *The Light appearing more and more towards the perfect Day* (1651) explained the purpose of the tract as showing '*how happily the Lord carrieth on his work there*' and 'to remove such false surmises and aspersions, suggested on purpose to retard the work.' To those who questioned New England's 'affections' towards Parliament, he asserted that both the rulers and the people of New England were 'faithful and cordial' to it. '*Others endeavour more directly to prejudice the work, by suggesting that the charity of the wel-affected hath been abused, in that there is no such work, or that there is a greater noise made of it in the world then there is cause.*' To this Whitfield answered that no business could be carried out with greater truth, that he had seen the accounts and that they were ready to be shown to Parliament 'if need require'.[1] Similar assurances were reiterated in *Strength out of Weaknesse* (1652).

John Eliot himself, although 'the principal instrument' in the Indians' conversion, was also in some respects a liability. In the first place, Eliot was a master of the begging letter. Before the Society was founded he had solicited assistance which was sent to him direct and after 1649 he saw no reason for discontinuing his efforts. This resulted in a number of private collections which were a constant irritation both to the Society and to the Commissioners of the United Colonies. Edward Winslow, in a letter dated 5 April 1652, expressed this irritation when he wrote:[2]

> Wee are very much troubled by pryvate Collections sent by Mr Butcher and procured by him to the greate prejudice of the Worke, wee endeavoringe to purchase Lands of Inheritance and to mayneteyne the Worke with the Revenue, Hee sendinge over what hee getts, & wee knowe not but by accident what hee sends nor to whome, soe that wee are like to bee att noe certayntyes.

On 19 July 1652, Eliot wrote to Jonathan Hanmer, minister of Barnstaple, Devon, who had collected some money privately, asking him to buy strong linen, canvas and other good hempen cloth 'because in the hot sumors the Indians delight to goo in linnon, and work, if in any garment, only a linnon garment, if they can get it.' He further in-

[1] *Op. cit.*, 'The Epistle Dedicatory'.
[2] Bodleian, Ms. Rawlinson C934, f. 16.

structed Hanmer that if the goods were sent from London 'there is a faithfull friend of mine Mr. Butcher, who will conveigh any such things to me.' Cloth to the value of £52, including carriage, was sent to Eliot by Hanmer in 1653. He also received through Hanmer a gift of £5 from Ferdinando Nicolls of Exeter and another gift from Mr. Spragot or Spegot and 'his religious familie.'[1]

Jonathan Hanmer was not the only person who conducted private collections on Eliot's behalf, to the intense annoyance of the Society. Thomas Thorowgood also collected for Eliot in Norfolk. While the Society could 'bee att noe certayntyes' as to what was being sent to New England, the contributors to those unofficial collections themselves became suspicious: as one would expect, the private collector was not obliged to render accounts, so that contributors never knew whether their gifts had reached the proper destination and were unlikely to feel charitably disposed towards the Society's collection. Thomas Thorowgood found it necessary to publish the following receipt in *Jews in America* (1660)[2]:

> *Received by the hand of Mr.* Thomas Thorowgood *forty pounds in good goods to be conveyed unto Mr.* Eliot *in* New-England *from several Knights, Ladies and Gentlemen* of Norfolk, *for his encouragement in his happy endeavours to gospellize the Indians*:
>
> August 30, 1652.
>
> *This, the danger of the Seas excepted, is acknowledged*
>
> By me
>
> Ri Thurston.

But Eliot caused even greater grounds for anxiety by writing to friends in England complaining that he received only £20 a year from the Commissioners, with the result that he was constantly in debt and was unable to give his children the education they deserved. Hugh Peter, who had never been very sympathetic towards the conversion of the Indians,[3] used this information as a weapon with which to attack the

[1] Rendel Harris, 'Three letters of John Eliot and a bill of lading of the "Mayflower"', *Bulletin of the John Rylands Library*, 5 (1918–20), 105–6, 109.

[2] *Op. cit.*, 2–3.

[3] M.H.S. *Collections, 4th series*, VI, 116.

whole project and even told Winslow 'in plaine tearmes hee heard the worke was but a plaine Cheat and that there was noe such thinge as Gosspell conversion amongst the Indians.' The Society was particularly concerned at Peter's reaction because he had been a member of a committee in the army for the promotion of the work, although he had 'protested against contributing a peny towards it in his person'. The Society, in writing to the Commissioners of the United Colonies, said that the news that Eliot was receiving only £20 a year 'flyeth like lightening and takes like tinder, men being extream glad to meet with any thing that may Couller over theire Covetiousnes and dull theire Zeale in soe good a worke.' The Society believed the work would 'suffer some Thousands of pounds by itt.' Accordingly, the Commissioners of the United Colonies, while justifying themselves in their previous conduct, doubled the salaries of both Eliot and Mayhew.[1]

Although from the meagre records which have survived it appears that the Society's integrity was without blemish, Englishmen in the 1650s were accustomed to fraudulent collections and suspicion came to them naturally. On 9 September 1653 Parliament took up the question of fraudulent collections and ordered that it be referred to the Council of State 'as well for the suppressing of such as are now on Foot, as for preventing the like Abuses, and Deceit of the People, for the future.'[2]

On 17 July 1655, the Council of State ordered the Society to take the most effective means at its disposal to recover money still in the hands of collectors and to explain the reasons for the delay in the Society's collections. The Society was further ordered to make a return showing all the money collected, how it had been disposed of, and how its growing revenues were employed.[3] The Society's Court approved on 10 November a letter and accounts to be signed by every member and presented to the Council of State forthwith. In December the Council of State was still ignorant of the Society's doings and the Court ordered that the accounts should be submitted without further delay and that copies of the Indian tracts should be given to each member of the Council.[4]

The Society made its return to the Council of State on 11 January

[1] *Acts*, II, 118. [2] *Journals of the House of Commons*, VII (1813), 316.
[3] *C.S.P.Col., 1574–1660*, 426. [4] Ms. 7952, 10 Nov., 18 Dec., 1655.

1655/6.[1] It was very much on the defensive and, although the accounts showed a total income for the period of its existence exceeding fourteen thousand pounds, it dealt at length with the difficulties that had been encountered in carrying on the collection. The first difficulty was that of 'finding out meete and fitt Instruments to carrye on the worke in the respective Citties and Counties.' The Society's minutes bear full witness to its plight, which continued throughout the decade 1650–60. In fact, suitable treasurers were so difficult to find that it was often forced to send blank commissions to one trustworthy person and allow him to appoint his own colleagues. Nor did it always succeed in making a happy choice when it appointed treasurers itself. Richard Lobb, treasurer for Devon, wrote to the Society explaining that the contribution of Falmouth would have been larger 'if fish in our County had not fayled as itt did' and added as a warning that another treasurer, Mr. Sampson Bond, was 'a notorious, Insynuatinge Hypocrite' liable to cause money to 'miscarry.'[2] Wales presented particular difficulties, and although the Society considered the matter of promoting collections there, nothing was achieved. In November 1656, application was made to Whitehall for the names of suitable treasurers, and nearly two years later a Mr. Cox was found who was prepared to undertake the work, but apparently either Mr. Cox thought better of his offer or the Society thought better of Mr. Cox.[3]

The return to the Council of State also complained of the 'want of zeale and activitie in the Ministers of many places, to publish and stirr up the people thereunto.' Then it raised another difficulty: 'ye Moneys that have beene Collected through the remisnesse of some & dissatisfaction of other of the Treasurers and Collectors (though Wee used our utmost endeavours to make use of the fittest persons therein) have not beene returned as they ought According to the Instructions sent them.' To cope with this contingency the Society found it necessary to employ messengers whose job it was to encourage the collection and to bring in the money from those treasurers and ministers who were loath to part with it. These messengers were paid thirty shillings a week

[1] Ms. 7943.
[2] Bodleian, Ms. Rawlinson C934, f. 22.
[3] Minutes (M.H.S. Ms.), 19 June–30 Aug. 1658.

while on tour and were provided with a horse which the Society bought for them. By 1658, however, the two messengers then in the Society's employ were no longer satisfied with their pay and demanded two shillings and sixpence in the pound on all money collected. Sometimes even the messengers failed in their task and the Society had then to invoke the law's assistance.

Yet, in spite of all difficulties, the collection was successful. The total amount collected, from the Society's foundation in 1649 to the Restoration, reached the remarkable sum of £15,910. 15s. 6½d. Of this, nearly £1,242 came from personal contributions sent direct to the Treasurer. The army was far the most generous benefactor, giving over £3,000. Yorkshire came next with over £1,100, followed by London with almost the same amount. London had suffered particularly from the aftermath of the Weld and Peter episode, so that as late as September 1659 the Society ordered one of its messengers to visit ministers in the City whose parishes had not contributed 'and in case they desire satisfaction concerninge this business that they would repare unto Mr Richard Floyde or att the meetinge of this Court att Coopers Hall'; however, those ministers who had refused to support the Society remained adamant. Devon and Somerset contributed more than £900 each while Kent, Essex, Suffolk and Wiltshire all contributed over £500.[1]

But there was another source of income which yielded about £4,000 between 1653 and 1660 — rents. The act of 1649 provided for the purchase of property and as early as April 1651 the Society determined to invest 'that soe the Prinsipall bee not eat up as it comes but som Money bee layed out to purchase a standing Revenew.'[2] The purchase of property and the urgency for its purchase were used as arguments for the encouragement of contributors. In fact nearly £12,000 was laid out for this purpose.

Early in 1652 the Society opened negotiations with the Committee for Sequestered Estates, on which two of its members, Edward Winslow and William Molines, served, and on 3 August 1652 concluded the pur-

[1] Compiled from the Society's Ledger, 1650–60, printed by G. P. Winship: *The New England Company*, lxviii–lxxxiv, and from Accounts, 1653–64 (M.H.S. Ms.).

[2] *Acts*, I, 194.

chase of certain fee farm rents in Northumberland. With the Mercers' Company it acquired the moeity of the tithes arising from the parish of Woodhorne and with the trustees of the parish of Hampstead it acquired half the rents from the rectory of Woodhorne, half the income of the prebend of Binchester and half the rent of a mill at Binchester. Thus for the modest outlay of £250. 19s. 5d. an annual return of £44. 11s. 4d. was received. In theory this investment carried little responsibility as the Mercers' Company, landlords of great experience, and the trustees of the parish of Hampstead dealt with the collection of the rents and undertook to pay the Society its share twice yearly.[1] In practice, however, the arrangement was not altogether satisfactory, as both the Mercers' Company and the Hampstead Trustees were very remiss in making over the money. In fact, the Society must have realized the disadvantages of this investment from the beginning, for when it next approached the Committee for Sequestered Estates on 27 November 1652, it asked for assistance in purchasing, by private contract, delinquents' estates to the value of £350 per annum.[2]

In the following year the Society received an annuity of £20, the gift of William Littleton, gentleman, of the Moor, Shropshire. Littleton had been appointed a Commissioner for better propagation of the Gospel in Wales in February 1649/50, probably in the hope that he would support that cause from his own pocket.[3] He had during his lifetime 'often declared his great desire' to encourage the Indians' conversion and had told 'severall persons that debated or discoursed with him thereaboutes' that he would make a gift to the Society, either before he died, or in his will.[4] He was as good as his word; in his will dated 29 May 1653, he bequeathed to the Society a rent charge of £20 per annum arising out of landed property at Aston, in Herefordshire.[5]

But the Society's biggest acquisition was made in 1653. This was the purchase of the manors of Eriswell and Chamberlains in the county of

[1] Ms. 7945, rent account, 1652–4.

[2] Letter from William Steele to 'trustees at Drury House', 27 Nov. 1652 (Bodleian, Ms. Rawlinson C934, f. 7).

[3] C. H. Firth and R. S. Rait, eds., *Acts and Ordinances*, II, 343.

[4] P.R.O. C5/62/27 mem. 3.

[5] P.C.C. 247 Brent.

Suffolk from the delinquent Colonel Thomas Bedingfield. The Society paid £6,500 on 29 September 1653, and concluded the purchase with another £500 on 23 November of the same year. The property consisted of two manor houses, a water mill, 2,460 acres of arable land, 152 acres of meadow and pasture, 17 acres of boggy or carr ground, two free warrens of about 2,000 acres and four fold courses with liberty of folding 2,240 sheep. With small additional purchases at a later date the property totalled about 6,665 acres. The Society estimated that this would bring in rents to the value of £470 per annum,[1] but it was reckoning without the inevitable misfortunes of the landlord and without foreknowledge of the Restoration.

From the beginning, the administration of the manors of Eriswell and Chamberlains proved troublesome. It was found necessary to employ an agent to collect the rents and keep an eye on the estates. Every year a committee of three members went down to Suffolk to view the property and report to the Court. But the Society was unfortunate in its tenants; one was constantly applying for a reduction in his rent, and another, the tenant of Chamberlains, not only fell into great arrears but had no stock on the property so that it seemed he would never be able to pay. By December 1659, the tenants were £500 in arrears and the Society's patience was at an end. At the instigation of the agent the tenants' goods were seized but, as the Society forlornly noticed in its minutes, the corn seized was worth only £100; the 900 sheep and other cattle belonged to sub-tenants and the Society felt itself obliged 'to deal favourably with the Sheep masters' provided they had done the property no harm. This was not the end of the worries these properties caused: to find suitable tenants remained no easy business. In February the Court advised its agent to try to find a tenant for the whole of Chamberlains at the reduced rent of £200 per annum. If he could not let it as a whole, he should let it in two parts rather than in three, and should charge £10 more per annum. If he could not let the property at all, he was to find 'an able and sufficient bayly' to manage the farm. By June 1660, Chamberlains was still unlet and the agent had had no suc-

[1] G. P. Winship, *The New England Company*, lxxi; Accounts, 1653–64 (M.H.S. Ms.); Rent account, 1652–4 (Ms. 7945); Ms. 7952, Committee for surveying the manor, 30 April 1714.

cess in finding a suitable bailiff, so that the Society was prepared to sell the corn and grass standing to anyone who would buy it. But these troubles were minor ones compared with the recovery of Eriswell and Chamberlains after the Restoration.[1]

Meanwhile the Society acquired a number of properties in London. In October 1654, it purchased three houses in Bucklersbury from Samuel Vassall, Esq. for £2,100, and these brought in £160 per annum in rents. In April 1655, it bought a house in the parish of Holy Trinity the Less from James James, citizen and apothecary, for about £650. In 1659 it bought another house in Distaff Lane for the same price with an annual rent of £50. A certain Captain Coysh gave the Society houses in St. Paul's Churchyard, but apparently these were in poor repair, as in 1657 the rents were reduced from £50 to £40 per annum. The last important purchase made by the Society was the farm of Suffolk Place at Plumstead in the county of Kent. This was bought in 1656 for £1,700 from Sir Robert Josselyn and in 1659 a small piece of land adjoining the farm was acquired for a further £40.[2]

The Society worked hard in its search for suitable investments. The Court continually appointed members to view property, who then reported on the advisability of purchase. Houses all over London and estates in all the Home Counties came under consideration. If the chosen member reported favourably, then the property would be viewed by a committee of three who would make a further report. The work involved was considerable when added to the administration of the estates already purchased. By 1658 the Society was able to write to the Commissioners of the United Colonies that it had an assured annual revenue of £600.[3] Rents received in 1653 were a mere £22. 15s. 0d. but they rose as the company acquired more property, reaching just over £800 in 1656 (although this included arrears). In the following year they totalled over £515 and in 1658 £676, but after this the troubles at the manor of Chamberlains and then a general reluctance of all tenants to pay anything more until the political weather was set fair,

[1] Minutes (M.H.S. Ms.), May 1657–June 1660 *passim*.

[2] Ms. 7945, rent account, 1652–4; Ms. 7944/1; Accounts, 1653–64 (M.H.S. Ms.).

[3] *Acts*, II, 201.

brought the rents down with a crash to £272 in 1659 and less than half that amount in 1660.[1]

But the Society was not merely concerned with the collection and investment of money. As will be seen in a later chapter, it took a keen interest in the way the money sent to New England was spent.

[1] G. P. Winship, *The New England Company*, lxviii–lxxxiv *passim*; Accounts, 1653–64 (M.H.S. Ms.); Accounts, 1659–72 (Ms. 7944/1).

3

The Company, 1660–1691

CHARLES II returned to England in the spring of 1660. The Convention Parliament which had voted for his return proceeded to make the enactments necessary to complete the Restoration. The acts and ordinances of the Interregnum were swept away by the Act of Oblivion and Indemnity and with them was swept the act of 1649 which had created the Society for Propagation of the Gospel in New England.

It was not until the autumn of 1660 that the Society took the first steps to insure its continued existence. At a Court held on 28 September 1660, a meeting was arranged with ministers of Sion College. All those members present at the Court, namely Henry Ashurst, Richard Hutchinson, John Rolfe, Thomas Speed, Thomas Bell, Joshua Woolnough, William Molines and George Clarke, together with Erasmus Smyth, were 'desired to attend Dr. Reynolds, Mr. Calamy, Mr. Ash, Mr. Baxter, Dr. Spurstow and Mr. Mantuam to consult with them about the Corporacions busines.'[1] These ministers were all interested in the Society's work and some of them had been of considerable assistance in publicizing it. Edward Reynolds had signed the letter from Oxford University in 1649, and had edited and written the dedicatory epistle to John Eliot's *A further Accompt of the Progresse of the Gospel amongst the Indians* (1659). Edmund Calamy and Simeon Ash had both given support to the Indian tracts of 1648, 1652 and 1655 and Calamy had also subscribed to Castell's petition of 1641, while William Spurstowe had lent his name to the tract of 1652 as well as to the Cambridge letter of 1649. But the Society's staunchest ally was Richard Baxter, a close friend and admirer of Henry Ashurst, the Society's Treasurer, and a correspondent of John Eliot.

[1] Minutes (M.H.S. Ms.).

Many years later Baxter wrote an account of the steps which were taken to obtain a charter: 'Mr. *Ashurst* (being the most exemplary Person for eminent Sobriety, Self-denial, Piety, and Charity, that *London* could glory of, as far as publick Observation, and Fame, and his most intimate Friends Reports could testifie) did make this (and all other Publick Good which he could do) his Business: He called the Old Corporation together, and desired me to meet them: where we all agreed, that such as had incurred the King's Displeasure, by being Members of any Courts of Justice, in *Cromwell's* days, should quietly recede and we should try if we could get the Corporation restored, and the rest continued, and more fit Men added, that the Land might be recovered.'[1] Probably at this meeting between the members of the Society and the ministers, a petition was drafted 'of Divers of his Majesties Subjects, Ministers and others for propagateing the Gospell among the miserable Heathens in America.' The petition set forth 'the hopefull proceedings of that worke' and prayed that the Society for Propagation of the Gospel in New England might be continued. It also asked that the lands formerly belonging to the Society might be recovered from those who had unlawfully taken possession of them.[2] It is possible that the Honourable Robert Boyle took part in drafting this petition, for Baxter had written to him on 20 October: 'Having some speciall use for your favourable assistance in the worke of propagating the Gospell among poore barbarous infidells, I intreate you by this messenger to send me word when I may find you at home, that I with 3 or 4 of my friends may waite uppon you.' One of these friends was Thomas Foley, the wealthy iron manufacturer, who was ready to support the Indians' cause.[3] On 14 November 1660 the petition was read before the Privy Council and the Attorney General was ordered to prepare a draft for a charter and to report to the Privy Council.

On 1 December 1660, six members of the Society, Henry Ashurst, Richard Hutchinson, George Clarke, John Rolfe, Thomas Bell and Erasmus Smyth met together at what was probably the last formal

[1] Matthew Sylvester, ed., *Reliquiae Baxterianae* (1696), lib. I, pt. II, 290.

[2] *Acts of the Privy Council, Colonial*, I (1908), no. 493.

[3] Royal Society, Boyle Letters, I, 31. Baxter's letter was written: 'From Mr Foley's house in Austin fryares in Bread Street'.

Court held by the Society. Unfortunately no minutes survive other than the bare list of names of those present, but there can be little doubt that the meeting was as important as any in the Society's history. It must have been at this meeting that proposals for the terms of the charter were discussed. The draft was actually made by Erasmus Smyth, who no doubt adopted the Court's proposals. The Attorney General, Sir Geoffrey Palmer, perused it early in 1661, charging £10 for his trouble.[1]

To obtain a charter is normally a lengthy process and in the Society's case it was particularly difficult as the grant was opposed in several quarters. An especially formidable opponent was Colonel Thomas Bedingfield, from whom the Society had purchased the estates of Eriswell and Chamberlains; he had ordered the Society's tenants to pay their rent to him, and was doing everything in his power to recover his title to those estates. In his efforts, he was fortunate in having the strong support of the Attorney General. In about November 1660, Bedingfield petitioned the King: he pointed out that he had raised and maintained a regiment for Charles I, had sold his estates to do so, and had been banished from England; in particular, he had sold the manors of Eriswell and Chamberlains to the Society, but had never been paid for them, and as the Society was unlawfully constituted he had now taken possession of the manors. In conclusion he asked that care might be taken to protect his title in any future charter granted to the Society.[2]

Others, too, had little time for the Society or its works. Edward Godfrey, formerly Governor of Maine, had suggested in 1659 that some of the Society's funds might be spent in his colony and that payments might be made to a minister of his naming.[3] Neither of his suggestions was acted upon, so that when, several years later, he met Erasmus Smyth at the Attorney General's office in the act of soliciting a charter for the Society, he saw an opportunity for retaliation. Accordingly he made a statement to the effect that the Society had done everything on behalf of Massachusetts and that the other colonies in New England had received no benefit from a charity intended for New England in general. To sharpen his criticism he added: 'None either there or heer had any

[1] Minutes (M.H.S. Ms.), 1 Dec. 1660; Ms. 7944/1, 5 Jan. & 5 Feb. 1660/1.

[2] *Calendar of State Papers, Domestic, 1660–1*, 390.

[3] Minutes (M.H.S. Ms.), 19 March 1658/9; *Acts*, II, 217.

acting in these affayres that did not idolise the Church Covenant.'[1] But more highly coloured accounts of the Society and its affairs were also current in Whitehall; for instance, one attributed the collection for the Indians to the efforts of Hugh Peter and claimed that the money collected had gone into private pockets.[2]

But this tittle-tattle was far less harmful to the Society's interests than the powerful opposition of Bedingfield. It was of vital importance to the members of the proposed corporation that the property formerly belonging to the Society should be recovered, and of this property that claimed by Bedingfield was the most valuable. In fact the Society's annual revenue apart from donations had derived from its estates, so that if the charter did not specifically settle the title to this property upon the new corporation it would be destitute from its inception. Yet when, on 10 April 1661, the Attorney General reported to the Privy Council as he had been ordered to do, no such property clause appeared in his draft.[3]

The omission did not go unnoticed, for Baxter had interested the Lord Chancellor himself in the cause. Indeed, the Lord Chancellor approved of 'the Work, as that which could not be for any Faction, or Evil end, but honourable to the King and Land' and had told Baxter that '*Beddingfield* could have no right to that which he had sold, and that the right was in the King, who would readily grant it to the good use intended.' He also promised 'his best assistance to recover it.'[4] So on this occasion the Attorney General was ordered by the Privy Council to insert a clause in the charter which would settle the property upon the new corporation. The Privy Council also ordered that the new corporation should have power to purchase property to the value of £2,000 per annum and Lord Valentia was ordered to examine the list of names submitted for approval. On 17 May 1661 the Privy Council ordered that the new names should be inserted into the charter.[5] But all was not

[1] P.R.O. COi/15/19; *C.S.P. Col., 1661–1668*, no. 33.

[2] *C.S.P. Col., 1661–1668*, p. 26.

[3] *Ibid.*, 23; *Acts of the Privy Council, Colonial*, I, no. 510; a copy of the Order in Council is preserved amongst the Company's records (Ms. 7952).

[4] Matthew Sylvester, ed., *Reliquiae Baxterianae*, lib. I, pt. II, 290.

[5] *C.S.P. Col., 1661–1668*, p. 31; *Acts of the Privy Council, Colonial*, I, no. 514.

well, for the Attorney General had done nothing to repair his omission of the property clause from the charter. Several of the nominated members of the new corporation petitioned the King to rectify the omission, bewailing the fact that the Attorney General was absent in the country and asking that a charter should be speedily granted.[1] Yet no mention was made of the property clause on 7 August, when the Privy Council ordered letters patent to be prepared constituting Robert Boyle the first Governor.[2] And finally on 7 February 1661/2, when the charter itself was sealed, it lacked the vital clause, undoubtedly to the intense gratification of Bedingfield and the acute disappointment of Ashurst and his friends. There can be little doubt that Bedingfield's 'friendship of the Attorney General', as well as the latter's natural sympathy with a royalist, had stood him in good stead.

The only passage in the charter which could possibly be regarded as referring to the property formerly held by the Society was contained in its introduction. Here the royal intention was declared: 'to the end that such our livinge Subiects, as either have already byn aydinge herein, or as shall hereafter bee willing to Contribute hereunto, may not bee discouraged in theire intended Charitie for want of sufficient authority and Patronage from us, faithfully to Order and dispose all and every sum and sums of money, goods, Chattells, lands, Tenements or hereditaments, that have byn, or shall or may bee given for the purposes aforesaid.' The clause which dealt with property merely empowered the Company 'to purchase, take, have, hold, receive and enioye, any Mannors, lands, Tenements, liberties, Priviledges, jurisdiccions, and hereditaments, whatsoever, of what kinde, quality or nature soever they bee' not exceeding the yearly value of two thousand pounds.[3]

The main argument of the charter's preamble was that through commerce and 'the paines and industry of certaine English Ministers of the Gospell' many natives had been brought over from 'the power of darknesse and the Kingdome of Sathan, to the Knowledge of the true and only God and to an owninge and professing of the Protestant Religion.' It continued by pointing out, as had the preamble to the act of 1649, that 'unlesse some due and competent Provision bee made to lay a

[1] Royal Society, Boyle Papers, Miscellaneous, XL, 7.
[2] *C.S.P. Col., 1661–1668*, no. 152.
[3] Ms. 7908, mem. 1.

foundation for the educating, Cloathing, civilizinge, and instructinge the poor Natives, and alsoe for the supporte and maintenance of such Ministers of the Gospell, Schoolmasters and other Instruments, as have byn, are, or shall bee sett apart and employed for the Carryinge on of soe pious and Christian a worke, the same may bee much retarded, and a worke, soe happily begune, discouraged, those Planters whoe first began and Contributed largely thereunto, beinge of themselves unable to beare the whole Charge thereof.' The 'Royal resolution' was to seek the welfare of the colonies 'by puttinge an industrious People into a way of Trade and Comerce . . . but more especially to endeavour the good and Salvacion of their imortall Soules, and the publishing the most glorious Gospell of Christ amongst them.'

The corporation created by the charter was to be known 'by the name of the Company for Propagacion of the Gospell in New England, and the parts adjacent in America.' With a name so long, it is not surprising that in time it became known as the New England Company, as it is still called today. However, in New England the Company was usually referred to as 'the Corporation', just as the Society had been before the Restoration.

In the eyes of the law the Society had never existed. It was not mentioned in the charter and when members of the Company referred to it, they always spoke of 'the late pretended Corporation'. Yet there was definite continuity between the old Society and the new Company. Indeed, nine members of the Society were amongst the forty-five members named in the charter. This meant that only seven members of the Society were not put forward by Baxter and Ashurst for membership of the Company. Of these William Steele was not only unacceptable but unavailable as he had taken the precaution of going to Holland in 1660. Thomas Ayres and Abraham Babington were also unacceptable as they had both been appointed Commissioners for a High Court of Justice in 1650, while William Molines had been prominent in public affairs throughout the Interregnum. It was, no doubt, on similar grounds that Major William Puckle was overlooked by Baxter and Ashurst, although he was to remain interested in the Indians' conversion to the end of his life. Captain Mark Coe, on the other hand, may have been passed over because he had never shown great interest in the

Society's work. The nine members of the Society who were nominated proved acceptable to the Privy Council and as Baxter put it: 'many other godly, able Citizens made up the rest: Only we left the Nomination of some Lords to His Majesty, as not presuming to nominate such.'[1] In fact this task was left to the Earl of Anglesey, who chose the Lord Chancellor, the Lord Treasurer, the Lord Privy Seal, the Duke of Albemarle, the Lord Steward, the Lord Chamberlain, Viscount Saye and Sele and himself. The choice was impressive on paper but, with the exception of the Earl of Anglesey who attended Court twice, the lords did nothing to direct or influence the Company's affairs.

Amongst the 'many other godly, able Citizens', none threw himself into the Company's affairs with more energy than the newly named Governor — the Honourable Robert Boyle. The Company was indeed fortunate in securing for its first Governor such a man; well known for his scientific works, he was also distinguished in other fields. His extensive notebooks bear witness to his interest in the propagation of the Gospel, while his knowledge of the Scriptures was remarkable for a layman, even in an age of Biblical scholarship. In spite of a self-declared aversion to learning languages, he knew enough Hebrew, Greek, Chaldee and Syriac to read the Scriptures in the original. His belief in the significance of the Bible is shown by his support of its translation into foreign tongues. He paid either the whole or part of the expense of printing the Bible in Irish and Welsh, the New Testament in Turkish and the Gospels and Acts in Malayan.[2]

Boyle was well suited to the position of Governor of the New England Company from almost every point of view. In particular, his interest in the American colonies and their affairs made him an excellent choice. As a member of the Council for Foreign Plantations he was well informed on the subject of the colonies and on occasion closely associated with affairs in New England. In 1664 the Governor and Court of the Massachusetts Bay colony begged him to use his influence to ensure that the Commissioners sent by Charles II would not encroach upon their religious liberty and in 1673 he was again asked to protect New England's interests. Although he often used his influence on the colonists'

[1] Matthew Sylvester, ed., *Reliquiae Baxterianae*, lib. I, pt. II, 290.
[2] *Dictionary of National Biography*, VI, 118–123.

behalf he was not above censuring them: in 1681 he wrote to Eliot saying that he had heard of the 'great severity to some Dissenters' shown by the Massachusetts colony. He continued: 'This severe Proceeding seems to be ye more strange and ye less defensible in those who haveing left their native countrey & crossd ye vast Ocean to settle in a wilderness that they may there enjoy ye liberty of worshipping God according to their owne Consciences, seem to be more engagd than other men to allow their brethren a share in what they thought was so much all Good mens Due.'[1]

Boyle had many correspondents in America who wrote to him on a variety of subjects. For example, William Avery wrote of natural phenomena in New England, of the clay at Martha's Vineyard, and of his alchemical discoveries and speculations; William Penn described the Indians, natural ores and the wild flowers; John Winthrop wrote describing the death of fish in a pond at Watertown. Some of his friends sent him specimens, and on one occasion the Company paid the carriage 'of certaine Harts Hornes sent as a present from New England to Mr Robert Boyle Governour of this Company $00^{li}04^{s}0^{d}$.'[2]

It was particularly fortunate for the Company that Boyle was a moderate Anglican. On the one hand he was fully conversant with, and often sympathetic to, nonconformist views and these, of course, were held by most of the Company's members. On the other hand his religious convictions and his strong family ties with the Anglican church did something to obscure the Company's true religious complexion and helped to make it more widely acceptable.

Equally valuable to the Company was his outstanding ability in managing its affairs and his remarkable conscientiousness. Unlike the President of the old Society, the new Governor hardly ever missed a meeting. It is true that the charter required the Governor's presence, but Boyle was so genuinely concerned in the Company's affairs that he had every question referred to him for his consideration. The charge for horse hire to take one of the Company's officers to Pall Mall in order to consult him was a normal sundry in the Company's accounts.

Baxter had no doubt remembered, when he suggested Boyle as

[1] Royal Society, Boyle Letters, VI, 94.
[2] Ms. 7944/2, Ms. 7911/1, 12 July 1676.

Governor, that he was a wealthy and generous bachelor. At the Restoration Boyle had obtained from Charles II the confirmation of a grant, originally made by Cromwell, of expropriated church property in Ireland. But he had many scruples about its use and had assured Michael Boyle, Bishop of Cork, that two thirds of the income would be used 'by releeving the Poore in those Places, & contributing, if need be, towards the Maintenance of Ministers' in Ireland or elsewhere. In the same letter he reported the news of his appointment as Governor of the New England Company and continued: 'soe pious a Designe, as is pursu'd by this Corporation, is now in danger to miscarry for want of Maintainance, soe that ye Worke being soe charitable, and I having a peculiar Call to promote it, I think, after having advised with the Bishop of Lincolne in ye case, that it becomes me, on such a Juncture of Circumstances, to apply ye other 3d part, or thereabouts of what ye Kings Grant will yeild me for 6 or 7 Years at least, to ye carrying on of soe unquestionably good a Worke.'[1] Although he did not immediately give money to the Company, and was never able to use his Irish estates for this purpose, he did give the sum of three hundred pounds in 1679 and also gave two small sums to Eliot.

If Boyle was the Company's master, Henry Ashurst was its most devoted servant. He was also the most active member of the old Society to become a member of the new Company. Treasurer of both, he did more than anyone to establish the Company during years which were crowded with difficulties. From 1662 onwards he gave £100 per annum towards supporting the ejected ministers of Lancashire, his native county. In 1663 he tried to persuade pious Londoners to contribute towards the same cause and he sent Baxter to Lord Chancellor Clarendon 'to acquaint him with it and get his consent, that it might not be taken for a fomenting of faction.' It is not surprising to find that this project received no support from the Lord Chancellor and had to be abandoned. 'Since then,' Baxter relates, 'he and others set up a Conventicle, which methinks, might be tolerated by Bishops themselves.' In 1668 Ashurst was elected Alderman of London and avoided holding office by paying a fine of £420. He was criticized for showing a lack of public spirit, but Baxter defended him on the grounds that 'it was only

[1] Royal Society, Boyle Letters, I, 158–9.

to keep the peace of his Conscience, which could not digest, 1. The Corporation Declaration and Oath; Nor 2. The execution of the Laws against Nonconforming Ministers and People.'[1] At least six other members of the Company also found it impossible to hold the office of Alderman for the same reasons.

The members of the Company were, with the exception of the peers, predominantly merchants. Almost all of these belonged to one or other of the livery companies of the City of London: usually one of the great twelve, the Drapers' Company and the Merchant Taylors' Company having the largest share. This alone is some evidence of the prosperity of those whom Ashurst and Baxter chose for membership.

Several of the new members had held office or served on the Committees of the East India Company and the Levant Company. As a rule they do not seem to have used their positions to interest these companies in the propagation of the Gospel. But Boyle, who was a member of the East India Company, did attempt to persuade it to convert the natives 'in whose countries we have flourishing factories.' On 5 March 1676/7 he wrote to Robert Thompson, a member of both the East India Company and the New England Company, excusing himself on the grounds of illness from attending East India House, but professing himself happy that the subject of conversion was to be raised again. He also told Thompson that he had discussed the whole question with Lord Berkeley, another member of both companies.[2]

Three physicians were named in the charter; all were outstanding members of their profession and all of them took an extremely keen interest in the Company's affairs. Thomas Cox served as a physician in the Parliamentary Army and was one of the original members of the Royal Society; he became physician to the King in 1665 and President of the Royal College of Physicians in 1682. Sir John Micklethwaite was also physician to Charles II and held the office of President of the Royal College of Physicians from 1659 until 1682. Edmond Trench, less eminent than Micklethwaite or Cox, was, like them, a fellow of the Royal College of Physicians.

[1] R. Baxter, *Faithful Souls shall be with Christ*, 45, 47; A. B. Beaven, *The Aldermen of the City of London*, I, 118.

[2] *The Works of . . . Robert Boyle* (1772), I, cviii–cix.

Despite the Company's increased membership — forty-five as opposed to the Society's sixteen — it was no more active than the smaller body had been: although at first meetings were held as frequently as they had been before 1660, they were no better attended. The charter authorized meetings to be held whenever necessary 'in some convenient Place within the Citty of London.' This convenient place was once more the Coopers' Company Hall until it was burned down in the Great Fire in 1666; then private members' houses were used instead — in particular Ashurst's house, 'the Golden Key' in Watling Street. The Company also met occasionally at East India House and at the house of Boyle's sister, Lady Ranelagh, although this was in Pall Mall and outside the City boundaries.

The Company held its first Court on 27 March 1662. Eighteen members were present. This comfortably exceeded the quorum which was specified by the charter for most purposes: the election or removal of the Governor required thirteen members; the election of new members or the discharge of old ones required the presence of the Governor and twelve members as did the election of officers. The management of estates and the passing of by-laws required a quorum of the Governor and eight while the Governor and five members had 'power from time to time upon all emergent occasions, to allow of all incident charges.' After the reading of the charter, John Hooper and Anthony Trafford were reappointed clerk and messenger respectively; each had received his full salary for the year 1661, although the Society had ceased to exist and the charter had not yet been granted; there can be no doubt that, whatever the legal position, Ashurst himself regarded the Society and the Company as one and the same thing. At the same Court 'the Seale of ye late reputed Corporation' was ordered to be altered 'as soone as Conveniently it may: and as much of ye Title of ye new Charter put into ye Inscription thereof as it will admitt of.'[1]

[1] Ms. 7952. The inscription on the seal now reads: THE.SEALE.OF.THE CORP: FOR. PROMOTING.THE.GOSP: IN.NEW.ENGLAND.1661. The seal depicts a standing Indian holding a book in his left hand to which he is pointing with his right hand. Above him a ribbon contains the text: COME OVER.AND HELPE VS. An example of the seal is contained in the British Museum's collection of detached seals — CXXX, 27.

The Court also appointed a committee to examine and audit the accounts of Henry Ashurst. These were duly approved on 3 April 1662 and Henry Ashurst was elected the Company's first Treasurer. The accounts that survive are not very satisfactory in showing the disposition of the Society's funds between September 1660 and March 1662, but they appear to be in order except for one cancelled entry in the rough accounts between 10 and 17 November 1660, which reads: 'Paid Mr. George Clarke 500^{li}' and in the margin: 'To be lefte out.'[1] This may merely refer to the fact that Clarke held £500 for the Treasurer and returned it when required — a normal practice at the time.

Receipts during the period had fallen away to just over £400. The balance in hand on 28 September 1660 was £1,154; rents amounted to about £286; a hundred pounds owed by Floyd's executors was returned, and the Society raised £18 by lending £400 each to John Harwood, a London merchant and Samuel Thomson, stationer, at six per cent. Ashurst had seen that a request for £800 from New England in September 1660 was duly paid. The other payments made were the salaries of the clerk and messenger, and of the printer employed by the Society in New England, and of course the expenses of obtaining the new charter which amounted to over £90. This meant that the balance when the accounts were audited in April 1662 amounted to about £491.[2] Thus the financial position of the new Company was far from satisfactory. At its first meeting the Earl of Anglesey announced that Sir William Morice, Secretary of State, who had obtained the royal consent to the Company's charter, had made a gift of £100 and that he would add £50 to it.[3] But, however welcome this windfall, it did not solve the Company's financial predicament.

To some members of the Company a new collection seemed the easiest and most satisfactory way to restore its fortunes. On 10 April 1662 Governor Boyle was asked by the Court 'to use ye best of his Endeavours with ye Lord Chauncellor for a generall Contribution for ye carrying on the good worke of propagating ye Gospell.'[4] The Company petitioned the King for a brief to enable it to make a fresh collection, and on 2 July 1662 this was read before the Privy Council. The

[1] Ms. 7944/1.
[2] Ms. 7911/1; Ms. 7944/1.
[3] Ms. 7952.
[4] *Ibid.*

case presented gave an outline of the work done by the Society and continued: 'His Majesty considering ye Consequence of soe glorious a Worke hath lately erected a Corporacion to carry on and perfect this worke, who at their first entrance cheifley by meanes of Collonel Bedingfield for ye space of neare two yeares past, interrupting their possession and receiving ye profitts of Lands purchased of him with ye greatest parte of ye moneyes received by the former Collections doe finde their charges have of late much exceeded their incumbs, and their Revenue much to smale at present, to enable them to carry on soe chargeable, as well as charitable a worke.' The Company therefore asked for another collection 'which they hope wilbee lesse scrupled at because ye benifit intended by ye first Collections was not received, there being divers Countyes in the Kingdome, and Severall parishes in ye Citie, in which noe collections for this worke have yet bene made.' The Privy Council recommended the matter to the Lord Chancellor who was asked 'to take the same into his particular care and give order for a Briefe accordingly.'[1]

But no further reference to the brief is to be found apart from a cancelled entry in the Company's minutes for 19 August 1663: 'Ordered that John Hooper Doe procure the Coppy of the briefe prepared for the Colleccon accordinge to the order of the Councell.'[2] The brief itself was apparently never issued. During 1662 there was a small trickle from the collection of the Interregnum — nearly £68 from Shropshire, about £9 from Norfolk and £6 'of Mr Edmund Calamy late minister of Aldermanbury London severall Summes of money which were given him by divers persons at severall tymes.' As late as January 1668/9 the accounts record the receipt from Mr. Whiteway of Dorchester of £4 formerly collected and in December 1669 a further £3. 10s.[3]

The Company's failure to obtain a brief for another collection must have been due to the success it was having in the recovery of its property. The Bedingfield affair was, of course, the most urgent problem confronting the newly formed Company. It had sought to remedy the

[1] Bodleian, Ms. Clarendon 74, f. 263; Royal Society, Boyle Papers, Theology, IV, 122; *C.S.P. Col., 1661–1668*, 95–6; P.R.O. CO5/903/6–9; CO1/16/70.

[2] Minutes (M.H.S. Ms.).

[3] Ms. 7944/1; Ms. 7911/1.

omission of the property clause from its charter by obtaining an Act of Parliament but when the Solicitor General, Sir Heneage Finch, was asked for an opinion he apparently advised against it.[1] The Company decided that all tenants should be warned by letter that rents due must be paid only to the Treasurer and that '3 or 4 more (besides ye Lord Chauncellor) of the Lords names, members of this Corporation, bee inserted in ye Letters to bee written to ye Tennants.' It no doubt considered that this would lend authority to its proceedings, but unfortunately more than lords' names was needed to recover the property in Bedingfield's hands. Ashurst and John Rolfe were consequently ordered to apply to the Attorney General for advice as to whether a bill against Bedingfield should be presented in Chancery or Exchequer and to act accordingly.[2]

The bill of complaint, filed in Chancery by Richard Hutchinson, William Molines and the Company against Thomas Bedingfield and others recited the terms of the purchase of the manors of Eriswell and Chamberlains — how Bedingfield, after payment of £7,000 for the property free from all encumbrances, had quit but had now re-entered. Not only did he withhold the property from its rightful owners and refuse to render any account of the rents he received, but he had done everything in his power to delay the grant of the Company's charter. Bedingfield answered in November 1662: he and his father had lost £60,000 in the late rebellion; he had raised 'A regiment of Foote and a troope of horse which he conducted in his said Majestyes service & for his defence till by the fortune of Warr he was over powered Most of his soldiers slaine or taken prisoners and himself alsoe sore wounded [and] taken prisoner by ye Rebells.' His lands had been sequestered by a committee of which Edward Winslow and William Molines were members. The sale of Eriswell and Chamberlains to Winslow, Hutchinson and Molines in the name of the late pretended Society had, Bedingfield contended, been on the understanding that the deed of sale would become void when the monarchy was restored to power.[3]

However, by 6 July 1663 the Company had obtained a decree in its

[1] Ms. 7944/1, 12 March 1661.
[2] Ms. 7952, 3, 24 April 1662.
[3] P.R.O. C6/160/107.

favour; four days later at the Lord Chancellor's request it considered what allowance should be made to Bedingfield out of the rents which he had been receiving. The Company suggested that he should buy back the property for the original purchase money, £7,000, with interest and that a separate agreement should be made about the profits which had been derived from the property. Bedingfield was not ready to accept this offer and again pleaded great suffering in His Majesty's service. The Company considered that its offer remained a fair one and on 31 July 1663 appointed a committee to treat with him. He finally declared his submission to the decree on 23 November, and the Company was able to take full possession of its estate.[1] Yet it was no nearer extracting from Bedingfield the rents which had been paid to his nominees, amounting to about £2,000. Boyle in a letter to the Commissioners explained the difficulty: 'wee having had to doe with a man who hath as little estate to recompence the wrongs done us, as he made scruple to doe the same.'[2] Not until 1669 was a settlement finally reached, the Company taking proceedings in Chancery against Thomas Wharton and others, who, as Bedingfield's nominees, had received the rents during 1660 and 1661.[3] Although the Company's title was now secure the tenants did not pay regularly and were constantly in arrears. At times they owed as much as a thousand pounds — more than twice the total annual income of the Company at this period. In 1668 John Cheston, tenant of Eriswell, was prosecuted, as he owed nearly £600.[4] But the Company was at the mercy of its tenants for, even if the tenants' goods were distrained, these were often worth less than the amount owing, and better tenants were not easy to find.

Apart from Eriswell and Chamberlains, the Company succeeded in securing its former property without difficulty. Its title to Suffolk Place farm, at Plumstead, in the county of Kent, and to the London properties in Trinity Lane and Bucklersbury were uncontested, though the London properties were both devastated by the Great Fire in 1666. The Company managed to rebuild in Bucklersbury with the minimum of

[1] Minutes (M.H.S. Ms.), 10, 31 July, 25 Nov. 1663.
[2] Ms. 7936, f. 4.
[3] P.R.O. C10/120/80.
[4] Minutes (M.H.S. Ms.), 6 Oct., 16 Nov. 1688.

delay, but Trinity Lane proved a constant source of worry to the Court for a minute financial return; by the 1680s the houses there were yielding a total rent of twenty pounds per annum, and out of this two rent charges under the will of Sir John Gore had to be found — one of four pounds per annum to the parish of Holy Trinity the Less and the other of nine pounds to the Merchant Taylors' Company: after taxes had been paid only six pounds per annum was left.[1]

But the Company did have trouble in securing William Littleton's annuity which was payable from the rents of property at Aston, Herefordshire. In February 1666/7 it filed a suit in Chancery against Tymothy Littleton and Edward Littleton. In November Edward Littleton offered to buy off the annual rent charge for three hundred pounds, and to make up the arrears; the Company rightly refused the offer but enquired whether the Littletons would accept a private ruling from the Lord Keeper. This they refused but in due course the Company secured a decree in Chancery awarding it all the arrears owing and costs of Court. Finally in June 1688, the Company agreed to sell outright for four hundred pounds.[2]

It is not surprising that the Company's financial position from the Restoration to about 1690 was far from satisfactory. Much litigation, the Great Fire and the general hazards of landed property as a form of investment combined to make its revenue far smaller than it had been before the Restoration. Although in the years before the fire its income was about six hundred pounds a year, this was partly made up of arrears. The annual income totalled only about four hundred and forty pounds until the 1690s.

While gifts to the Company helped it through this difficult period, even one of these caused trouble. Theodore Herringe, minister of the Gospel in York, left the Company fifty pounds, to be paid within five years of his death. Although his will was proved on 1 March 1657, it was not until April 1668 that the Company managed, after taking proceedings in Chancery, to recover the money. Fortunately other gifts

[1] *Ibid.*, 1666–77 *passim*; H. Ashurst to Boyle, 24 Oct. 1666 (Royal Society, Boyle Letters, I, 12); Ms. 7911/2.

[2] Minutes (M.H.S. Ms.) 5 May, 21 Nov. 1670; P.R.O. C5/62/27; Ms. 8000 contains several indentures relating to this annuity

caused no difficulties and reached the Treasurer's hands without mishap.[1]

The largest gift of money received during the seventeenth century came from France. The Court minutes recorded that 'Monsieur Mowsche of the Citie of Paris in Fraunce hath (by the meanes and incouragement of the honourable Robert Boyle, Governor of this Companie) contributed & made over to the said Governor the somme of 360ll: sterlinge to be employed for the maintenance of one or more preachinge Ministers for the conversion & instruccion of the Native Indians.'[2] Ashurst was ordered to receive the money and make it over to New England. Care was taken — 'that ye effect of his charity should not be confounded with ye contributions we received from others to advance the same worke.' It was remitted to New England as a lump sum to be 'kept by it selfe under ye name of Monsr Mousche's Gift'. The interest, amounting to 8 per cent, was to be laid out rather 'for Preachers to ye Americans than any of those other uses upon which ye Corporation is obligd to employ a good part of their money.'[3]

The Company received £10 under the will of Lady Mary Armine, who had given an annuity of £20 for the work, even before the Society was founded. Several members of the Company either made gifts or remembered the Indians in their wills. Thomas Stanley made a free gift of twenty pounds in May 1674; in January 1673/4 Benjamin Albin gave fifty pounds, and a year later another fifty pounds.[4] Albin had been elected a member of the Company in 1668, and on the day after his election had been discharged from the office of Alderman of London on the payment of the usual fine of £420. He was a prominent member of both the East India Company and the Levant Company. Andrew Dandy bequeathed two hundred pounds 'for the good of the College, for the Promoteing of learning there as the Governor and Corporation here shall order and appoint soe that it may doe most good for spreading the gospell amongest the Indians and others for God's glorie.'[5] Five

[1] Will dated 13 Aug. 1655 (P.C.C. 16 Wootton); Ms. 7952, 7 May 1662, 7 March 1663/4; Ms. 7911/1, April 1668.

[2] Minutes (M.H.S. Ms.), 22 March 1668.

[3] Royal Society, Boyle Papers, Theology, IV, 121.

[4] Ms. 7944/2; Ms. 7911/1.

[5] P.C.C. 122 Pye.

years later, in July 1679, Boyle gave the Company three hundred pounds; two further bequests of £50 were received under the wills of Henry Ashurst and Christopher Boon in 1682 and 1688.[1]

In November 1670 William Pennoyer promised to give £600 for building new houses upon the site in Trinity Lane to replace those destroyed four years earlier in the Great Fire of London. The Company was to pay £60 per annum to him during his lifetime and after his death £20 per annum to Harvard College and £25 per annum to his wife, Martha Pennoyer, until her decease. The members were delighted with the offer and promptly ordered that three or four houses be built with provision for one large room suitable for meetings and for housing the Company's books. When he made this offer, Pennoyer had only been a member of the Company for two years, but from the first he proved himself extremely useful and was, indeed, a most suitable choice, both as a staunch nonconformist and as a wealthy merchant with interests and relatives in New England. He had as close friends a number of other members — Sir William Thomson, John Bathurst, John Joliffe, Michael Davison, Samuel Crispe and Benjamin Albin, all of whom were remembered in his will. He had also had business dealings with various members — Abraham Babington had sold him East India Company stock, Edward Parks had purchased property in Stepney from him, and so on. With his partner, Maurice Thomson, sometime governor of the East India Company, he had, during the Civil War, subscribed £6,000 to reducing Ireland (for which he received a share of confiscated estates), and had purchased saltpetre from the East India Company and sold gunpowder to the state with great success. He owned fishing rights at Cape Ann, sugar works in the Barbados and had invested in a number of colonizing ventures. Like several other members of the Company, he had been elected an Alderman of London and had avoided holding office on payment of £420.

Unhappily Pennoyer died before the £600 which he had promised had been paid to the Treasurer. His will was proved on 13 February 1671 and on the next day the Company ordered that a copy of the agreement made with him should be shown to his executors. The executors, however, were unable to comply with the agreement.

[1] Ms. 7944/3–4; Ms. 7911/2.

Nevertheless, the Company was not altogether denied the benefits of Pennoyer's wealth, for his will, made on 25 May 1670, provided it with an annuity of £10 arising out of a farm at Pulham in Norfolk; the residue of the rents he bequeathed to Harvard College to found a scholarship fund. The farm was left to the care of twelve trustees, amongst whom the Company was represented by Henry Ashurst and William Kiffin. By 1684, however, the Company's influence had waned, for the trustees questioned whether the annuity was due to the Company at all, as Pennoyer had not named it correctly in his will. But the annual payment continued to be made even after 1708 when, in consequence of a decree in Chancery, the trusteeship was transferred to Christ's Hospital, also a beneficiary under the will.[1]

During the seventeenth century the Company was, on the whole, fortunate in its employees, although they were not always without fault. For example in 1664 John Hooper, the clerk, fell sick and wrote to Henry Ashurst: 'I did take to my owne use out of the moneyes as recd. 29^{li} 10^{s} 0^{d}.' The Company seems to have taken the matter lightly for it treated Hooper kindly. In March 1668/9 he was given £10 on the grounds that he had 'beene longe visited with sicknes & is still in a weake Condicion & in greate want, and Consideringe how willinglie he waved such Sallarie as was or might be due unto him for his service upon the losses happened to this Companie by the Late dreadfull fire in London & otherwise.' In 1670 he was given £5 'as a gift towardes his reliefe being at present in greate want.'[2]

More serious was the muddle occasioned by the death of John Rolfe, who with his son Edmond to help him became, after John Hooper's illness, receiver of rents and clerk in all but name. When he died in 1686 it was found that the Company's accounts were in a deplorable mess. Henry Ashurst had seen that the accounts kept formed an adequate

[1] Minutes (M.H.S. Ms.), 21 Nov. 1670, 14 Feb. 1670/1; P.C.C. 25 Duke; S. E. Morison, *Harvard College in the Seventeenth Century* (Cambridge, Mass., 1936), II, 383–5; R. W. Lovett, 'The Pennoyer Scholarship at Harvard', *Harvard Library Bulletin*, IV (1950), 213–38; *Report of the Charity Commissioners*, XXXII, pt. 6 (1840), 142–3.

[2] Ms. 7956, 21 Dec. 1664; Minutes (M.H.S. Ms.), 22 March 1668/9, 21 Nov. 1670.

record, but William Ashurst, who had been appointed Treasurer in 1681 after his father's death, had left most of his duties to John Rolfe and his son. In fact, there is no evidence that Rolfe was in any way dishonest, but he did not keep separate accounts for the Company or, at all events, no accounts could be found after his death. This meant that John Bellamy, his successor as clerk, had to reconstruct the Company's payments to New England for the period 1682 to 1686 by going through Rolfe's business ledgers. Bellamy wrote in January 1686/7: 'I find Mr. Rolfe the late Clerk has not bin so exact in his Accounts as he ought to have bin.' He added primly: 'I am likely to be your Clerke for the Future and hope that I shall be so care full in my Accounts that you may never have any further Trouble of this nature.'[1]

Paid servants were easier to find than new and willing members. The first election was held at the Vulture in Winchester Street in September 1668; the 'divers members' present ate a dinner costing the Company £2;[2] nineteen new members were elected to take the places of the twelve who had died and of seven others who 'Did seldome or never appeare upon sessions by reason of their habitacion in the Countrie & other occasions.'[3] Of the new members, less than half were to take any interest in the Company and its affairs. Amongst them, however, there were a number of wealthy men — William Pennoyer, Benjamin Albin, William Moses and John Joliffe. Lord George Berkeley, also a member of the East India Company, and interested in the Indians' conversion, was no doubt introduced by Boyle. The law was represented by Sir Orlando Bridgeman, Lord Keeper, and John Fountaine, Serjeant-at-Law. The nonconformist element was strong, five of the members having avoided the office of Alderman of London by paying the fine; William Kiffin was a well-known Baptist preacher, while William Moses had been encouraged by Baxter, without success, to present the nonconformist point of view at the Savoy Conference in 1661. In 1677 another election dinner was held at the Company's expense, the accounts recording: 'Paid to Mr Levett the Cooke in full of his Bill for the dinner at his house when the Company chose Members and officers . . .

[1] Ms. 7956, letter to Edmund White; Ms. 7945, 'The Corporacon & Mr Rolfes Account 1687'.

[2] Ms. 7944/2; Ms. 7911/1.

[3] Minutes (M.H.S. Ms.), 23 Sept. 1668.

5^{li} 9^{s} 0^{d}.'[1] But these two election dinners seem to have been the only occasions on which any money was spent on behalf of members throughout the Company's history.

Twenty-five years after the charter was granted, almost all the original members were dead, and those still living took small interest in the Company's affairs. Only the Governor, Boyle himself, was still active, and after the death of Henry Ashurst, in particular, it was his interest which kept the Company alive. However, by 1688 so taxing was he finding the pressure of everyday life that he issued to the public a remarkable advertisement: in it he asked to be excused from receiving visitors as he was sick and wanted to set his writings in order. It was in this overburdened frame of mind that on 22 August 1689 he wrote to the Company resigning his position as Governor. Sadly he began his letter:

> As it has not been without great Satisfaction that I have for many years served such Worthy Persons, as I now write to, in promoteing so excellent a Worke, as the Propagation of the Gospell among Savages, that were utter Strangers to it, and worshipp'd the grand Enemy of it; so tis not without much trouble, that I am now oblidg'd to Resigne so Honourable, & to me Gratefull, an Employment.

He went on to plead his unfitness for the role of Governor on the grounds of 'almost continual sicklyness' coupled with reduced means, describing himself as 'a Person that wants his Health, and is for the present deprived of all his Estate in Ireland . . .' and adding 'it may justly lessen my Griefe, for parting with my Employment that my doing so may very probably turn to the Advantage of the Honourable Corporation . . . and that your next Governor may be as faithfull and affectionate as your last, but much more capable and prosperous.'[2]

Prosperous, faithful and affectionate future governors may have been; Boyle remains the most capable and distinguished man ever associated with the New England Company.

[1] Ms. 7911/1.

[2] Ms. 7956; Boyle's rough draft of this letter is contained in Royal Society, Boyle Letters, I, 148, and was printed in *The Works of . . . Robert Boyle*, I, cxxviii–ix.

4

The Commissioners of the United Colonies, 1649–1684

BOTH the pre-Restoration Society and the post-Restoration New England Company were served on the American side of the Atlantic by a single body of men — the Commissioners of the United Colonies. It was in 1643, six years before the Society came into being, that the colonies found it necessary to form a confederation. Isolated as they were from England, the pressure of Dutch and French expansion and the increasing threat of Indian hostility as the Indians were pushed further inland had brought the colonies of Plymouth, Connecticut, New Haven and Massachusetts together in an attempt to protect their common interests. Each of the four member colonies elected two commissioners annually who met on the first Thursday in September at Plymouth, Hartford, New Haven and Boston in rotation. So, when the Society for Propagation of the Gospel in New England was first mooted, and it was obvious that such a body would need agents to disburse in New England the money collected at home, the Commissioners must have presented themselves to Winslow's mind as the most obvious choice. Accordingly, the act of 1649 which created the Society laid it down that the Commissioners, or those they should appoint, were to receive and administer such funds as the Society might send them.

In two important respects, Winslow's choice of the Commissioners for this work was a wise one: they could be said fairly to represent the greater part of New England; and they were drawn from the ablest men taking part in colonial affairs at this period; moreover it was, of course, convenient that the machinery for their annual meetings already existed. As against this, it must be admitted that, since one of their prime functions was to protect the United Colonies against the Indians, they may not have been sufficiently concerned with the main object of the Society — the conversion of the Indians themselves. Indeed, the Society was to be uneasy on this score more than once — an uneasiness reflected in recurrent proposals that the constitution of the body responsible for distributing the funds should be improved by the addition to it of ministers of God. Thus in 1656 Thomas Weld and Hugh Peter proposed: 'that for ye better carryinge on of the busines in N.E. some Ministers there might bee ioyned, vizt 2 in every Coloney with the Commissioners there, vizt 4 in ye Massachusettes Coloney & One a peece in ye other 3 Colonyes.'[1] John Wilson, Richard Mather and Samuel Stone were among the seven ministers suggested for this work: each was to receive £20 per annum for his advice. But the Society rejected this proposal, no doubt on the grounds that the Commissioners were authorized by the act of 1649 to distribute the funds and that the Society had no power to force co-opted members upon them; added to this the outlay of £140 per annum which the proposal of Weld and Peter entailed made it unacceptable on every count. The Society had contented itself on this occasion, therefore, with the general suggestion that the Commissioners might seek the advice of ministers, a suggestion which they were to repeat in later years.

All this, however, is to anticipate. The Commissioners received official confirmation of their new duties at their meeting in September 1650. No doubt they had heard of the passage of the act through Parliament in July of the previous year and had probably already seen a copy of it so that the letter which came to them from President Steele, written in the name of the newly founded corporation, would have caused no surprise. The naming of the Commissioners in the act constituted the only occasion on which they were officially recognized by the English government, and the only authority exercised by them in their own right was that given them under the act — the authority to spend the Society's money.

Money, then, became the main theme of the letters which, from this time onward, passed between the Commissioners in New England and the Society in London. It is hardly surprising that, with such a theme, the tone was at times testy and querulous and that there was an almost

[1] Minutes (M.H.S. Ms.), 25 Nov. 1656.

constant undercurrent of argument and disagreement even when, as usually happened, the letter was polite and patient on the surface. The Commissioners wrote every year at their annual meeting in September; the Society too wrote annually, or oftener, and it is from these slow exchanges that the material of this chapter is drawn.

The first letter — that from President Steele in March 1649/50 — initiated the first dispute; while it contained no news of money to be sent across the Atlantic in the near future, it did suggest that Edward Winslow should receive financial support from New England. The Commissioners for Massachusetts pointed out that their colony had already paid three or four hundred pounds towards his maintenance. The jealous neighbours of Massachusetts promptly argued that Winslow was not their liability, having been appointed by Massachusetts alone. This first dispute was temporarily solved by the Commissioners' suggestion that, as Winslow had been so valuable to the Society, it should pay him £100 from its funds.[1]

The Commissioners now began to tell the Society how it should spend its money. They recommended that £100 should be paid to John Eliot and that £1,000 in goods should be sent to New England by Winslow and Herbert Pelham. They specified what the goods were to be: shoes of all sorts, strong stockings, with a preference for those of Irish make, canvas for summer clothing and bedding, blankets, light axes, broad and narrow hoes, spades, saws, nails, hooks, hinges and haberdashery, especially thread. The Commissioners took the precaution of appointing the Governor and Court of Massachusetts to act on their behalf in the coming year in dealings with the Society. With undue optimism they recommended that the Massachusetts Court should write for more goods if the collection in England should prove successful. Provision was to be made for the safe keeping of any goods which arrived during the year, and authority was given for the sale of one hundred pounds' worth. The other colonies were to be kept informed of all actions taken.[2]

The first cargoes were shipped by Edward Winslow to John Cotton and John Wilson at Boston. On 12 April 1651 the master of the *New England Marchant* signed the Society's first bill of lading for 'twelve

[1] *Acts*, I, 161–5.

[2] *Acts*, I, 165–7.

grindstones, two bundles of spads, three bundles of sawes, on[e] barrell and six kilder kings.' A detailed account accompanied the bill of lading showing more precisely the nature of the goods as well as their cost. In fact the whole cargo consisted of hardware: nails, hatchets, felling axes, broad axes, narrow and broad hoes, spades, hand saws, two handed saws, augers, chisels, drawing knives, carpenters' hammers, adzes, and gimlets. The value of this consignment totalled over £70. The second bill of lading, signed by the master of the *Mayflower of New England* and dated 12 June 1651, enumerated 'five bailes, tow hoggeds and one punchyon.' The accompanying accounts showed these to contain: twenty dozen green and blue hose for men and the same number for women; more than one hundred and eighty pounds' worth of cloth purchased from Richard Hutchinson and Abraham Babington, both members of the Society; and

	li	s	d
One & twenty doz & a halfe of Neates Leather Lyquored Shooes att ij^s vj^d per paire comes to	032	05	00

The most varied part of this consignment was supplied by the Society's Treasurer, Richard Floyd, at a total cost of £28. 14s. 04d.: it consisted of haberdashery, fish-hooks, knives, scissors of various kinds, needles, pincers and whetstones. Included in the same hogshead were a number of items

> sente by a well wisher to the furtherance of the gospell which hee giveth and sendeth to bee at the disposeing of Mr. Elliott for the use and Bennefitt of the Indians that receive the gospell which are as followeth
> Item one book cald the phisicall directorie
> Item 3 dossen & 8 primers of a new makeinge
> Item ½ dossen of English spelling bookes in a box in the same hogshead
> Item 12 potts of Ballsom with directions for the use there of in the box afore said written in a booke
> Item 4 oz of Methredate
> Item 4 oz of allowes
> Item ½ li of London Treakell } with directiones there with for the use & vertues of them
> Item 1 oz of Safferon
> Item 1½ oz of Worm seed
> some Cardus seeds
> some Angellico seeds } which may bee soed though late in ye yeare when they come
> Item 1 pece of Tape
> Item 1½ m of pines } for Mr Eliots wife

The third and fourth bills of lading, dated 26 April and 3 May 1652, were now made out to Edward Rawson at Boston by the Masters of the *Cannary Marchant* and the *New England Marchant*. The goods sent included writing materials, 190 quarto Bibles costing 2s. 10d. each, 10 large quarto Bibles costing 3s. 4d. each, six dozen spectacles at 3s. 6d. a dozen and two dozen at 1s. 6d. a dozen, all of which had been purchased by Richard Floyd, and more than a hundred pounds worth of cloth sold to the Society by Abraham Babington and Joshua Woolnough. One of the barrels in which the goods were sent contained a gift to the Indians from Richard Andrewes to be delivered to John Eliot and Thomas Mayhew and distributed by them. Its resemblance to the gift of the 'well wisher' in the previous year suggests that Eliot had specified some of his needs. Andrewes' present consisted of:

Item 6 dozen of rackes or spindells to spinn one the knee
Item 2 oz of Angellica seeds
Item 2 oz of Cardus seeds
Item 2 dozen of smale books Cald the rule of ye New Creature
Item 8 litell books against swareing
Item 1 booke of phisicall directions
Item a litell box of pipin kernills for ye Indians to sett
Item some Cherrie stons for the Indians to sett
Item some bay berries for the Indians to sett
Item 3 booke against drunckennes
Item 3 bookes of Englands Unthanckfullnes.[1]

If the Commissioners had imagined that they would be given a free hand in distributing the money collected in England, without interference, the Society's letter of April 1651 must have disillusioned them quickly enough. It asked them to confer with Eliot and Mayhew in estimating what buildings, meeting houses and so on would be needed by the Indians, what salaries should be paid to ministers and schoolmasters and how much all this would cost: furthermore it declined to pay Winslow's salary on the grounds that there was insufficient money in hand, and added that Winslow would prefer payment from the Commissioners. (The Society was obviously astute enough to see that a

[1] Ms. 7947.

payment to one of its members might be hard to justify in its much advertised account books, and that the colonies might be slow to keep their part of the bargain and might fail to pay the money to the Commissioners when it was needed.) The letter also pointed out that Herbert Pelham and Winslow were a poor choice as agents for the purchase of goods: Pelham because he lived in the country and was seldom in town, and Winslow because he would 'by no means be perswaded to meddle with the Receipts of Money.' Elsewhere in the letter it was announced that invoices would be supplied of all goods sent, and that the Commissioners should return an account of all goods received, as well as an annual account of how the funds had been distributed. It was suggested that they should appoint a steward to attend to affairs between annual meetings. The most irritating news of all from the Commissioners' point of view was the Society's stated intention of purchasing property in England as soon as possible, in order to achieve a regular annual income.[1]

The Commissioners realized that it was futile to object to the Society's interference. Although the act gave them the power to spend, this was of little avail until there was some ready money. The only hope of extracting funds from the Society was to dance to the Society's tune. With considerably less enthusiasm than in the previous year, they wrote to the Society complying with most of its requests; they promised to send a receipt for all goods received and an annual statement of accounts. Meanwhile Simon Bradstreet and Captain William Hawthorn, the two representatives of Massachusetts, were ordered to confer with Eliot concerning what should be undertaken in the next year, and Edward Rawson, 'a man well approved in the Massachusets who lives at Boston', was appointed to act as agent or steward.[2]

The problem of transferring funds from England to the colonies was one which exercised both the Society and the Commissioners. Obviously, where goods for distribution amongst the Indians were concerned, direct shipment by the Society was satisfactory enough; but where the Society shipped goods for sale in Boston, the proceeds of which would pay for the Indian work, there were several obstacles to

[1] *Acts*, I, 193–5.

[2] *Acts*, I, 195–6.

be faced. In the first place, the sea voyage was hazardous and the possibility of loss or damage to the goods while in transit was considerable; moreover, this procedure lent itself to personal profit on both sides of the Atlantic: many members of the Society were involved in commerce and even if the added business which came their way through belonging to the Society did not enrich them unfairly, it did give grounds for criticism and suspicion; finally, currency was in such short supply in the colonies that it was difficult to find customers who would or could pay in cash for the goods they purchased. This meant that customers were usually given credit and so debts were incurred, debts which the Commissioners sometimes found impossible to recover.

However, for five or six years the shipment of goods was the normal method adopted by the Society for sending funds to New England, and nearly every consignment provoked some kind of disagreement between the senders and the receivers. For example the Commissioners complained that the brass goods sent in 1654 and the woollen and linen goods sent in 1655 were too dear, and that they would be forced to sell them at a loss. The Society apologized and assured the Commissioners that it had endeavoured to buy the goods at the lowest rates possible 'and never Charged one peney more upon them then in truth they cost.' Again, in September 1656, when accounting for stock in hand, the Commissioners complained that part of a consignment consisting of hoes, hatchets, twibills and other goods which, incidentally, they had not asked for, were of such poor quality as to be unfit for use and not 'like to bee put off without much losse or offence.' On this occasion the Society excused itself on the grounds that, at the time of sending, it had not received any instructions from the Commissioners, and that in any case the implements were not intended for sale but for distribution amongst the Indians; inquiries had been made of the person who had supplied the goods and it was found that he was 'willing upon som reasonable alowance to take them againe.' The Society instructed the Commissioners, therefore, to return the implements if they were still unsold.[1]

The goods which the Commissioners asked for most often were textiles of various descriptions — canvas, linen, serge, cotton, 'good black

[1] *Acts*, II, 162, 164, 184.

broad cloth', dowlas, locram, Irish and Jersey stockings, as well as Maidstone, brown and coloured threads, buttons and silk tape. More occasionally demands were made for fine holland, cambric and lawn. Tools were also in demand, these having a double purpose, being suitable either for sale or for distribution amongst the Indians. The Society warned the Commissioners to be careful in what they requested as it purchased the goods for ready cash and then had to 'beare the adventure.' However, there was one other commodity which had always been in short supply since the founding of the colonies and which the Commissioners considered admirable as a form of merchandise, if carefully controlled — namely, arms and ammunition.

Indeed, to ensure a supply of arms and ammunition was an important part of their primary function — the protection of the colonies from the French, the Dutch, and the Indians themselves. No written request for arms survives, but in July 1652 Edward Hopkins, a former Commissioner who had just arrived in England, petitioned the Council of State, together with Edward Winslow and Francis Willoughby, for permission to ship arms to New England; and this must have been, at least in part, on the Society's behalf. The Council of State readily acceded to the request, recommending that a ship be sent to New England with ammunition, barrels of powder and shot and a thousand swords, with which the colonists might defend themselves against the Dutch.[1] It was not until 11 September 1652 that Thomas Bell, one of the Society's members, obtained bills of lading for a consignment of arms and ammunition from Richard Thurston, master of the *Johns Adventure*. The consignment consisted of twenty barrels of musket shot, sixty barrels of powder, two barrels of flints, eighty muskets costing eleven shillings each, one hundred snaphance locks, eighteen bullet moulds and one hundred swords with basket hilts. Only one barrel contained goods intended for the Indians themselves and these were tools and implements and seven bells for oxen.[2] In a letter to Winslow, written at their meeting in 1653, the Commissioners acknowledged the safe receipt of

[1] *C.S.P. Col., 1574–1660*, 386.

[2] Ms. 7947. The text of the bill of lading dealing with this consignment has been printed in *The Journal of the Arms and Armour Society*, III, no. 7 (1960), 198–203.

the ammunition and arms which, they added, would be very acceptable 'as things stood betwixt England and the Duch in Europe; and betwixt us and the Duch att the Monhatoes.'[1]

The Commissioners ordered the division of the arms and ammunition between Massachusetts, Connecticut, New Haven and Plymouth on 17 May 1653. Payment by the colonies was to be made to the Commissioners' agent, Edward Rawson, in money, barley, wheat, peas, pork or beef at current prices, and the proceeds were to be devoted to the Indian work. In September the Commissioners ordered Rawson to receive payment from the colonies but, although the total value of the consignment amounted to only £358. 12s. 8d., the order proved difficult to put into practice: in other words the colonies would not pay. This piece of disquieting news reached the Society's ears in February 1653/4 and the failure to recover this debt became one of the recurrent complaints made to the Commissioners. Three years later in September 1656 the Commissioners asked for a hundred pounds' worth of 'good fine gunpowder' and hastened to assure the Society that this might 'in severall Respects . . . further the Indian worke and account as much as any other English comoditie but to prevent offence and mistake wee shall neither devide it among the Collonies nor for any Respect (not Requset for the worke) alter the propertie.'[2] But now the Society proved hesitant in supplying ammunition, whether because it feared that it would not be paid for, or for other reasons, it is impossible to say.

In general this means of transferring funds to the colonies was bound to create friction, the more so when the Commissioners only met once a year. They were regularly brought to book for the unsatisfactory nature of their annual accounts. In September 1653 they wrote to Winslow telling him that Rawson, their secretary, had sent his accounts to the Society: 'wee hope in a more satisfying forme then formerly.' In the same letter they protested that they took no goods for their private use. But the Society saw fit to write to the General Court of each colony begging that the colonies might end all dissension amongst themselves, and at the same time asking that accounts should be rendered by the Commissioners in order to clear the Society of charges being made

[1] *Acts*, II, 104.

[2] *Acts*, II, 33–4, 165–6.

against it at home. In fact it warned its correspondents that if they failed to distribute the funds sent over: 'wee shall receive a Mandamus from the State to send noe more but bee accomptable to them ab initio.' In September 1655 the demand for careful accounts was reiterated and to it was coupled a demand for a general receipt covering all goods sent to New England; but there was a particular and urgent reason for these demands at this time: the Society had been ordered to present its own accounts by the Council of State. The subsequent presentation of the return in January 1655/6 evidently served to show members that things were not as they should be and so, in April of the same year, the request for a general discharge for all goods sent over to New England was again repeated, this time with the reminder that the sum in question totalled over £1,722. To prevent future embarrassment the Society urged the Commissioners to appoint someone in London with powers to give the Society a receipt for goods sent. This the Commissioners were reluctant to do and the demand, like that for better accounts, became perennial. To attract attention to its wishes the Society, in April 1656, pointed out that the Commissioners had £1,259 in stock and that, for this reason, the full complement of goods asked for that year would not be sent. The Commissioners rejoined that, on the contrary, they had only £553 in stock, part of which consisted of goods which had not been asked for; they insisted that the work could scarcely be carried on unless funds were sent from England and proceeded to ask the Society to send £1,000 in goods according to invoice, in order that they might build up a stock. This they recommended in spite of the Society's intention to restrict moneys sent to New England and to purchase landed property at home instead.[1]

This letter of 1656, more than any other from the Commissioners, must have caused the Society to reconsider the whole problem of sending funds to New England. Whatever the views of the Commissioners, the Society remained determined to invest in England most of the money accruing from the collection; accordingly in April 1657 it wrote to the Commissioners announcing its continued intention to purchase property; the Commissioners' proposal to build up a stock in New England involved sending money or goods across the seas and this was

[1] *Acts*, II, 104, 162–6, 432.

impracticable, it was argued, because those seas were dangerous 'in regard of pyrates which continually enfests the same'; furthermore there was no one in London to give the Society discharge for goods sent; therefore, the letter stated, goods would not be purchased by the Society in future. Instead, the Commissioners were to supply their needs by bills of exchange, not exceeding £500 per annum, to be drawn on the Society in London.[1]

In theory, the Society had hit upon the obvious solution, but in practice its control over the amount spent by the Commissioners was now diminished since it was obliged to honour whatever bills of exchange the Commissioners might draw upon it. The Commissioners themselves clung to the view that it was unnecessary for the Society to invest in land and that the stock would be better employed if held by them and invested in New England. In February 1656/7 the Society discussed the matter and it was decided to take legal advice. But this decision was probably not arrived at without heated discussion in the Society's Court for it was ordered 'that ye Transaccions of ye Court this day bee not entred.' In April 1658 the Society referred to its duty to invest according to the 'Judgment of learned Councell of the land.' The Commissioners grudgingly acquiesced in the Society's view and in September of the same year wrote explaining that it was 'never our desire or intent to hinder the purchasing of Lands; . . . we yet see not that the Act of Parliament or the trust imposed therein obliges you to the purchasing of 2000 li per annum.'[2] But here the matter rested, for the Society had already purchased most of its property and in future it was to have little surplus to invest.

The Commissioners were in fact comparatively restrained in drawing bills of exchange, although the restraint was not sufficient to prevent the Society from constantly begging them to be more careful. The Society's letter of April 1658 stated that two bills of exchange for £500 and £700, drawn by Hezekiah Usher, the Boston merchant with whom the Commissioners dealt, had been paid. A little sadly it added that the second bill, for £700, had prevented the purchase of some property and that large bills of exchange could not be accepted, as the clear revenue amounted to only £600 a year.

[1] *Acts*, II, 185. [2] Minutes (M.H.S. Ms.); *Acts*, II, 201; Ms. 7936, f. 3.

The Society's anxiety at the results of having passed the purse strings to the Commissioners was considerable. Nor was it happy about the rate of exchange given on money advanced to Hezekiah Usher; it claimed that Usher gave only six per cent on money advanced, and in April 1660 a letter was written to the Commissioners stating that overtures had been received from 'some in New England and alsoe heer' who were prepared to serve the Society and who offered not less than twenty-five per cent. By now quite familiar with the Commissioners' reactions to its suggestions, the Society added: 'this wee offer not with the least disrespect to Mr. Usher.' At the same time the Society hit upon the plan of shipping £500 in pieces of eight 'to bee parte of the account of the Indian worke; which wee conceive wilbee alsoe advantageus to the countrey, hopeing the Government there will allow the binifitt of the Coynage wee paying the charge of workmanship.'[1]

The Commissioners' reply to the Society, written in September 1660, was mild. They vindicated their choice of Usher, praising his 'sufficiency to discharge what hee undertakes; and the full satisfaction he gives in his payment both for prise and choise of goods to all that Receive upon this accounte . . . neither have wee heard of any man that would undertake it upon better tearmes.' The Commissioners had their way and continued to deal with Usher. As far as the pieces of eight were concerned, they would accept them, currency being very short in the colonies, provided the Society in its turn accepted a bill of exchange for £800. They doubted, however, whether the consignment of pieces of eight would prove profitable: 'unlesse they bee very good; there wilbee Rather losse then gaine by the coyning as the mint master doth informe us though the Government doeth expect noe proffitt therby.'[2] Nevertheless, the idea seemed a particularly seductive one to members in England — so much so that, at the Restoration, when members of the Society were seeking a charter, they obtained an order in council for the inclusion of a clause authorizing the export of 'Spanish or other forraigne silver coines' not exceeding the yearly value of £1,000.[3]

The Commissioners of the United Colonies seem to have taken little

[1] *Acts*, II, 240–1.

[2] *Acts*, II, 243–4.

[3] *Acts of the Privy Council, Colonial*, I, no. 510; *C.S.P. Col., 1661–1668*, 23; Ms. 7952, 10 April 1661.

interest in English affairs. The return of Charles II was a distant event: the idea that their duties under the act of 1649 would come to an end with the new régime does not appear to have long occupied their minds. But in 1661 they received a letter from John Hooper, the Society's clerk, signed in the name of 'Youer loveing ffrinds' which ran:

> Wee suppose you are not strangers to the condition of affaires; and particularly with respect unto our selves being now noe Corporation; though not without good hopes that the same wilbee renewed and confeirmed by his Majestie though posibly the busines may bee acted by other persons; and therfore not knowing in whome this trust wilbee reposed wee thinke fitt and advise that before you draw any more bills you first understand the persons appointed heer for carrying on the same which wee shall endeavor to give you notice of by the first oppertunitie.

The Commissioners did continue the work and, pleading shortage of money, promptly sent to Henry Ashurst and Richard Hutchinson another bill of exchange for £800 to be drawn upon whoever was responsible for the funds. With remarkable confidence one of the Commissioners wrote to Usher telling him that they had issued a bill of exchange for £800 and remarking: 'Wee are enformed by a letter from the Corporation that there is some change made concerning theire power.'[1] It nowhere appears that the Commissioners doubted that they would be reappointed under the new dispensation. In the event they were proved right, although the charter did not in any way recognize their existence.

In fact the charter, unlike the act of 1649, empowered thirteen members of the Company to appoint 'such and soe many fitt and meete Person and Persons, residinge in or neere any of the Collonies or Plantations in New England . . . to bee Commissioners for and on the behalfe of the said Company.' At the first meeting of the Company, on 27 March 1662, a committee consisting of six members, all of whom had been members of the Society, was ordered to meet 'Mr. Broadstreete and Mr. Norton and others lately come from New England and desire them to give their Opinions whoe are ye fittest persons to bee employed as Commissioners in New England.' The case for reappoint-

[1] *Acts*, II, 255, 264.

ing the Commissioners of the United Colonies was presented with success by Simon Bradstreet, himself a Commissioner, so that a fortnight later the committee, which was sympathetic anyway, reported to the Company's Court and 'in Conclusion found it most expedient that for this yeare ye said worke should bee carryed on as formerly.'[1]

It would indeed have been strange if the Company had not reappointed the Commissioners: not only had they about ten years experience of distributing the funds but they were prepared to do so without payment. And although they only met once a year, they did so regularly in September. But in 1664 the position altered slightly. The Commissioners decided to discontinue their annual meetings and instead to meet only once every three years. Indian affairs were more settled and the Commissioners and those they represented strongly favoured triennial meetings except in cases of emergency, should such arise. As far as the Company's affairs were concerned it was decided that three Commissioners of Massachusetts and Plymouth were to meet annually at Boston or elsewhere; these three were to dispose of the Indian stock and report their actions both to the Company and also to the triennial meetings of the Commissioners.[2]

And on the whole the Company was well served. Immediately after the Restoration and for the following decade there was a sadly diminished annual income to remit to the Commissioners. The discussion of how the money should be transmitted continued — taken up where the Society had left off. The Company wrote to the Commissioners in April 1663 informing them that one hundred pounds worth of pieces of eight had been sent 'haveing obtained this privilidg in our Charter; that what wee shall send over shalbee without any charge or Custom payed for the same.' To this was appended the pious wish that a considerable profit would be made in recoining. The Company was, no doubt, looking forward to further shipments of a similar kind, for it purchased a warrant from the officers and farmers of the Customs for the transport to New England of one thousand pounds worth of foreign coin.[3]

If the Company inherited from the Society its enthusiasm for this

[1] Ms. 7908, mem. 2; Ms. 7952.
[2] Ms. 7936, f. 6; *Acts*, II, 319.
[3] *Acts*, II, 291; Ms. 7944/1, 6 & 7 April 1663.

plan, the Commissioners' attitude remained unaltered: there is a touch of the 'told-you-so' air in their annual letter of September 1663 in which they reported that the sum realized was only £117. They told the Company that they had discussed the matter with Usher; he formerly gave six per cent interest and allowed three pence in the shilling discount on goods purchased from him; he now agreed to give twelve per cent and to keep the accounts gratis. This, the Commissioners argued, was far more satisfactory than the shipment of either goods or coin. The Company remained unconvinced but with a surprisingly good grace it accepted the Commissioners' advice, although it asked that Usher should be persuaded to pay at least fourteen or fifteen per cent.[1]

Pleas for financial restraint were reiterated in the Company's letters during the next ten years. In April 1663 the auditors appointed by the Company to examine the Commissioners' annual accounts reported that money was laid out for books and gratuities to several people which, in view of the Company's small income, might well be forborne: 'unlesse it bee thought by you that some unavoydable prejudice might happen to the worke for the want thereof.' After the Great Fire of London the income was even further reduced and the appeal to the Commissioners for economies stronger than ever. In June 1668 the Company asked them to carry on for a year without any income at all. While hoping that the situation would improve by the following year, the Commissioners were asked in the meantime 'to abate all charge that is not essentiall to the being of this good worke; as printing & Binding of bookes, and salaryes to Governours & Gratuityes to those that doe not Actually Contribute to the worke.' The Company added its hope that those who were engaged in the work would continue with abated stipends. The Commissioners in their reply of 10 September 1668 promised to exercise the greatest frugality. However, they hastened to point out that they knew of no salary paid to any Governor, although payments were sometimes made to individual Commissioners for distribution to deserving Indians in their colonies.[2]

The financial difficulties of the Company at this time made it less certain of its former policy of investing capital in landed property in

[1] *Acts*, II, 292–3, 313.

[2] *Acts*, II, 291; Ms. 7936, f. 7–8.

England and sending the interest to New England. The set-backs which this plan had received by the contested possession of property, the recalcitrance of tenants and the destruction of the London property in the Fire, made the Company more ready than at any time before to consider transferring capital to New England for investment there. The gift made by the Parisian lawyer, Mouche or Mousche, in 1669, provided an opportunity to try out the new policy. In its annual letter to the Commissioners, dated 28 April 1669, the Company commented: 'It hath been judged very probable that heerafter our Remitting Monyes att 25li advance (which we are now offred) will augment the Revenew more Considerably then now it is: your drawing bills uppon us amounting not to above 15 or 16 per cent. But however we have suspended our positive determination heerin till we shall heare from you by the next.'[1] In May 1669 it had arranged for the transfer of Mouche's gift, without waiting for further word from the Commissioners. The £360 which constituted the gift was to be paid in two parts: £300 was to be paid to Thomas Glover of London, and his partner in Boston was to pay the Commissioners' agents, John Leverett and Hezekiah Usher, £375 in New England money. The other £60 was paid to Robert Thompson of London whose partner in Boston, John Richards, was to pay £75 in New England currency.[2] In September 1669, in their annual letter to the Company, the Commissioners commented upon these arrangements for transferring funds: they argued that there was no one to whom the bills in New England could be addressed with safety, that many merchants would fail to honour the advance promised, and that they themselves would have to pay a salary to someone to receive and disburse the funds. In a postscript to the same letter the Commissioners reported that the £450 New England which constituted Mouche's gift had been 'put out upon improvement at 7 li per cent into such hands where it will be secured to the ends proposed.'[3]

In spite of the fact that neither Company nor Commissioners were satisfied with the other's actions, and in spite of the continued wrangle over the percentage which the Mouche gift should yield, this transaction did provide the basis of the Indian stock out of which the missionary

[1] Ms. 7936, f. 9. [2] Ms. 7911/1, 7 May 1669.
[3] Ms. 7936, f. 11. Postscript dated 22 Sept. 1669.

work was partly financed throughout the rest of the colonial period. The Company wrote in January 1669/70 informing the Commissioners that it thought fit 'to make further tryall of the way they have begun for remittinge monie & that they intend this yeare to remitt 300^{li}.'[1] From the Commissioners' point of view, the Company's determination to remit money to New England in this way now appeared to be a mixed blessing. Although they could decide upon how to spend what was sent they could not, as before, decide how much they would spend and send the bill in to the Company. Moreover, Boston merchants who had been able to draw bills of exchange on the Company in London would no longer be able to do so. On the other hand if the Indian stock became large enough, the Commissioners would gain some measure of independence. But this, as they correctly foresaw, was unlikely to happen.

Major Robert Thompson, a member of the Company and a merchant who did a great deal of trade with New England, wrote to Governor Leverett in 1674 saying that he had heard that the Commissioners 'did not incoredge the sending any stocke into the country' but that nevertheless: 'If you please to advise with them and others, and find a way of certain improvement by buying lands, mortgages or other security, I am confident the corporation may be inclined to goe in debt here to remitt a good some over.'[2] By 1679 the Indian stock stood at over £1,500. The Company ordered on 27 May 1679 that enough should be sent over to make it up to £2,000. In the following year it was added to by £300, the gift of Robert Boyle. But this was to be disposed of 'from time to time according to the desire and good intent of the said Governor & to noe other use.' Major Thompson's prediction was proved correct in 1681 when the Company borrowed from William Ashurst in order to make further investment in New England; the Court ordered 'soe soon as the . . . [£100] shall or may be received and gotton in by and out of the Rents and arreares of Rents due to this Company [it] shall be paid to Mr. William Ashurst.' Ashurst, on this and several later occasions, received six per cent interest for his loan. By

[1] Minutes (M.H.S. Ms.).

[2] Thomas Hutchinson, *A Collection of original papers* . . . (Boston, Mass., 1769), 449–50.

January 1681/2 the Indian stock stood at £2,230, and the Company formulated the optimistic policy: 'that there may be such a stock in New England as that the improvement thereof may carry on the work if a Supply should fail from hence.'[1]

But, as always, the Company expected a greater return on its money than was in fact forthcoming. Early in 1672 the Company heard that Mouche's gift might yield less than had been expected. It was at once ordered 'that if the Gent: which hath the monie now in his handes shall not thinke fitt to hold it longer the Commissioners may finde other good securitie in New England for the same who will give as good an allowance for it as that Gent now doth.' Again, in the following year the Company expressed surprise that the Commissioners should have difficulty in improving Mouche's gift, some members of the Company 'knowinge that private men can finde meanes to make a good improvement of their particuler monies there.'[2] This criticism of Captain John Richards, the gentleman concerned, not only offended Richards but also offended the Commissioners. On 20 December 1677 they wrote to Boyle: 'Wee have shewed Captain Richards your Letters and have received of him as per account, though wee finde him somewhat troubled at your intimation, referring to his Service therein, of which wee suppose you will heare from him, with intimation of his desire to dispose the mony into some other hand, which wee cannot advise, knowing no more meete person to bee betrusted therewith.'[3] The Company were apparently silenced by this answer, but still continued to expect greater returns. In March 1683/4, however, the Commissioners reminded the Company that it was mistaken in assuming that Mouche's gift was still in Richards' hands as the latter, more than three years before, had declined 'the service of Treasurer & improver of your Stock.' It had been taken over by William Stoughton, one of the Commissioners, 'where it hath since bin increased by all those considerable annual additions which your honour and the Honourable Company have made thereto.'[4]

By March 1683/4 the stock stood at just over £3,410 but the interest

[1] Minutes (M.H.S. Ms.), 4 May 1680, 14 Oct. 1681; Ms. 7946/15.
[2] Minutes (M.H.S. Ms.), 12 March 1671/2, 30 April 1673.
[3] Ms. 7955/1, no. 1. [4] Ms. 7936, f. 28.

during the previous year was only £156. The Company, on auditing the Commissioners' accounts, was 'a little surprized' that the return on the Indian stock was so small.[1] William Stoughton rendered 'An Account of the Indian Stock under improvement as it now stands disposed of' on 1 April 1685. This showed a total of £3,435 disposed amongst fifty-three people in amounts ranging from £416 to less than £6. Nearly all the money was loaned either on bond or mortgage, the only notable exception being a house leased by Edward Rawson, valued at £300. Stoughton added at the end of the account: 'What the summe total above, falls short of compleating the whole stock as in this years accounts it stands made up, is partly not yet receaved, & partly lyes ready for the next responsible person.'[2]

The Commissioners of the United Colonies held their last meeting in 1684, and after that date the Company had to look for individual officers to act on its behalf. It was perhaps only when this happened that the value of the Commissioners' work became apparent: they laboured at least as conscientiously for the Company as did the individual men it later chose to do its bidding. Considering their honorary status and their infrequent meetings, the fact that sometimes half the Commissioners' time at those meetings was devoted to the Company's affairs is remarkable, and on the whole they received with tolerance the Company's interference in matters where it could have little grasp of the issues involved — an interference at least as irritating as their own obstinacy was frustrating to the Company. In short, they did their job; they kept things going for thirty-four years, acting as middlemen between a Company with whose instructions they did not always agree and a body of missionaries with whose work they did not always sympathize.

[1] Ms. 7946/17; Minutes (M.H.S. Ms.), 8 Aug. 1684.
[2] Ms. 7946/18.

5

Missionaries and Indians, 1646–1690

IT is difficult to imagine the New England Company without John Eliot. It was his devotion to the task of converting the Indians which provided the early promoters of the Society with an example of what was being done for the Indians — even with proof that something really was being done for them; it was his continued devotion and enthusiasm which lent distinction to the New England mission in the seventeenth century.[1]

When Eliot began his missionary labours in 1646 he was nearly half-way through his long life. He was born at Widford, Hertfordshire on 5 August 1604. His father, Bennett Eliot, was of comfortable yeoman stock, owning property in both Hertfordshire and Essex; he died in 1621 having provided in his will for the education of his children. Two years before his father's death John matriculated as a pensioner at Jesus College, Cambridge, and in 1622 took out his B.A. Nothing is known of his life at Cambridge, but tradition has it that he was particularly interested in Greek and Hebrew and that he found philological studies absorbing. In 1629 he became usher at a school kept by Thomas Hooker at Little Baddow, near Chelmsford, Essex, thus coming under the influence of one of the most distinguished nonconformist ministers of the day. It has been suggested that Eliot was ordained at this time, but it seems unlikely that so fervent an admirer of Hooker would have sub-

[1] The first biography of Eliot was Cotton Mather's *The Triumphs of the Reformed Religion, in America. The Life of the Renowned John Eliot* (Boston, Mass., 1691), reprinted in *Magnalia Christi Americana* (1702). By far the best modern life is contained in S. E. Morison's *Builders of the Bay Colony* (1930), 289–319, to which I am greatly indebted. I have also drawn extensively upon the same author's *The Founding of Harvard College* and *Harvard College in the Seventeenth Century*.

scribed to the Thirty-Nine Articles.[1] Nevertheless, he was determined to serve God as a minister and, holding views incompatible with those of the Church of England, he naturally looked to New England. By November 1631 he had arrived in Boston and in November of the following year was ordained, in the Congregational manner, pastor of the first Roxbury church.

In a recently discovered letter to Sir Simonds D'Ewes, written during his first year at Roxbury, Eliot gave a lively account of the state of New England. He incidentally referred to the Indians, but it is clear that he did not at this time envisage his future work amongst them: 'we are at good peace with the . . . natives,' he wrote, '& they doe gladly intertaine us & give us possession, for we are as walls to them, from theire bloody enemise, & they are sensible of it, & also they have many more comforts by us; & I trust, in Gods time they shall larne Christ.'[2] But Eliot, who was urging D'Ewes to found a college in New England, did not take the opportunity of coupling the project with the conversion of the Indians, which he certainly would have done twelve years later.

It is difficult to explain what, during those twelve years, made Eliot turn his attention to the Indians. Contact between the Englishman and the Indian was having quite the reverse effect to that predicted by colonial propagandists. Eliot explained to Baxter that when Indians visited English homes they disliked any talk of God: so much did they dislike it, in fact, 'that if any began to speake of God, & heaven & hell, & religion unto them, they would presently be gone. So that it was a received & knowne thing to all English, that if they were burdensome and you would have them gone, speake of religion & you were presently rid of them.'[3]

The inevitable hostility of the colonist towards the aborigine was intensified in New England by the fact that, to the Puritan, paganism and satanism were identical. Indian life was dominated by the powwows, described by Gookin as 'partly wizards and witches, holding

[1] No record of his ordination has been found in the archives of the Diocese of London.

[2] *Harvard Library Bulletin*, VIII (1954), 272.

[3] Dr. Williams's Library, Baxter Letters, II, 274a.

familiarity with Satan, that evil one.'[1] In fact, nothing in the Puritans' experience more vividly illustrated the powers of the devil than the life of savages. Here Satan could be seen at work before their very eyes and the sight was a repulsive one. This feeling of repulsion together with prevailing theological views was not conducive to evangelical endeavour. John Cotton and others had argued that it would be unreasonable to expect the Indians' conversion until after the Jews had been converted. But Eliot managed to find a place for the Indians' conversion within the framework of the New England Way. He argued that the Indians were one of Israel's lost tribes which must be gathered in before the general conversion of the Jews. He was familiar with this idea before reading Thorowgood's *Iewes in America* (1650) but this so completely convinced him of its truth that he committed his own views to print in Thorowgood's second tract: *Jews in America, or Probabilities, that those Indians are Judaical, made more probable by some Additionals to the former Conjectures. An Accurate Discourse ispremised* [*sic*] *of Mr John Eliot . . . touching their Origination, and his Vindication of the Planters* (1660).

Eliot saw the conversion of the Indians as something ordained in the Scriptures and as something which would hasten the time when the Son of God would rule directly over the world. But one of the greatest obstacles in the path was language. Eliot maintained that Hebrew should become the universal language, as it was the language of God's own making. He himself was proficient in it and had assisted Thomas Weld and Richard Mather in translating the famous Bay Psalm Book (1640). Yet even he balked at the idea of teaching Hebrew to the Indians; instead he learnt their language.

It cannot have been before 1643 that he began this task. He was by no means the first Englishman to attempt it, but was probably the first to preach to the Indians in their own tongue. Algonquian, which was spoken in Massachusetts, was like most primitive languages, difficult to master, as there was no written language and no systematic grammar.[2] Its lack of affinity with any European tongue made it doubly

[1] M.H.S. *Collections, 1st series*, I, 154.

[2] There was, of course, Roger Williams's famous *Key into the Language of America* (1643), which was the first vocabulary of North American Indian words to be printed. However, it is not known how much use Eliot made of it.

difficult to learn: the French Jesuit, Sébastien Râle, admitted that his own speech was made fun of by the Indians (a confession never made by a Puritan missionary). Cotton Mather remarked that, although female demons could master Latin, Greek and Hebrew, Algonquian was beyond them. The greatest problem, however, was the lack, in the Indian vocabulary, of the abstract words so vital to an understanding of religious ideas. Eliot employed a young Indian to teach him, and before long had embarked upon the translation of the Lord's Prayer. According to Governor Winthrop he 'took great pains to get their language, and in a few months could speak of the things of God to their understanding.'[1]

In September 1646 he went, with Richard Mather and John Allen, to visit the Indians under the sachem Kitshomakin.[2] Little is known of the meeting, but it is possible that he tried his hand at addressing his audience in Indian, although probably most of the meeting was conducted through an interpreter. Eliot's first sermon in the Indian language was preached four or five miles from his home at Nonantum on the river Charles near Watertown. The meeting lasted for three hours, and began with prayers in English: 'we . . . being not so farre acquainted with the *Indian* language as to expresse our hearts herein before God or them.' The prayers were followed by Eliot's sermon, and the author of *The Day-Breaking* found it 'a glorious affecting spectacle to see a company of perishing, forlorne outcasts, diligently attending to the blessed word of salvation then delivered.' The sermon lasted for an hour and a quarter — the length of sermons is usually noted by those who hear them — and contained 'all the principall matter of religion, beginning first with a repetition of the ten Commandements, and a briefe explication of them.' God's wrath at those who broke his commandments, Jesus Christ the redeemer of sins, the Last Judgement, 'the blessed estate of all those that by faith beleeve in Christ', the Creation, the Fall of Man, Heaven and Hell — these things and more were expounded — 'not medling with any matters more difficult, and which to such weake ones might at first seeme ridiculous, untill they had tasted and beleeved more plaine and familiar truths.' Then came question time. For this Eliot and

[1] J. K. Hosmer, ed., *Winthrop's Journal*, II, 276, 319.

[2] *Ibid.*, II, 276; *The Day-breaking if not the Sun-rising*, 3.

the three ministers who accompanied him used an interpreter, although Eliot tried to answer the questions in Indian. The questions asked on this occasion compare very favourably with those asked on many later occasions. For example, it was asked: 'How may wee come to know Jesus Christ?' and the answer was given: through the Bible, which the Indians must consequently learn to read; through what they were taught, and through prayer and repentance. Again, the Indians asked: 'Whether English men were ever at any time so ignorant of God and Jesus Christ as themselves?'; 'How can there be an Image of God, because it's forbidden in the second Commandement?' 'How all the world is become so full of people, if they were all once drowned in the Flood?' The children were then given apples and the men tobacco. The Indians asked for ground on which to build a town and for more teaching, both which requests were found very encouraging by Eliot and his companions.[1] The pattern of this first meeting was, in most respects, adopted by Eliot in subsequent meetings though in time, as he became more fluent, he prayed in the Indian language.

The Indians' request for land brought Eliot up against one of the most difficult problems confronting the missionaries of New England and one to which no satisfactory solution was ever found, namely, how to secure Indian reserves against English encroachments. The English asserted that the only land to which the Indian had any inherent right was that which he cultivated; uncultivated ground was public domain in the Crown's gift. In theory at least the Indians might receive allotments made over to them by the agents of the Crown, in exactly the same way as the English. But to the nomadic Indian the allotment must have seemed as incomprehensible as the English claim to the soil of America by right of discovery. Eliot never expressed himself fully on the theoretical aspects of Indian title to land; to the practical issue of how to secure land for the Indians he devoted himself tirelessly.

Writing in 1648, he held that the Indians must have land of their own properly fenced off to prevent English cattle from eating their crops, and that where possible, they should be instructed in 'Letters, Trades, and Labours, as building, fishing, Flax and Hemp dressing, planting Orchards &c.'[2] Early in 1650 he wrote: 'they long for to proceed in

[1] *Op. cit.*, 1–7. [2] E. Winslow, *The Glorious Progress of the Gospel*, 8.

that work which I have in former Letters mentioned; namely to cohabit in a Towne, to be under the government of the Lord, and to have a Church and the Ordinances of Christ among them.'[1] He explained to the Indians how necessary it was, that first they should become civilized, by living together in a community. In the summer of 1650 the Dorchester Indians selected a site, but Eliot anticipated strong opposition from some English settlers who had an interest in the place, and refrained from pressing this claim. The place finally decided upon was called Natick, lying about eighteen miles south-west of Boston on the Charles River. This choice did not please the Dorchester Indians; they thought that Eliot had let them down, and were consequently unwilling to settle there. Thus was dashed Eliot's original plan that all the 'praying Indians' live together in one large community. Nevertheless, work began immediately at Natick, first upon a house and then upon a bridge to span the Charles River which divided the site; a fort was also completed by the middle of 1651. But the title to Natick was almost immediately disputed by inhabitants of the neighbouring township of Dedham. In October 1651, Eliot petitioned the General Court of Massachusetts on the Indians' behalf: the Court ordered that 2000 acres should be allowed to the Indians provided that they surrendered all claims to land in Dedham itself and provided also that they set no traps on unenclosed land; if Eliot should demand from Dedham more land for the Indians, it should be yielded, nearby towns compensating Dedham for the gift.[2]

A year later, in October 1652, the General Court reiterated the principle that the Indians had a right to any land they held 'by possession or improvement, by subdueing of the same'. For their encouragement it was added that if any of them were civilized enough to live among the English, they would be given allotments or, if there were enough of them to form a township, the necessary land would be granted.[3] On the strength of this order Eliot successfully petitioned the Court on a number of occasions during the following decades, and land grants were

[1] H. Whitfield, *The Light appearing*, 31.

[2] N. B. Shurtleff, ed., *Records of the . . . Massachusetts Bay*, III, 246; IV pt. i, 75–6; *Acts*, II, 423–4.

[3] N. B. Shurtleff, ed., *Records*, III, 281; IV pt. i, 102–3.

made for forming further townships on the Natick model. They were made always upon the condition that the Indians should not dispose of the land without the consent of the General Court, this proviso being intended to ensure that the Indians' interest would be protected and that they would be prevented from selling their land and then demanding more.

Yet Eliot viewed his efforts with no satisfaction and was fully aware of the difficulties of maintaining Indian title against the increasing land hunger of the English settlers. He expressed his views in the dedicatory epistle of his *Indian dialogues* (1671) addressed to the Commissioners: 'My earnest request unto your selves, is, That in all your respective Colonies you would take care that due Accommodation of Lands and Waters may be allowed them, whereon Townships and Churches may be (in after-Ages) able to subsist; and suffer not the English to strip them of all their Lands, in places fit for Sustenance of the life of man.'[1] Writing in August 1673, Eliot claimed that the Indians showed great reverence for the English 'but the business about land giveth them no small matter of stumbling.'[2]

Eliot's labours at Natick met their first reward in August 1651: '(their Pallizadoe Fort being finished) they had a great meeting, and many came together from diverse parts . . . and finally they did solemnly choose two Rulers among themselves, they first chose a Ruler of an Hundred, then they chose two Rulers of Fifties, then they chose Ten or Tithing men.'[3] The Indians were thus initiated into a system of government devised by Eliot for the world at large but only essayed by the red Indian. Eliot had conferred with Mr Cotton and others concerning the government of the Indians and had decided that 'they shall be wholly governed by the Scriptures in all things both in Church and State; they shall have no other Law-giver; the Lord shall be their Law-giver, the Lord shall be their Judge, the Lord shall be their King, and he will save them.'[4] In a period famous for theocratic theories of government, Eliot's was certainly outstanding for the extreme nature of its provi-

[1] *Op. cit.*, sig. A2b.
[2] M.H.S. *Collections, 1st series*, X, 128.
[3] H. Whitfield, *Strength out of Weaknesse*, 9.
[4] H. Whitfield, *The Light appearing*, 23.

sions. His views, most fully experienced in a tract entitled *The Christian Commonwealth: or, The Civil Policy of the Rising Kingdom of Jesus Christ* [1659], were based upon the concept that Christ is the King of Kings before whom temporal power must give way. The law of God is revealed in the Scriptures and nowhere else; for this reason there is no need of an authority for making law as the law is already made. Nor, when monarchy is overthrown, will there be any distinction between temporal and spiritual rulers. All that will be needed is a system of rulers based on the common multiple of ten: elected rulers of tens, fifties, hundreds and so on.

Although, at the Restoration, copies of the *Christian Commonwealth* were publicly burned and Eliot signed a recantation, his views did not radically change. In 1665 he printed for private circulation a small tract entitled *Communion of Churches* in which he set forth his theories on government. This time he argued that a hierarchy of Councils elected on a system of twelves, instead of tens, should determine the affairs of the whole world, whether civil or spiritual. These councils should be absolute in their power, and to disobey them would mean death, for: 'It is a greater good to preserve Order, then to preserve the lives of the wilfull and obstinate violaters thereof.'[1]

But this book attracted little attention to itself either in America, where it was printed, or in England, whither several copies were sent. Baxter, a recipient of one of these, wrote to John Woodbridge saying: 'I would faine know whether his Method of Councills be yet Communicated, and how it taketh.' To this request Woodbridge answered: 'Truely, Sir, I thinke it better took with himself than with any of his Bretheren, not because of his pride, I suppose you know him better, but the peculiar Cut of his Genius. While some were smiling at it, others whispering about it, the booke, as I understand, was called in Agen, & now none of them seen walking Abroad.' However, Baxter himself considered the work worthy of his criticism, which he accordingly sent to Eliot soon after receiving his copy. But when he answered Woodbridge's letter late in 1671, he remarked: 'I am sorry that Mr Eliots propositions tooke no better with you. For though I am not for his conciet of founding such synods on ye 24 Elders &c., yet every man

[1] *Op. cit.*, 33.

may have leave to go his own way, in point of unnecessary notions, while they agree in ye same practise.'[1]

New England's elect were prepared to allow Eliot to impose his system of government upon the Indians without interference. But to the proposal for forming the first native church at Natick there was sharp opposition. Church members unprepared to admit their unregenerate fellow countrymen were naturally even more sceptical of Indian claims to regeneracy. The step from paganism to regeneration was so enormous as to be almost impassible. It seemed inconceivable that the savage mind could sufficiently grasp the intellectual framework within which the highly sophisticated process of regeneration operated.

But to form a church at Natick was Eliot's avowed aim. He was particularly anxious that not only should the Indians be fully prepared for this solemn occasion but that the English settlers should realize that they were fully prepared. Both the preparation of the Indians and the convincing of the English caused the long delay in forming a church. Eliot described how the Indians at Natick had 'come under Civil Order; and fixing themselves in Habitations, and bending themselves to labor, as doth appear by their works of Fencings, Buildings, &c. and especially in building without any English Workmans help, or direction, a very sufficient Meeting-House, of fifty foot long twenty five foot broad, neer twelve foot high betwixt the joynts, wel sawen and framed.' The meeting house being completed, Eliot began in the summer of 1652 to encourage them 'to make confession before the Lord of their former sins, and of their present knowledg of Christ, and experience of his Grace.' He wrote down these confessions and, in October 1652, several ministers from Boston came to Natick to hear them read. The result was a disappointment to Eliot because it was decided that the Indians were not yet ready to form a church. Nevertheless Eliot, Mayhew and the Society all agreed that the confessions were suitable material for the next Indian tract entitled *Tears of Repentance* (1653).[2]

Early in the summer of 1654, Eliot arranged another public examination at Roxbury. An outbreak of drunkenness before the examination confirmed the examiners, ministers and elders in their opinion that

[1] Dr. Williams's Library, Baxter Letters, II, 239, 234, 240.

[2] *Op. cit.*, 1–2.

the Indians of Natick were unready for church estate.[1] It was not until five years later that they began to relent in their view and even then it was with the greatest reluctance. In July 1659 the third examination was held; eight Indians read confessions of faith which were then translated for the ministers and elders. This time it was decided that a few Indians should 'be seasoned in Church-fellowship in communion with our *English* Churches, before they should be Churches among themselves.'[2] They were therefore admitted to membership of the church at Roxbury strictly on trial, and obviously in opposition to the wishes of a substantial part of the Roxbury congregation. Eliot must have felt that it was at least a beginning. It is interesting to notice that he strongly championed the idea of mixed congregations many years later, but qualified his arguments characteristically: 'I am quiet in the plea of the diversity of language.'[3]

It was not until 1660 that a sufficient proportion of the conservative Roxbury elders were persuaded to allow the Natick Indians to form their own church. No other Indian community had a comparable struggle to attain church status, partly because Natick created a precedent and partly because Puritans of the second generation were less critical than their fathers had been. But although the resistance to a church at Natick may have been partly prejudice against the whole Indian race, it was primarily based upon profound doubts as to the effectiveness of Eliot's efforts. Probably no saner or more balanced judge can be found than Daniel Gookin, himself a worker amongst the Indians: 'And for my own part, I have no doubt, but am fully satisfied, according to the judgment of charity, that divers of them do fear God and are true believers; but yet I will not deny but that there may be some of them hypocrites, that profess religion, and yet are not sound hearted.'[4]

Far different was the opinion of the Commissioners appointed by Charles II to report on the state of New England. According to their view the Indians of Massachusetts were converted 'by hiring them to

[1] J. Eliot, *A Late and Further Manifestation of the Progress of the Gospel* (1655), 2, 22.

[2] J. Eliot, *A further Account of the progress of the Gospel* (1660), 1–2.

[3] M.H.S. *Collections*, *1st series*, X, 127.

[4] *Ibid.*, *1st series*, I, 183.

come & heare sermons, by teaching them not to obey their heathen Sachims, and by appointing rulers amongst them, over tenns, twenties, fifties &c. The lives, manners, & habits of those whom they say are converted cannot be distinguished from those who are not, except it be by being hired to heare sermons, which the more generous natives scorne.'[1] But the Royal Commissioners seized upon anything which could be reported to the detriment of Massachusetts, and Eliot's efforts seemed as much to their purpose as any other subject.

From his first essays at converting the Indians Eliot had contended, in accordance with the generally accepted Puritan view, that it would be impossible to bring them to Christianity without civilizing them first and that to civilize them would cost money. Tools and implements would have to be bought and other ministers paid to enter the field. It was at this period that he began to pen letters to his friends in England asking for assistance. Although Thomas Thorowgood collected money in Norfolk and Jonathan Hanmer collected in Devon, Eliot hoped for greater assistance from England than one or two individuals could offer. He therefore received the news of the act creating the Society with a joy only equalled by his impatience to receive its first fruits. It was a bitter disappointment to him that no financial assistance was forthcoming from the Society during 1649 or 1650, and although he resolutely quoted, in a letter to the Society, John Cotton's advice to him, 'My heart sayeth go on, and look to the Lord onely for help', he still fretfully awaited the arrival of the first shipment.[2]

Over one thing the Society acted promptly — the purchase of two libraries for Eliot and Thomas Mayhew. Eliot had asked Winslow in 1649 if the Society would buy for him, at the cost of £34, the library which Thomas Weld had left in Boston when he went to England as the agent of Massachusetts. At the same time he asked that Thomas Mayhew, who 'being young, and a beginner here, hath extreme want of books', might be sent 'such books as may be necessary for a young Scholer' and added: 'I will name no books, he needs all.'[3] The Society not only purchased Weld's library but also bought, for £30, a library

[1] E. B. O'Callaghan, ed., *Documents relative to . . . the State of New York*, III (Albany, 1853), 112; *C.S.P. Col., 1661–1668*, 346.

[2] H. Whitfield, *The Light appearing*, 36.

[3] *Ibid.*, 24.

left in New England by Thomas Jenner.[1] Eliot received many gifts of books sent from England. In July 1652 he explained to Jonathan Hanmer that, apart from these two libraries: 'the reverend eld[er]s ministers of exon have sent unto us new supply, and this yeare they sent unto us the 2nd edition of the new annotations upon the whole bible.'[2] Henry Jessey, the famous Independent minister, sent him in 1657 a small parcel of books which was shipped by the Society,[3] and on a number of other occasions London ministers and well-wishers entrusted gifts of books for Eliot to the Society's care.

When in 1651 the first shipment of goods arrived at Boston, Eliot wasted no time in exerting his influence upon how they should be disposed and from this time onwards was always ready with advice as to what goods should be sent from England. The Commissioners, who were anyway out of sympathy with Eliot's aims, resented his interference in what they considered to be their domain; but they were at a disadvantage, for Eliot's letters to the Society and to his friends in England carried great weight. When the Commissioners were not prepared to give way to his proposals, a letter from Eliot in the right quarter usually tipped the scales in his favour. Yet on the whole they were reasonable in their dealings with him, though they did not refrain from offering him unwanted advice from time to time. They warned him that the Indians might 'onely follow Christ for loaves and outward advantage Remaining enimies to the yoak and goverment'. They advised him to confer with Simon Bradstreet and Captain Hawthorn concerning the distribution amongst the Indians of tools sent by the Society, and warned him that these should be given only to those Indians who were converted and that if they showed any signs of relapsing, no more should be given. To one subject, Eliot's salary, they returned on more than one occasion. Eliot himself admitted that he had received £20 for four years (Lady Armine's annuity which was paid to him by order of the General Court of Massachusetts), but the Commissioners had heard of £100 'sent from exeter or som of those Western parts' to

[1] The inventories of these libraries were printed by C. F. & R. Robinson, 'Three Early Massachusetts Libraries', *C.S.M.*, XXVIII (1935), 107–75.

[2] *Bulletin of the John Rylands Library*, **5**, 105.

[3] Ms. 7936, f. 2, Eliot to Richard Floyd, 8 Oct. 1657.

be divided among Eliot, Mayhew and the Indians themselves but in what proportion the Commissioners did not know. They therefore needed an account from Eliot both of his income and his expenditure.[1]

But if the Society found it difficult to extract satisfactory accounts from the Commissioners, the Commissioners found it difficult to persuade Eliot to submit any accounts at all. Eliot regarded the money and goods sent to him personally as exclusively his own affair. The Commissioners, on the other hand, were not prepared to pay him more than £20 per annum without knowing how much he received from other sources and this he regarded as unjust. The Society asked in 1653 that Eliot, Mayhew and all other ministers employed in the work might be paid more, but added for the Commissioners' peace of mind: 'wee are farr from Justifying Mr Elliott in his *Turbulent and clamorus proceedings* but the best of gods servants have theire faylings.' The Commissioners acquiesced by paying both Eliot and Mayhew £40 per annum but reminded the Society that Eliot had admitted receiving large sums from private sources of which he was 'slow to give any account' and that his salary from the Roxbury congregation was not less than £60 per annum.[2] Half of the £40 paid to Eliot by the Commissioners continued to derive from Lady Armine's annuity. His salary was later increased to £50 and this remained the normal amount that he received from the Company for the rest of his life.

He often complained about the infrequency of the Commissioners' meetings and pointed out that the goods sent over were liable to deteriorate between the annual meetings and that the work was held up for lack of funds. The Commissioners for their part were irked by the demands for goods which he made without consulting them. In 1653, after the receipt of brass and glass goods suggested by Eliot, the Commissioners told Winslow: 'wee have advised Mr Eliott and others that heerafter they forbeare such writing and consult with the Commissioners first what to send for; And wee desire you not to attend such private letters.'[3] The Society, answering in February 1653/4, agreed to send only such goods as the Commissioners asked for, yet Eliot continued to be sufficiently persuasive to get his own way. For example in

[1] *Acts*, I, 203–4. [2] *Acts*, II, 119–20. [3] *Acts*, II, 104.

1655 one bale of a consignment was directed to Eliot personally, and the Commissioners saw that they had lost yet another round when they wrote to the Society saying: 'One bale . . . which Cost there 34^{ll} 09^{s} 05^{d} and with the advance amounts to 45^{ll} 19^{s} 03^{d} directed to Mr Eliote for the use of the Indian worke but why it is severed from the Rest of the parsell and consigned to him is not expressed; It seems different from the Course youer selves approved and may prove Inconvenient if it bee Continued.'[1]

Another of Eliot's suggestions to the Society — that the ministers engaged in the work should be paid by bills of exchange — caused the Commissioners irritation: the idea was that the ministers, rather than the Commissioners, would have the benefit of the rate of exchange. The Society favoured the suggestion, on the grounds that it might quell the general complaints circulating in England that ministers and schoolmasters were 'very much discorraged for want of a competent maintainance' and the more particular remarks of Hugh Peter that 'those who carry on the worke are not lookt upon, but are constrayned to take course cloth att Boston.'[2] The Commissioners sulkily and somewhat naively replied that they did not understand why anyone should want to be paid in England 'unlesse to free themselves from the 4^{d} on the shilling advance.' If ministers employed untrustworthy assignees, the Commissioners pointed out, or if they met with losses 'some Inconveniencies may follow.' The Society compromised by asking them to pay the ministers' salaries in 'goods in kind according to the prise they Cost heer without any advance upon them and that they may not bee paied in Corne or any other Comoditie of the Countrey grouth which wee understand turnes to noe considerable account and give offence to divers well afected heerunto.'[3]

Although Eliot was not above complaining about the treatment he received from the Commissioners, he was very generous, if not careless, with his money. In 1666 he gave his whole annual salary 'to bee disposed unto such as Mr Ashurst & Mr Bell, who are to consult ye advice

[1] *Acts*, II, 138.
[2] *Acts*, II, 160; Minutes (M.H.S. Ms.), 25 Nov. 1656.
[3] *Acts*, II, 164, 186.

of Mr Carroll and Mr Brookes shall thinke fitt.'[1] Eliot probably specified that the money should be used to assist ministers ejected from their benefices in 1662 and it was for this reason that Bell and Ashurst were advised to consult two distinguished ejected ministers — Thomas Brooks and Joseph Caryl. However, by 1670 he was short of money, though he had been warned by the Commissioners that his salary would probably be abated because of the Company's difficulties in England. He wrote to Ashurst in November informing him that he had drawn a bill of exchange for £40 upon the Company. He assured Ashurst that the Commissioners would approve this action when next they met: 'especially considering that I touch none of the expences so much as with one finger. I reape nothing; it is expended only upon the work & that in a prudent & I hope we shall find in a successefull way.' In the event his confidence in obtaining the Commissioners' approval was completely misplaced. In September 1671 he informed them that 'by some intimation I had from worthy Mr Ashurst I tooke boldnesse to charge a bill of 40ll upon the honourable Corporation.' He explained that he had spent this money on sending messengers to many places and on providing entertainment for those who attended his lectures. He not only asked for their approval but also asked for an allowance: 'And the rather I am bold to propose it, because in all the Publik meetings, motions, jornyes, translations, attendances on the presse & other occasions that I have attended in this work, I have never had (to my knowledg & remembranc) the least acknowledgment from your selves, or one penny supply, save my bare Salary. And I am forced to move, because I am fallen into dept. I ow unto Mr Usher 100ll at least . . . And therefore I request you to pay this debt of mine. Did I not conceive that something is due unto me, I should not make so bold, for to beg I am ashamed.' The Commissioners did nothing and Eliot won his point by dint of enclosing a copy of his letter to the Commissioners in his letter to Henry Ashurst with the comment: 'but they are pleased to answer me with silence, as it is wont to be' and reporting that he had taken the matter into his own hands by drawing a bill of exchange for £80 upon

[1] Minutes (M.H.S. Ms.), 20 Feb. 1665/6; Ms. 7944/1 & Ms. 7911/1, payments to Thomas Bell and Henry Ashurst, 23 Feb. 1665/6, 10 April 1666, 22 Aug. 1666.

the Company. To consolidate his position he wrote to Boyle in similar vein.[1] At its meeting on 12 March 1671/2 the Company accepted the bills of exchange: 'for the incouragement of Mr Eliot in his faithfull & indefatigable labours . . . & in regard of the extraordinarie charges which he hath been at the last yeare.' It ordered that the Commissioners should be informed of its decision 'being unwilling to discourage soe worthy an Instrument in the worke . . . as Mr. Eliott is & hath been.' Heaping insult upon injury the Company proceeded to ask the Commissioners not to charge any more bills upon the Company 'but to reward Mr Eliott & other Ministers & Instrumentes . . . as the said Commissioners shall finde them & their labours respectively deserve & as their stock & monies remitted to them by this Company will affoard.'[2]

Eliot was not quite alone in the missionary field during the 1640s. At about the time that he was beginning his work, Thomas Mayhew, junior, took active steps towards converting the Indians of Martha's Vineyard. He was a man of less temperament than Eliot; whereas Eliot regarded the Indians' conversion as virtually impossible without assistance, Mayhew began and continued his work without thought of financial help. And because he lacked Eliot's gift for self-advertisement and because his life was much shorter, his efforts are sometimes forgotten.

He was born in 1620 or 1621, the only son of Thomas Mayhew, senior, later governor and proprietor of Martha's Vineyard, and probably accompanied his father to New England in 1631. He was ordained pastor at the early age of twenty-one or twenty-two; his father had purchased the proprietary rights of Martha's Vineyard, Nantucket, and fourteen smaller islands, in 1641, and in the next year the young man went to Great Harbour, Martha's Vineyard, and began his work as minister. It is not known how or where he gained his education, but at this time he knew some Latin and Greek and according to Thomas Prince was 'not wholly a Stranger to the *Hebrew*.'[3] He quickly realized that an effort must be made to assist the Indians in his father's domains and by 1643 he had made his first convert — Hiacoomes. Historians of Martha's Vineyard are quick to point out that this conversion took

[1] Ms. 7936, f. 15, 16, 21, 22. [2] Minutes (M.H.S. Ms.).
[3] E. Mayhew, *Indian Converts* (1727), 280.

place three years before Eliot began to preach to the Indians. Indeed some years later, the Commissioners referred to Mayhew as 'the first', and then as an afterthought, 'or one of the first whose hart god stired up effectually to laboure in this worke.'[1] Mayhew followed up his success with Hiacoomes by visiting the Indians from 1644 onwards, and with the assistance of Hiacoomes as interpreter, attempted to make further converts. It was not until 1647 that he held his first public meeting, and it is not possible to say at what time he began to learn the Indian language, but sooner or later he, too, was preaching to the Indians in their own tongue. Probably his main work was begun just after Eliot's, but the title of first Protestant missionary to the Indians in New England should be shared between them.

If Mayhew was not given to soliciting aid, he did not have much opportunity of doing so. Martha's Vineyard was far from any centre of population and, unlike Eliot, he lacked influential friends at home. He wrote an account of himself in November 1647 which was not printed until 1649. Winslow explained that it was included in *The Glorious Progress of the Gospel* 'lest the young man should be discouraged,' and more particularly as proof that ' 'tis not one Minister alone that laboureth in this great work.'[2] But the Society did not receive pressing requests for assistance from Mayhew. It was only chance, in the form of adverse winds, which brought Henry Whitfield to Martha's Vineyard to witness Mayhew's work there. But Whitfield was impressed and, like Winslow, a little relieved, to find a second worker in the field. When he returned to England he was able, in the Indian tracts, to draw attention to Mayhew's work, but he remarked: 'the man himself was modest and I could get but little from him.'[3]

In fact Mayhew's early efforts, if not spectacular, compared very favourably with Eliot's. By October 1651, 199 men, women and children 'had professed themselves to be Worshippers'. Three months later Mayhew opened a school for Indian children with such success that by October 1652 his converts numbered 282. It was Eliot himself who first recommended that the Society should help Mayhew by buying for him the library of Thomas Jenner. After this, of course, Mayhew received a regular salary from the Commissioners; initially £20 per

[1] *Acts*, II, 293. [2] *Op. cit.*, 3. [3] H. Whitfield, *The Light appearing*, 2.

annum, it was increased to £40 in 1654 and in the same year the Commissioners allowed £10 each to his two Indian schoolmasters and a further £10 to be distributed amongst the weak, sick or well-deserving natives. Other allowances made by the Commissioners at this time were £40 towards a meeting house and £8 for a boat to ply between the island and the mainland but 'onely for the service Intended and nott att the pleasure of the Indians Etc.'[1]

But the labours of Thomas Mayhew junior were already drawing to an end. In September 1655 he had proposed to the Commissioners that he should go to England to secure his title to some property there. The Commissioners had done their best to persuade him to send someone else in his place so that his work at Martha's Vineyard would not suffer. But Mayhew felt obliged to go himself and in November 1656 set sail from Boston with one of his Indian converts. Their ship was never heard of again and the Indians of Martha's Vineyard thus lost their first and most renowned teacher.[2] The loss was indeed serious but the Commissioners were able to inform the Society that Thomas Mayhew senior 'though ancient is healpfull with an other English man [Peter Folger] and two Indians that Instruct the rest upon the Lords day.'[3]

Peter Folger was only a schoolmaster and Thomas Mayhew senior was anxious that the Indians should have a minister. On his behalf the Commissioners promised to approach Abraham Pierson and John Higginson, but in the event neither of these gentlemen was anxious to move to Martha's Vineyard. However, in about 1663 the Commissioners found a minister for the Vineyard—John Cotton, son of the celebrated Boston preacher. Cotton became minister at Edgartown and hired an Indian at twelve pence a day for fifty days to teach him the Indian language: 'but his Knavish Tutor having received his Whole Pay too soon, ran away before *Twenty Days* were out.'[4] Undaunted, Cotton nevertheless tended the Indians and was duly paid by the Com-

[1] *Acts*, II, 124.

[2] The work of the Mayhew family as missionaries is dealt with fully in C. E. Banks's *The History of Martha's Vineyard* (Boston, Mass., 1911–25), 3 vol.; *D.A.B.*, XII, 456.

[3] *Acts*, II, 203; L.C.M. Hare, *Thomas Mayhew, Patriarch to the Indians* (New York, 1932); *D.A.B.*, XII, 455–6.

[4] Cotton Mather, *Magnalia*, III, 200.

missioners. His wife also received £10 for 'Physick and Surgery' dispensed to Indians. But the appointment of John Cotton proved unsatisfactory as he soon quarrelled with Mayhew and, in September 1667, the young minister appeared at the Commissioners' meeting, where he was severely reprimanded and told that 'hee was left to his libertie to dispose of himselfe as the Lord should Guid him.'[1] In fact he found a position at Plymouth and was soon employed once more by the Commissioners.

Whatever the grounds of dispute between Cotton and Mayhew, the blame cannot have been entirely Cotton's. Enough letters written by Thomas Mayhew have survived to show that, excellent though his good qualities were, he was strong-willed and often irascible and, unlike his son, kept a jealous eye upon the Commissioners' moneys. Early in 1658 he asked John Winthrop to support his cause before the Commissioners. He had worked for the Indians for ten years and on two occasions had received £10 or £20 which, though more than he expected, did not mean that he would be satisfied with this, or even with £30 per annum, if he were a regular salaried servant of the Commissioners. He insisted that the money at the Commissioners' disposal was meant to pay the salaries of those who tended the Indians and should be used for this purpose before all else. About a year later he wrote in similar vein and made no secret of his view that Martha's Vineyard was not receiving its fair share of the spoils.[2] It was no doubt from Thomas Mayhew himself that Samuel Maverick, one of the Commissioners appointed by Charles II to investigate the colonies of New England, heard of this grievance. Maverick incorporated it in his 'Description of New England.' The two Mayhews, son and father, had done much to convert the Indians, he wrote: 'Although (as I understand) they have had a small share of those vast summes given for this use and purpose or ye Revenues of it. It were good to enquire how it hath been disposed of. I know in some measure or at least suspect the business hath not been rightly carryed.'[3]

In his eightieth year Mayhew wrote on the same theme to the Com-

[1] *Acts*, II, 329.
[2] M.H.S. *Collections, 4th series*, VII, 34, 36–7.
[3] British Museum, Egerton Ms. 2395, f. 406–7.

missioners, adding characteristically: 'I suppose when I am gonne it will cost doubl to doe what I doe now or have done.'[1] He had, as a matter of fact, done a great deal, and it would be wrong to dismiss him as either acquisitive or cantankerous. Few, if any, of his contemporaries were equally successful in dealing with the Indian people; as he himself put it: 'tis hard to find amongst the English a Moderate Interpretation of the words & actions of the Indians.'[2] He did not even consider his own interpretation of them to be fair, and disarmingly enough he wrote: 'my error hath been, in all cases, that I am too favourable to English and it hath always been very hard for me to preserve myself from being drawn to deal over-hardly with the Indians.'[3] But the Indians themselves trusted him, and even wanted him to become their first pastor; he declined — 'conceiving that in his present capacity he lieth under greater advantages to stand their Friend, and do them good.'[4] And so, to the end of his days, Thomas Mayhew senior contented himself with supervising their religious affairs, teaching them and protecting their lands from English encroachments.

It was not until 1670 that the first church was gathered at Edgartown, Hiacoomes being ordained pastor and John Tackamash teacher. Two years later John Tackamash was ordained pastor of the second church at Chappaquidick. He was even more highly regarded than Hiacoomes and it is some evidence of his repute that the white population was prepared to accept the Lord's Supper from his hands.

The Society was extremely worried in the 1650s by the small number of ministers actually employed throughout New England in preaching to the Indians. The Commissioners, for their part, were well aware of the situation, and promised that they would not 'willingly neglect any oppertunitie to Increase the number of fitt Instruments.' But the Congregational minister was bound to his flock and having tended its needs had little time for those 'without the covenant.' Nor were New England's elect anxious to release those few ministers who were prepared

[1] Ms. 7936, f. 17, 23 Aug. 1671.

[2] Note appended to the accounts sent to the Commissioners, 21 Aug. 1671 (Ms. 7936, f. 17).

[3] M.H.S. *Collections, 1st series*, VI, 196–7. He expressed himself similarly to the Commissioners (Ms. 7936, f. 17).

[4] J. Eliot, *A Brief Narrative*, 4.

to preach to the heathen. In September 1656 there were only three of them and efforts to find others had proved unsuccessful. In the following year, Eliot and other elders informed the Commissioners that they had found three ministers willing to undertake the work. To these the Commissioners offered salaries of £20 per annum but in the event only one of them accepted. The Society itself made several recommendations: in 1657 it put forward John Blackleech 'whom wee thinke may bee usefull and serviceable in Civilliceing of the Indians and alsoe healpfull to enforme them in the knowlidge of the gosspell.' The Commissioners replied in September that they did not know him and had not heard that he was interested but would, nevertheless, 'close with him'.[1] The Society must have regretted its recommendation, as Usher, who was in England in February 1657/8, reported to the Court that Mr. Blackleech was a man with some general notions but 'not fixed and fitted for this worke.'[2]

As suitable ministers were so hard to find, the Commissioners undertook the education of several English youths in the hope that they would, one day, tend the Indians. Amongst those who received this support were John and Thomas Stanton, the sons of Thomas Stanton, the Commissioners' official interpreter, and Matthew Mayhew, the eldest son of Thomas Mayhew junior. When Thomas Mayhew's wife was convinced that her husband was lost at sea, she did her best to persuade the Commissioners to undertake the education of her three sons so that they could continue their father's work. The Commissioners were loath to follow her suggestion, as the boys were young and might well change their minds about their vocation later. However, in September 1658, they gave her £20 and began to pay for Matthew Mayhew's education. The Commissioners' experience with the Stanton boys, one of whom, it was reported in September 1659, 'doth greatly neglect his Studdy and hath Comitted many other misdemenors' made them wary of 'breeding up fit instruments.' In 1660 they wrote to the Society 'we shalbee slow to take many more English or Indian youthes upon our charge for education till wee have some experience of those on whom soe much hath bine bestowed.'[3]

[1] *Acts*, II, 164, 186–7.
[2] Minutes (M.H.S. Ms.).
[3] *Acts*, II, 205, 228, 242.

If the work of converting the Indians remained as the Commissioners styled it in 1664, 'a day of small thinges', this was still partly because so few people were employed as missionaries. Eliot remarked, in his dedicatory epistle to the *Indian dialogues* (1671): 'I finde few English students willing to engage in so dim a Work as this is.' He had endeavoured to find colleagues both in America and in England. In his search he had turned to Richard Baxter for assistance but Baxter wrote in November 1663: 'There are many here that would be ambitious of being your Fellow-Labourers, but that they are informed, you have access to no greater a Number of the Indians than you your self, and your present Assistants are able to instruct.' Boyle, he continued, had asked him to start a collection 'for the maintaining of such Ministers, as are willing to go hence to you . . . . But I find those backward to it, that I have spoke to about it, partly suspecting it a Design of those that would be rid of them . . . partly because they think there will be nothing considerable gathered. . . .'[1]

In the 1680s the Company sent two young men to New England to be trained there for the Indian service. Both were recommended by Charles Morton, an active dissenting minister, who ran a school at Newington Green. The first, Samuel Penhallow, was sent to this school by his father who was a friend of Morton's, and in 1686 the young man accompanied his former teacher to New England with an assurance from the Company that it would support him while he learnt the Indian language and afterwards employ him as a missionary. However, on arriving at Boston he changed his mind, perhaps realizing what such a life would involve. Many years later he did in fact serve the Company, in a much less onerous capacity, as a Commissioner for Indian Affairs.[2] The other young man recommended by Charles Morton was his own nephew, Nicholas Morton. In February 1685/6 the Company asked the Commissioners that he might be brought up for two years at Harvard as a missionary: 'he being a person well skilled in the Tongues.'[3] His skill in the Tongues seems to have been somewhat misrepresented for, after he had begun his studies at Harvard, his uncle found it necessary

[1] M. Sylvester, ed., *Reliquiae Baxterianae*, lib. I, pt. II, 295–6.

[2] *D.A.B.*, XIV, 427; M.H.S. *Collections, 2nd series*, I, 161. He served as a Commissioner for the years 1724–6 (Ms. 7930).

[3] Minutes (M.H.S. Ms.).

to apologize for his backwardness: 'especially in the Hebrew.'[1] Nevertheless the Company allowed him £20 a year for two years for learning the Indian language, judging this to be 'more then enough to ataine it.'[2] But once again the Company was thwarted: Nicholas Morton died in November 1689.

Of the English missionaries who were employed during Eliot's lifetime, apart from the Mayhews none was outstanding. The first minister to preach to the Indians in New Haven, or Connecticut as it later became, was Abraham Pierson; he began studying the Indian language in 1651, from which date he received a salary from the Society for preaching to the Indians in the neighbourhood of Branford. He is best remembered for his Indian Catechism which was printed in 1658. James Fitch senior, his immediate successor in Connecticut, wrote to Gookin in 1674: 'Concerning the Indians in this colony and at Long Island, I cannot understand that they have any inclination to learn the knowledge of God: but when Mr Pierson did frequently try, in the several plantations in this colony, they did generally show an averseness, yea a perverse contempt of the word of God; and at present they will not yield to any settled hearing or attendance upon the ministry of the word.'[3] Although Pierson did not die until 1678, he received no salary after 1667, because he had moved to Newark, New Jersey, in that year and had abandoned his efforts to convert the natives.[4]

Another of Connecticut's earliest missionaries was William Thomson, who received a subsidy from the Commissioners in 1659 for learning the language. But he made little use of this knowledge in their service as he was only employed for three years, mainly at New London but also at Sandwich.[5] Vastly different, at least in length of service, was James Fitch — 'the holy and acute Mr *Fitch*,' as Cotton Mather called him.[6] He began his work among the Indians of Hartford county in 1670 and when he later moved to Norwich, preached to the Indians there, receiving an annual salary of £31. 10s., the interest from Mouche's gift. Eliot was able to report to the Commissioners in Sep-

[1] Sibley, III, 366–7.

[2] Draft letter from the Company to the Commissioners, 12 April 1687 (Ms. 7956).

[3] M.H.S. *Collections, 1st series*, I, 208.

[4] *D.A.B.*, XIV, 587–8.

[5] Sibley, I, 354–7.

[6] C. Mather, *Magnalia*, III, 200.

tember 1671 that Fitch was holding a lecture at his own home once a fortnight and that Uncas and his son had promised to attend.[1] But whatever high hopes Fitch had had, a few years experience deprived him of all optimism. Although he did not abandon the work, his salary was drastically reduced in the 1680s but was usually £25 a year in the following decade. In 1701, the Commissioners, in answer to a 'Pathetical Petition', paid him £12 'to take leave of him: his age & Manifold Infirmities hindering his farther attendance on ye Indian Work.'[2] The only other English missionary in Connecticut during the seventeenth century was John Blackleech, who in 1669 received the approbation of that colony's Court to engage in the work of conversion. But despite the support of both John Eliot and John Winthrop, he never seems to have been in the Commissioners' pay.[3]

Thomas James, first minister of the Congregational church of East Hampton, Long Island, began learning the Indian language in 1660 and received ten pounds from the Commissioners with which to hire an Indian assistant and interpreter. He must have become proficient in that language, at least to his own satisfaction, as he was anxious to produce an Indian catechism as Pierson had done ten years earlier. In 1668 Governor Lovelace wrote to him approving of his 'composure of a catechisme' and assuring him that it would be sent to England to be printed. In the same letter Governor Lovelace suggested that James should compose a small primer for the Indians.[4] John Winthrop wrote to him during 1667 asking him to devote all his time to missionary work. James replied that he would consider Winthrop's wish, adding: 'I doe not repent me of the labour & pains I have taken to obtaine that portion of their language I have, for I am employed from one end of the Island to th'other about setling matters between English & Indians.' He had, he continued, been asked to become an official interpreter, but this task he was not willing to undertake. Nevertheless, only four years

[1] Ms. 7936, f. 16.

[2] Ms. 7953/1, 13 Oct.

[3] *The Public Records of the Colony of Connecticut, 1665–1678*, ed. by J. H. Trumbull (Hartford, 1852), 111; M.H.S. *Collections, 4th series*, VII, 151.

[4] E. B. O'Callaghan, ed., *Documents relative to . . . the State of New York*, XIV, 610–11.

later, in 1671, he received his last payment from the Commissioners.[1]

The first missionary in Plymouth colony was William Leveritch, first pastor of Sandwich church. At Eliot's invitation he entered the Commissioners' service and began learning the Indian language, although, as he himself admitted, he found this difficult and the actual work of teaching the Indians most discouraging. In about 1653 he moved to Oyster Bay, Long Island, and from thence to Huntington and finally settled at Newtown, Long Island. However, the Commissioners discontinued his salary after 1658. His place at Sandwich was taken by Richard Bourn who was not then known to Eliot. But on Eliot's recommendation the Commissioners in 1657 began to pay him a salary; during the twenty-five years that he served as a missionary his pay was usually between £25 and £35 a year.[2]

Because missionaries were so hard to find, Eliot looked for assistance of a different kind: in 1656 he asked the Commissioners to appoint agents in Massachusetts: 'to promote and forward the worke among the Indians; both in Respect of theire government & Incurriging meet Instruments for theire further healp and Instruction.' In September 1657, he and other elders asked that Captain Daniel Gookin and Major Humphrey Atherton might be encouraged to assist in carrying on the Indian work 'in respect of Civill Government.'[3] The matter was referred to the General Court of Massachusetts with the proviso that the Commissioners would be ready to offer encouragement to any magistrate who would undertake the work. Captain Gookin was appointed, but was sent to England almost immediately afterwards. It was not until 26 May 1658 that Major Atherton was appointed in his stead. The General Court of Massachusetts ordered that he should see that the Indians 'live according to our laws as far as they are capable.' He was authorized to appoint Indians as magistrates to hear cases amongst themselves. An Indian court at which Atherton was present was to have the same powers as a county court. At Eliot's suggestion, the Indians elected

[1] M.H.S. *Collections, 4th series*, VII, 485–6; Ms. 7946/6.

[2] S. E. Morison, *The Founding of Harvard College*, 387–8; H. Whitfield, *Strength out of Weaknesse*, 21–5; *Acts*, II, 205; Ms. 7946/1–16 *passim*.

[3] *Acts*, II, 168, 182.

their own magistrates who were then approved by the General Court. Atherton died in 1661, and was replaced by Gookin, who had by then returned from England.[1]

During the 1660s the Company suggested that Gookin's salary, at this time £15 per annum, might be stopped for the sake of economy. This suggestion provoked compliments for Gookin from both the Commissioners and Eliot. The Commissioners explained, in 1663, that on enquiry they had found Gookin's labours among the Indians 'to bee of much use and benifitt to them; and therfore could not but desire him to goe on in that worke.'[2] Five years later they again explained to the Company that Gookin's 'great labour and good success . . . is of such use that if not attended by him must bee by some other.'[3] Eliot asked that his salary might be 'honorable' as his work 'doth necessaryly bring much resort to his house, and of such as cannot in common civility and humanity be sent away without entertainment.'[4] By 1669 Gookin's salary had been raised to £20 per annum. The Company accepted Gookin but continued to question payments to Indian rulers: in March 1675/6 it enquired: 'why so manie sommes of monie & allowances are given to Rulers over & above Capt: Gookins sallarie' and why so many Indian rulers were employed.[5] The Commissioners replied, on 20 December 1677, that the amount paid to rulers was small, that Gookin could not live among the Indians and regulate petty misdemeanours or 'prepare business for the severall Sessions, which now usually are dispatched in a short time', and that to employ Gookin and other English magistrates to do this work would take longer and be more costly.[6] Eliot, when writing to Boyle in 1681, described Gookin as 'my only cordial assistant,' and again two years later as 'a pillar in our Indian work'.[7] Although no other magistrate took as much interest in the conversion of the Indians as Gookin did, several were appointed to hold court amongst the Indians and do the same sort of work; in particular Thomas Hinckley who as early as 1673 began to perform these duties in Plymouth colony.

[1] M.H.S. *Collections, 1st series*, I, 177–80; F. W. Gookin, *Daniel Gookin, 1612–1687* (Chicago, 1912).
[2] *Acts*, II, 294.
[3] Ms. 7936, f. 8.
[4] *Acts*, II, 384.
[5] Minutes (M.H.S. Ms.), 6 March 1675/6.
[6] Ms. 7955/1 no. 1.
[7] Ms. 7936, f. 25; Royal Society, Boyle Letters, II, 161.

To civilize the natives was avowedly the first aim of the missionaries but the task was not an easy one. The Indians were not only idle by nature, they were also greatly addicted to strong drink. Gookin observed that they had drunk water before the English came to America, and that their taste for alcohol had been acquired from the white settlers. The Massachusetts General Court made numerous orders in an attempt to prevent drunkenness. It was forbidden for anyone to sell intoxicating liquor to the Indians without authority, but the number of orders of this kind suggest how ineffectual they were. Fur traders supplied the Indians with arms and liquor and the orders of the Court to prevent unauthorized persons from trading with the Indians were completely ineffective. Thomas Mayhew reporting in 1678 on the Indians in his care found that although witchcraft was 'out of use', drunkenness was a serious menace. He was, nevertheless, 'not out of hope but that the generallity will be convinced of their folly & gyve it quite over, that is, the use of rum.'[1] But drink took its toll and remained not only the Indians' most vicious habit but the most serious threat to their health and life.

Only idleness seemed an equal hindrance to civilizing them. Eliot hoped that bringing them together in townships would cure this evil but a number of other schemes were devised to give them employment. One of these, 'Proposals concerning the Employing the Indians in New England' was presented to the Company by John Winthrop, junior, in 1662, when he was in London. The Company was quite ready to receive suggestions, for it wrote to the Commissioners in 1662 telling them that if the revenue increased 'wee should consider of some Imployment in the way of trade and manifactury to Imploy the Indians.'[2] Winthrop estimated that a stock would be needed of £3,000 for the first year and £2,000 in the second. This would be repaid to the Company in the third year or by the end of the fifth year at the latest, either with interest or with a proportion of the net profit which could be reinvested. In four or five years, Winthrop asserted, the scheme would be on its own feet and the whole of the capital repaid. Unfortunately there is no indication in the proposals as to exactly what the Indians were intended to do or exactly how they would be employed. But the ad-

[1] *N.E.H.G.R.*, IV (1850), 17; *Acts*, II, 405.

[2] *Acts*, II, 273.

vantages to be derived from the scheme were clearly set out: it would civilize the Indians and so bring them nearer to receiving a knowledge of religion. They 'would be furnished with such necessaries as may make their lives more comfortable, as civil people have.' They would provide a market for English goods — particularly clothing — and would be able to supply such commodities as hemp, flax, tar, wheat and prairie grass for the English market. And finally: 'A revenue for the maintenance of the chief business of the corporation may thereby out of their own labor be raised without any charge to the people of England, which is a principal part of the intendment of this proposal.'[1]

Winthrop's confidence in his proposals seems quite inexplicable in view of the generally prevailing notion in New England that the Indians were constitutionally useless for any kind of work. Whatever his motives in promoting this scheme may have been, the Company was at that time completely unable to put up any money, although it seems that the proposals met with approval. Winthrop, however, still hoped that his scheme might be put into operation when, in September 1664, he wrote to Boyle explaining that he had been unable to attend the Commissioners' meeting at Hartford, but had heard that the Company had a great stock for disposal. He supposed that the question of how this should be disposed of had been answered by the Commissioners 'yet I am bold to add this motion; that your honour would please to cause that paper, which I left with the honourable corporation in England, to be reviewed.'[2] Winthrop need not have written because the Company had no great stocks for disposal.

But the problem of how to employ the Indians remained constant, and there seemed no satisfactory solution. The Indians at Natick and the other Indian townships were employed in agricultural pursuits of various kinds, basket-making, spinning and weaving. Gookin who, apart from the ministers, was one of the few people to take active steps to employ the Indians, managed with Eliot's backing to persuade the Commissioners to supply materials for 'spinning or other manufactury.' It was often held that apprenticeship was the most efficacious means of teaching the Indians trades. But the Indians were too fond of their

[1] M.H.S. *Collections, 5th series*, IX, 45–7.

[2] British Museum, Add. Ms. 4228, f. 98; *The Works of... Robert Boyle*, I, lxxi.

children to be ready to part with them. In 1660 the Commissioners decided that, in order to encourage Indian parents to apprentice their children, each parent should be given 'yearly during theire childrens apprenticeship one coate out of the Corporation stocke.' The Indians, however, often managed to obtain a new coat by this ruling without being parted from their little ones. The Commissioners in 1678 revised their order, insisting that the apprentice must be under twenty-one years of age, that the master must be godly and prepared to teach him to read, and that the agreement should be approved by two Commissioners. The trouble was not only the Indian parents' unwillingness to be parted from the children; English tradesmen were equally unwilling to take Indian children as apprentices.[1]

Not only must the Indian be employed, he must also be educated — his powers of reasoning developed to master the intricacies of theology and logic. For according to the Puritan view regeneracy came only after the rigorous preparation of the mind. Long before Eliot began his work, Henry Dunster had expressed himself on this subject. Thomas Lechford, who disagreed with the Puritans on many issues, wrote of Dunster: 'he hath the plat-forme and way of conversion of the Natives, indifferent right, and much studies the same . . . He will make it good, that the way to instruct the *Indians*, must be in their *owne* language, not *English*; and that their language may be perfected.'[2] It is not known whether Dunster became proficient in the Indian language, but he did undertake the education of two Indians in 1645 without much success, for after a little more than a year he complained: 'wheras the Indians with mee bee so small as that they [are] uncapable of the benefit of such learning as was my desire to inpart to them, and therefore they being an hindrance to mee and I no furtherance to them, I desire they may be somewhere else disposed of with all convenient speed.'[3]

When Harvard College's charter was drafted in 1650, allowance was made for: 'All other necessary provisions that may conduce to the education of the English and Indian youth of this Country in knowledge: and godliness.'[4] But the mention of 'Indian youth' was probably opportunist. It will be remembered that in 1649 Parliament had rejected

[1] *Acts*, II, 251, 398. [2] *Plain dealing; or, Newes from New-England* (1642), 53.
[3] S. E. Morison, *The Founding of Harvard College*, 314. [4] *Ibid.*, 248.

an amendment to Winslow's bill which would have made the Society's primary object: 'the maintaining of the universities of Cambridge in New-England' and its secondary object 'the preaching and propagating of the Gospel among the natives.'[1] The Commissioners were no doubt well aware of the rejection of the amendment, but were still uncertain whether or not the College would be able to lay claim to any of the money collected by the Society. In September 1651 they wrote to Winslow: 'It is apprehended by som that according to the entent of ye Act of Parliament an eye may bee had in the distrebutions to the enlargment of the Colledge at Cambridge wherof there is great need and furtherance of learning not soe Imeadiately Respecting the Indian Designe though wee fully Concure not, yet desire to know what the apprehensions of the honered Corporacion are heerin.'[2] The Commissioners were of the view that, if the College received assistance from the Society, the Indian work would in time receive assistance from the College; then everyone would be satisfied.

Much as Winslow may have wanted to comply with the Commissioners' wishes, the Society could not fall in with such a facile diversion of the funds from their proper purpose. The idea was apparently quashed. However, the Society was very anxious to see some Indian youths educated, and in April 1651 suggested to the Commissioners that mixed schools of Indians and English would be well worth considering 'for the better obteining each others language.'[3] Later, it asked that six Indians might be put in the College to learn English and to teach the Indian language to the English. The Commissioners replied to this suggestion in September 1653: the College was full and it was therefore necessary 'to raise some building' for Indian students. They reckoned the cost would be £100 and desired that 'the building may bee stronge and durable though plaine.' The Commissioners for Massachusetts were asked by their colleagues to consider and order the building of 'one Intyre Rome att the College' for six hopeful Indians: 'which Rome may bee two storys high and built plaine but strong and durable the charge not to exceed one hundred and twenty pounds besides glasse which may bee allowed out of the parcell the Corporation

[1] L. F. Stock, ed., *Proceedings*, I, 209. [2] *Acts*, I, 198. [3] *Acts*, I, 193–4.

hath lately sent over upon the Indian account.'[1] The Indian College, as it was called, was of brick, and was probably completed in 1654 or 1655. The difficulty was — and this must have been anticipated by the Commissioners — that there were no Indian students to fill it. There were, however, English students, so that in August 1656 Charles Chauncy, President of Harvard, wrote to the Commissioners asking if the new building could not be used by them. The Commissioners agreed that the President, with the advice of the Massachusetts Commissioners and Mr. Eliot, should use it for English students during the ensuing year.

The Society asked, in May 1659, 'what number of Indians there are att the university and what progresse and profisiency they make in their learning; and to what degree and measure therin they have attained; which we hope wilbee such as will give good satisfaction unto divers well affected heerunto.'[2] The well affected were doomed to disappointment in spite of the Commissioners' cheerful reply: 'there are five Indian youthes att Cambridge in the lattin Scoole; whose dilligence and profisiency in theire studdies doth much encurrage us to hope that god is fiting them and preparing them for good Instruments'. President Chauncy had examined those at Mr. Corlets' school 'and for theire time they gave good Satisfaction.'[3] No mention was made of any Indians at the Indian College. As some tangible evidence of the progress of education, the Commissioners, in 1658, sent the Society a certificate signed by Charles Chauncy, which testified that Caleb and Joel, two students 'trained up at the Grammar-Schoole in Cambridge', were able to translate part of a chapter of Isaiah into Latin and then construe it. This pleased the Society's members and they consequently had it printed on the last page of John Eliot's *A further Accompt of the Progresse of the Gospel* (1659). In the following year another certificate was sent, this time signed by Chauncy and Elijah Corlet. They testified that Caleb and Joel had been examined in translating Buchanan's version of David's Psalms and that three other Indian youths had 'made some competent

[1] *Acts*, II, 105, 107. The Indian College is the subject of an article in *C.S.M.*, XV (1925), lxxxii–v, and is also dealt with by S. E. Morison, *Harvard College in the Seventeenth Century*, I, 340–60.

[2] *Acts*, II, 216.

[3] *Acts*, II, 217.

proficiency, for the short time they have been with us.' This certificate, like its predecessor, was in turn printed, this time on the last page of Eliot's *A further Account* (1660).

However, the Society was not happy about the Commissioners' efforts, at least partly because it was completely unaware of the problems involved. This lack of understanding is illustrated by its concern lest the Indians who were receiving education should forget their native tongue. The Commissioners wryly assured the Society that the Indian students 'have soe much exersice of theire owne Language as there is noe feare or danger of theire forgiting of it.' The point on which they could not convince the Society was that the education of the Indians was progressing satisfactorily. By April 1660 the Society realized that things were certainly not as it had hoped: a letter to the Commissioners of that date politely praised the progress made by the five students, and added: 'But it is wondered by some heer that in all this time there are noe more in regard it appeers by the account sent; that there are about twenty Teachers under sallary; wee desire therfore that . . . you would please to bee more particulare in youer next accounts.'[1]

In 1665 Edward Rawson reported: 'there are eight Indian youths, (one whereof is in the college and ready to commence bachellor of arts) besides another in the like capacity, a few months since, with several English, murdered by the Indians at Nantucket, and at other schools, some ready to come into the college.'[2] But no student was entered for his B.A. before 1660 and only four before 1700. Of these only one, Caleb Chesschanmuk, graduated, and in the following year, 1666, he died of tuberculosis. Joel Iacoomes was the unfortunate Indian murdered at Nantucket. The intellectual achievements of Joel and Caleb reached the ears of the Royal Society for, in November 1663, John Winthrop, Governor of Connecticut, wrote to Robert Boyle, sending him two letters in Latin written by Joel and Caleb: 'If your Honour shall iudge it worth the notice of the Gentlemen of the honourable corporation and the Royall Society, you may be pleased to give them a view of it.'[3] In

[1] *Acts*, II, 239, 242.

[2] M.H.S. *Collections, 2nd series*, VIII, 66; N. B. Shurtleff, ed., *Records of the . . . Massachusetts Bay*, IV, pt. ii, 198–9.

[3] M.H.S. *Collections, 5th series*, VIII, 85.

1668 the Commissioners wrote to Boyle informing him that one of the students at the College 'being wholly indisposed to follow learning wilbee took of & put upon some other occupation by sea which he mostly desires.'[1] By 1675 there was only one student at the College and one at the grammar school at Cambridge. Early in 1675, at Danforth's order, a Bible costing 5s. 6d., John Smith's *The Mysterie of Rhetorique Unveiled* costing 4s. 4d. and '1 Virgill' costing 3s., were supplied for the use of the Cambridge student.[2] Neither Smith's *Rhetorique* nor Vergil were fare calculated to encourage the Indians in their studies. Yet the Company persisted in the idea that Harvard College would train Indians as missionaries. As late as 1685 it noted that it heard of only one Indian at College and asked the Commissioners 'to make up the nomber Tenn in all to be educated mainteyned & brought up there.'[3] But the education of the Indians to university level was hopeless and the Indian College a failure: it was pulled down in 1698, its most notable use having been as a workshop for the first Cambridge press.

University education was hardly less successful than secondary education and even teaching the Indians the rudiments of reading and writing proved extremely difficult. Eliot himself set great store by education and often prayed '*That before we die, we may be so happy as to see a good School encouraged in every Plantation of the Country*.'[4] He started to teach his Indians reading and writing as soon as he was familiar with their language, and constantly reiterated the need for educating them so that they might more readily comprehend Christianity. But school teachers were almost as difficult to find as missionaries. And although English schools did on occasion take in Indian students, the teachers only did so in the hope of augmenting their small incomes. Chauncy suggested to the Company that all teachers both in schools and at Harvard should receive a salary from the Company: 'to incourage them in the worke, wherin they have to deale with such nasty salvages, and of whom they are to have a greater care and diligent inspection.' The Company was disturbed at this advice, but the Commissioners assured Boyle that 'y^{e}

[1] Ms. 7936, f. 8.

[2] Ms. 7946/10, J. Usher's bill, 11 Jan. 1674/5.

[3] Minutes (M.H.S. Ms.), 30 Sept. 1685.

[4] C. Mather, *Magnalia*, III, 187.

allowance made by us to ye Schoolemasters & Tutors have ben sufficient & equall.'[1]

The men and women who undertook the education of English and Indian students must, indeed, have had a hard time of it and payment for their pains, as well as reimbursement for the goods and clothing which they had to find for their students, seems to have been very erratic. In 1653 the Commissioners ordered that the wife of William Daniell of Dorchester, who had spent three years teaching several Indian children to read, had received only £6 and should therefore be allowed £9 for past work and a further £3 for the coming year. By 1661 there were a number of teachers at work, though teaching the Indians was only a side line: Thomas Danforth, Elijah Corlet and Daniel Weld all tried their hands at preparing Indian children for the College. During the 1660s and 1670s the cost of feeding and clothing an Indian scholar was £15 per annum while his school fees amounted to only £3. 8s.[2]

A number of proposals for educating the Indians were made at this time, the most interesting being those put forward by Daniel Gookin. In 1674, he wrote a book entitled *Historical Collections of the Indians in New England* which he dedicated and sent to the Company in London. Intended as one of the series of Indian tracts, it was never published by the Company, although publication was seriously considered by a committee assisted by John Collins, the famous lecturer at Pinners' Hall and former fellow of Harvard.[3] It was to this work that Gookin appended: 'Proposals, as an Expedient for Civilizing the Indians, and Propagating the Gospel among them.' Here he stoutly endorsed the principles of education and apprenticeship for the Indians; and as a result of conversations with Eliot, he put forward a plan whereby the Indian village at Marlborough should be set aside for a school. The land would be walled off and the schoolhouse would contain accommodation for the schoolmaster, who would live there and farm the land — thus saving the expense of paying him a salary. Such a school would also be open to the English children of Marlborough. The cost to the Company, according to Gookin's estimate, would be about £200. The Indians

[1] Ms. 7936, f. 56. [2] *Acts*, II, 106; Ms. 7946/4, 8, 10.
[3] Minutes (M.H.S. Ms), 24 March 1674.

would feed and clothe their own children, but each child would be given a blue coat as an incentive to attend school. Gookin concluded his proposals by stressing that greater encouragement was needed for the success of the work and that a further collection should be taken up in England to this end.[1]

The Commissioners wrote to Boyle in December 1677 informing him that they had a surplus of funds which they were saving in order to build schools for the Indians' instruction 'in the English tongue.'[2] They had not, they admitted, yet decided exactly how to set about this project, but were full of confidence that it would be a success, and would be an important step forward in furthering conversion. In March 1678/9 the Commissioners approved a motion made 'for the erecting of English Scooles amongst the Indians wherby they may be brought up to Learne the English Toungue . . . as being most probable to Reduce them to Civillity.'[3] The Company appointed a committee to consider the question, which moved 'that this Companie doe soe far approve of Mr. Gookins proposicion concerning the building of a Free Schoole that they thinke it more convenient to have severall small Schooles in severall Townes for teaching & instructing of the Indians Children in the English Tongue.'[4] Nothing seems to have come of these schemes.

From his earliest experience of the work of converting the Indians, Eliot had realized that little help would be forthcoming from English ministers and teachers. He therefore determined to find ministers and teachers among the Indians themselves and of course they had to be paid. Amongst the earliest disbursements made by the Commissioners were small sums paid to Indians at Natick and Martha's Vineyard and during the 1650s and 1660s an increasing number of Indians appeared on the Commissioners' pay roll. In *A brief narrative of the progress of the Gospel* (1671), Eliot stated his views on the matter: 'I find it hopeless to expect *English* Officers in our *Indian* Churches; the work is full of hardship, hard labour, and chargeable also, and the *Indians* not yet capable to give considerable support and maintenance. . . . They must be trained up to be able to live of themselves in the ways of the Gospel of Christ.' The Indian teacher had the further advantage of knowing

[1] M.H.S. *Collections, 1st series*, I, 219–22.
[2] Ms. 7955/1, no. 1.
[3] *Acts*, II, 368.
[4] Minutes (M.H.S. Ms.), 6, 15 May 1679.

Indian perfectly, whereas the Englishman had to learn it and could only do so with the greatest application. Eliot aimed at teaching the Indians 'some of the Liberal Arts and Sciences, and the way how to analize, and lay out into particulars both the Works and Word of God.'[1]

Eliot sent out Indian missionaries from Natick to tribes in the western part of the colony beyond the reach of any of the English missionaries. In 1670 and for the three years following, his missionaries founded nine more Indian towns in the Nipmuc country. These towns, which lay from 50 to 70 miles west of Boston, were visited by Eliot and Gookin in the summer of 1673 and again in the following year. During these visits teachers were settled in each town and an attempt was made to bring them into line with the other Indian towns.

According to Gookin, Massachusetts contained in 1674 fourteen towns of praying Indians, with a total population of about 1,100. In the same year, Plymouth colony, together with Martha's Vineyard and Nantucket, was supposed to contain 2,500 converts. Both of these figures were, no doubt, rather on the optimistic side. In any case there were never as many again for, in June 1675, the disastrous Indian war — King Philip's war — began. This was the biggest setback which the work received either during the life of Eliot or, indeed, after his death.

Both Gookin and Eliot made suggestions for the employment of praying Indians in defence measures. Gookin suggested, for example, that the Indian towns, strengthened with one third English, would form excellent forts. In fact, in July 1675, Gookin was ordered to form a troop of Indians, and in accordance with this order, he sent fifty-two Indians to Mount Hope. Indians were also used as scouts, interpreters and guides, apparently with some success. However, the general feeling of the English towards them was one of mounting hatred. The praying Indians were ordered to stay in their villages, and then in October 1675 the inhabitants of the main Indian towns were shipped to Deer Island in Boston Harbour. In November the General Court of Massachusetts ordered that they were to be supplied with provisions to prevent them perishing from lack of 'absolute necessaries.' Six months later, as in fact the Indians on the Island were 'ready to perrish for want of bread', the Court ordered that they should be allowed to fish and plant corn and

[1] *Op. cit.*, 5.

that they could, under certain conditions, seek employment.[1] Eliot wrote to Boyle on 17 December 1675 describing the 'bleake bare Island' on which the Indians had been interned, and the sufferings and hardships they had to endure without food or fuel. He also reported that a company of Indians, possibly a hundred or more in number, '& sundry of them right Godly both men & women' had been surprised by the enemy and carried off captive, just as they were setting out for Deer Island.[2] In May 1676 the Indians on Deer Island were allowed on the mainland, but it was not until the following year that they were able to return to their homes.

The Company was able to do little to relieve the sufferings of the Christian Indians but on 6 March 1675/6 it ordered that 'some reasonable part' of that year's revenues should be spent on their relief.[3] Eliot had already procured, in 1675, 200 bushels of Indian corn for this purpose, and in the following year a further payment of about £30 was made for corn and fish.[4] In June 1676 the Company sent an additional £50, and some assistance was also received from a collection taken up in Dublin churches.[5] In 1680 the Company asked the Commissioners to distribute £100 'amongst Fiftie of such praying Indians as were serviceable in the late warre by Fortie shillings a peece or otherwise to some more and to others lesse.'[6] The Commissioners considered that this was either extravagant or that there were not enough Indians who had been 'serviceable', for in the years 1681–2 and 1682–3 they distributed a total of only £46.[7]

The blow dealt to the praying Indians by the war was enormous: in Massachusetts, where they suffered most, only four out of fourteen Indian towns survived it. As though this were not serious enough, the war had the further effect of bringing both Indian and missionary into greater contempt in the eyes of the white population. At a time when to defend the rights of the Indians was to bring upon oneself social ostracism, if nothing worse, Eliot had petitioned the Governor and

[1] N. B. Shurtleff, ed., *Records of the . . . Massachusetts Bay*, V, 64, 84.

[2] Ms. 7936, f. 22.

[3] Minutes (M.H.S. Ms.).

[4] Ms. 7946/10, 11.

[5] Minutes (M.H.S. Ms.), 28 June 1676; M.H.S. *Collections, 4th series*, VIII, 690–2.

[6] Minutes (M.H.S. Ms.), 4 May 1680.

[7] Ms. 7946/15, 16.

Council at Boston against selling Indians into slavery: Christ's design, he argued, was 'not to exstirpate nations, but to gospelize them.' To sell souls for money seemed to him 'a dangerous merchandize' and an act which would hinder the enlargement of Christ's kingdom.[1]

Eliot and Gookin were most severely critized for supplying the praying Indians with arms. Before the war they had given them several small amounts of ammunition: in 1665 they had distributed ammunition worth £4. 12s. 6d., which the Commissioners carefully explained was 'for ye Indians to bee imployed only for their necessary defence against ye Mohawks which are professed Enimies to all our neighbouring Indians & have slayne sundry of them.'[2] In 1669 the accounts show £10 spent on ammunition and provisions 'for Sundry praiing Indians that were greatly distressed by the Mohaukes.'[3] The Commissioners in their letter of September 1668 referred to £20 spent on ammunition and cards for preparing cotton: 'which ammunition' they wrote 'is by the care & prudence of Mr Eliot kept for their supply upon any occasion.'[4] The Company, however, was quite clear that funds should not be spent on ammunition: 'wee conseave it is not within our trust & soe can doe nothing in it. But are of opinion that the Collony in which those Indians are is as equally bound to protect them as others they being now his majesties subiects & as wee are informed all the Collonys by your Asotiation are ingaged to assist in such cases.'[5] In spite of this letter, one further small payment of £6. 8s. was made for ammunition on Eliot's orders in 1671.[6] But in 1675 the arms issued to the praying Indians were not paid for by the Company and were issued on the authority of the Massachusetts government.

Even before the war, Gookin's interest in the Indians brought him a certain amount of unpopularity. In 1671 it was rumoured that he had spoken to a Natick Indian urging him to 'animate Philip and his Indians' against Plymouth. Gookin wrote a letter of protest to Governor Prince denying the rumour and received a somewhat haughty letter of apology in reply.[7] In 1676, however, Gookin, who had been elected an Assistant

[1] *Acts*, II, 451–3.
[2] Ms. 7946/3; Ms. 7936, f. 6.
[3] Ms. 7946/4.
[4] Ms. 7936, f. 8.
[5] Ms. 7936, f. 10.
[6] Ms. 7946/6, account of H. Usher, senior.
[7] M.H.S. *Collections, 1st series*, VI, 198–201.

on the General Court annually since 1651, was not re-elected. By 1677 tempers had cooled sufficiently to allow his election. At this time Gookin thought it worth while to pen a defence of the Christian Indians and incidentally of Eliot and of himself. It was entitled: 'An historical account of the doings and sufferings of the Christian Indians in New England in the years 1675, 1676, 1677'. On Eliot's advice this was sent to the Company, but the Company wisely considered it unsuitable for publication.[1]

The most violent and unwarranted criticism of the praying Indians came from Edward Randolph who was sent to Massachusetts in 1676 to report on the colony. During the next decade, he never rested for long in his attacks on the Company in England and the Commissioners and missionaries in New England. In a report to the Committee for Trade and Plantations in 1676, he accused the praying Indians of being 'the most barbarous and cruel enemies to the English.' He also hastened to point out that the cause of the war was imputed by some 'to an imprudent zeal in the magistrates of Boston to christianize those heathen before they were civilized and injoyning them the strict observation of their lawes, which to a people so rude and licentious, hath proved even intollerable.'[2] William Stoughton and Peter Bulkeley, agents for Massachusetts, answered these charges before the Committee for Trade and Plantations, concluding: 'for though some very few of them have not so closely adhered to the English, yet the rest of them have been upon all occasions very faithfull.'[3]

To Eliot the criticisms of Randolph and the disasters of the Indian war must have been hard to bear. As the years went by he found it more and more difficult to devote himself to the Indians with the fervour of earlier years. Even when his missionary labours were at their most onerous he never neglected his ministry at Roxbury. And although he had Samuel Danforth as an assistant from 1650, the care of the Roxbury flock proved a constant burden to him, a burden greatly increased after Danforth's death in 1674. There is reason to believe that at one

[1] It was first published in *Archaeologia Americana*, II (Cambridge, Mass., 1836), 423–525.

[2] R. N. Toppan, ed., *Edward Randolph* (Boston, Mass., Prince Society, 1898–9, 5 vols.), II, 243, 245.

[3] *Ibid.*, III, 13.

time he wished to devote himself exclusively to the Indians. In a letter to Baxter, written on 5 February 1670, he seemed to imply that he had considered doing so but that his Roxbury congregation or part of it was opposed to releasing him. Indeed, the view of ordination held in New England at this time — that the bond between pastor and flock was indissoluble — would alone have deterred him from pressing his wish further.[1]

Eliot, like most fathers, had wanted his children to follow in his footsteps, but none lived long enough to make any considerable mark in the missionary field. Benjamin, Eliot's youngest son, assisted him for some years but was not even regarded worthy of a salary by the Commissioners. Eliot's eldest son, John, pastor of a small English congregation at Cambridge, was proficient in the Indian language and preached to the Indians once a fortnight at Natick and elsewhere, but died in 1668. Eliot described him to Baxter as 'a good workman in the vineyard of Christ, my assistant in the Indian work, a staffe to my age.'[2]

But it was not until fourteen years later, in 1682, that Eliot began to need physical support; the Commissioners 'found it Needful to allow Reverend Mr Elliot (now growne very aged in this service) a Servant to attend him when he goes his Journies amongst the Indians.' They also allowed him a horse. At the same time they made 'some allowance to a Wel-deserveing person Mr. Daniel Gookin, who hath entred upon Preaching to the Indians at Natick in the English tongue.'[3] Gookin was minister of Sherborn and the son of Captain Daniel Gookin. The allowance made him, however, amounted to only £5 until sixteen Natick Indians wrote to Eliot, in March 1683/4, asking him to use his influence on Gookin's behalf. They preferred his preaching in English rather than Indian on the grounds that English people came to hear him and this raised the tone of the services. The Indians' plea was successful and Gookin was thenceforth paid £10 a year.[4] Eliot then preached only once every two months at Natick. But he still persevered with his translations and in about 1685 produced a small tract entitled: *The Dying*

[1] *Bulletin of the John Rylands Library*, **15**, 151.

[2] Dr. Williams's Library, Baxter Letters, I, 55; C. Mather, *Magnalia*, III, 173–4.

[3] Ms. 7936, f. 26; Ms. 7946/15–16.

[4] Ms. 7936, f. 29.

Speeches of several Indians (Cambridge, Mass.). But the Natick Indians, who, out of respect for him, had never elected a minister of their own race, did so for the first time in 1687. In the following year Nehemiah Walter was ordained as Eliot's colleague at Roxbury which relieved the old man of most of his labours there.

On 21 May 1690 Eliot died. He had been for more than forty years the often exasperating but indispensable mainstay of the Company. His energy and his will-power had overridden Company and Commissioners alike, so that in the end it was he who decided at almost every point what steps should be taken to convert the Indians. Perhaps more than any other missionary, he persisted to the end in believing that their conversion was possible. William Hubbard cautiously summed up the fruits of conversion, remarking that 'some judicious persons have conceived no great harvest is to be expected of reall converts . . . there being little progresse made that way for the present, notwithstanding that many endeavours have been made in that kinde.'[1] These endeavours were more Eliot's than anyone else's, but Eliot himself was well aware of their imperfection. Cotton Mather reports Eliot's words on his deathbed: '*There is a Cloud . . . a dark Cloud upon the Work of the Gospel among the poor* Indians. *The Lord revive and prosper that Work, and grant it may live when I am Dead. It is a Work, which I have been doing much and long about. But what was the Word I spoke last? I recal that Word.* My Doings! *Alas, they have been poor and small, and lean Doings, and I'll be the Man that shall throw the first Stone at them all.*'[2]

[1] M.H.S. *Collections, 2nd series,* V, 29. For further details of Indian towns, see F. L. Weis, 'The England Company of 1649 and its missionary enterprises', *C.S.M.*, XXXVIII, 134–218.

[2] C.Mather, *Magnalia*, III, 207.

6

The Indian Library

OF all Eliot's doings the most renowned was his translation of the Bible into the Indian language. But scarcely less remarkable was his achievement in getting that translation printed. Although he had little or no encouragement and often direct opposition, he persuaded the New England Company that to finance publications in the Indian language was one of its most important functions. And indeed the Company spent a considerable proportion of its revenue during more than half a century on what Cotton Mather called 'The Indian Library'.[1]

Eliot was not the first to envisage books for the Indians: in 1642 Thomas Lechford had argued that to civilize the Indians 'a Presse is necessary, and may be obtained, I hope, so that wise men watch over it.'[2] In fact, Harvard College already possessed a printing press when Eliot began his work, but there was no move on foot to use it for the Indians' edification. In July 1649, after nearly three years' experience as a missionary, Eliot wrote to Winslow to acquaint him with the need: 'I do very much desire to translate some parts of the Scriptures into their language, and to print some Primer in their language, wherein to initiate and teach them to read . . . and printing such a thing will be troublesome and chargable.' In the same letter he explained that he considered translating the Scriptures a sacred work —'to be regarded with much fear, care, and reverence.' The Society was not yet in

[1] Most histories of printing in America deal with this subject to a greater or lesser extent. The most recent detailed treatment for the period prior to 1692 is to be found in G. P. Winship's *The Cambridge Press, 1638–1692* (Philadelphia, 1945). Wilberforce Eames' *Bibliographic Notes on Eliot's Indian Bible* (Washington, D.C., 1890) was included in J. C. Pilling's invaluable *Bibliography of the Algonquian Languages* (Washington, D.C., 1891).

[2] *Plain dealing; or, Newes from New-England* (1642), 35.

existence, but the act which created it was pending and, no doubt anticipating its passage through Parliament, he added: 'and all this is chargable; therefore I look at that as a special matter on which cost is to be bestowed, if the Lord provide means, for I have not means of my own for it.'[1]

It requires little imagination to visualize the difficulties encountered by Eliot when he started his work: his religion was based on the printed word; if the Indians' was to be likewise based, they must be taught to read. Whether they should read in English or in Indian was a question which was not at first debated; Eliot decided the matter and determined upon Indian, probably feeling that it would be too difficult for them to master a new language as well as a new religion. Indeed, President Dunster explained to Professor Christian Ravius: 'We doe not trouble the Indians to Learn our English' and added that some books sent over for the Indians' use would be 'of more use to the English, then Indians, being above their capacity for the present especially being writ in the English tongue.'[2] But while Eliot was more than prepared to translate the Holy Word into the Indian language, someone was needed to print it. And until books in Indian came from the press, the rudimentary business of teaching the Indians to read and to write was excessively arduous. However, by October 1650 he had taught one Indian to write: 'so that I can read his writing well, and he (with some paines and teaching) can read mine.'[3] This was Job Nesutan, an Indian of Long Island, who took the place of Eliot's first instructor and in due course assisted with much of the translating. In April 1651 Eliot was able to report that many others had learnt to read and write during the winter, and later in the year that he had compiled a primer or catechism from which he taught them both reading and writing. He also expressed the hope that the Indians would be able to transcribe as much of the Scriptures as he could translate 'for I have no hope to see the Bible translated, much lesse printed in my dayes.'[4] So hopeless a view so early in the story was not like Eliot: one can only suppose that he intended his words to sting

[1] H. Whitfield, *The Light appearing*, 17.
[2] M.H.S. *Collections, 4th series*, I, 253.
[3] H. Whitfield, *The Light appearing*, 43.
[4] H. Whitfield, *Strength out of Weaknesse*, 7.

the Society into action. Meanwhile he continued with his translation so vigorously that in the same year, 1651, John Wilson described a service at which a metrical psalter translated by Eliot was in use: 'all the men and women, &c. singing the same together in one of our ordinary *English* tunes melodiously.'[1]

It was only two years after this that printing for the Indians began and the first work to be printed was Eliot's primer or catechism. The sponsor of this printing was of course, the New England Company, Eliot's zeal having won the day. From now on, printing for the Indians occupied much of the Commissioners' time; in September 1653 they wrote to Winslow informing him that they were arranging an edition of five hundred or a thousand copies of Eliot's catechism to be paid for out of stock. However their letter implied that they were not altogether happy about the quality of the translation and that, in order to minimize errors, they would try to encourage Thomas Stanton, 'the most able Interpretor wee have in the countrey for that Langwige', to assist in seeing it through the press.[2] The printer employed by the Commissioners was Samuel Green, printer to Harvard College, who was operating the only press in New England at that time.

During 1654 the catechism or primer was completed, but it was completed without the assistance of Stanton. In September of that year the Commissioners wrote to Eliot: 'Wee desired that Thomas Stantons help might have been used in the Cattachisme printed and wish that noe Inconvenienc bee found through the want therof.' They advised him to seek assistance before proceeding with the translation of the Scriptures. Eliot's reply to this letter can only be surmised from the Commissioners' letter to him, written in September 1655: 'the Commissioners never forbade you to Translate the Scriptures . . . but advised that what you ment to print or sett forth upon the Corporation Charge might bee donn with such Consideration of the Language and Improvement of the best healpes to bee had therin that as much as may bee the Indians in all partes of New England might share in the benifitt; which wee feare they can not soe well doe by what you have alreddy printed.'[3]

The Commissioners' anxiety lest the Indian translations should be incomprehensible to those for whom they were intended persisted

[1] *Ibid.*, 19. [2] *Acts*, II, 105. [3] *Acts*, II, 123, 140.

throughout the century and into the next. But neither Eliot nor the members of the Society in London paid any serious attention to their worries. Thomas Stanton was almost certainly more proficient at the language than Eliot at this time, but he was a rough frontiersman who had little understanding of the Scriptures and who probably held the notion of converting the Indians in the contempt which was general amongst nearly all who came into contact with them. Eliot, no doubt, expressed himself on the subject of Stanton's character in writing to England. His opinion was supported by Hezekiah Usher who appeared before the Society's Court in London on 6 February 1657/8 reporting 'that Mr Stanton is a knowen man in the Indian tongue' made use of by the Commissioners but that he considered him 'not [to] bee Godly & soe qualified for the spirituall parte of this worke as hath beene suggested.'[1] Although Eliot had the complete confidence of the Society, the Commissioners remained unconvinced of his competence, but their last protest on this score during Eliot's lifetime was made in September 1660 when the Indian Bible was already in the press: 'Wee shall attend youer advice for the Impression of the whole bible without which wee should have rested in our former determination that the coppy might have bine fully perused and perfected by the most skilfulest healpes in the Countrey.'[2] After this the Commissioners let the matter drop, presumably because to dwell further upon what was now a *fait accompli* would be futile.

If Eliot went his own way, the Commissioners were at least not thwarted by Abraham Pierson. By 1654 Pierson was preparing a catechism 'to sute these southwest partes where the languige differs from theires whoe live about the Massacheuesetts.' In September 1656 the Commissioners had received part of Pierson's Catechism 'framed and propounded to convince the Indians by the light of Nature & Reason that there is onely one God.' The Commissioners advised that 'it bee perfected and turned into Narragansett or Pequott language' and that Thomas Stanton and Pierson were to co-operate in its translation. How Pierson and Stanton got on together with this task is not known, although they did manage to produce a translation which was duly presented to the Commissioners. The annual letter of September 1658

[1] Minutes (M.H.S. Ms.).

[2] *Acts*, II, 243.

to the Society explained that they had intended to send the manuscript to England to be printed there: 'but upon further consideration in regard of the hazard of sending and difficultie of true printing it without a fitt overseer of the presse by one skilled in the language wee have chosen rather to have it printed heer . . . and hope it wilbe finnished within three monthes.'[1]

The estimate was optimistic, for three months later only one sheet had been completed. A copy of this sheet was sent to England in December 1658 to show that the work was progressing and it was subsequently included in Eliot's *A further Accompt of the Progresse of the Gospel amongst the Indians* (1659). By September 1659 the catechism was still not quite finished and the Commissioners wrote explaining that 'by reason of Mr. Piersons sicknes the worke may have bin retarded; and wee and you suffer a disapointment.'[2] It was finished by the end of 1659 but the date 1658 on the title page bears witness to how long it was in the press. The title itself suggests the Commissioners' preference for the translation compared with Eliot's:

> Some Helps for the Indians Shewing them How to improve their natural Reason, To know the True God, and the true Christian Religion. 1. By leading them to see the Divine Authority of the Scriptures. 2. By the Scriptures the Divine Truths necessary to Eternal Salvation. Undertaken at the Motion, and published by the Order of the Commissioners of the United Colonies. By Abraham Peirson. Examined and approved by Thomas Stanton Interpreter-General to the United Colonies for the Indian Language, and by some others of the most able Interpreters amogst us. Cambridg, Printed by Samuel Green, 1658.

The text was, of course, in Indian but an interlinear English translation was also supplied. This translation makes such turgid reading even to English eyes that the Indian version must have been completely incomprehensible to the audience for which it was intended. A title page differing from the one above is to be found in a copy in the British Museum. In this copy the mention of Stanton is omitted and instead it has the words: 'Examined and approved by that Experienced Gentleman (in the Indian language) Captain John Scot.' Scot, a notorious

[1] *Acts*, II, 120, 176, 204.

[2] *Acts*, II, 216–17.

fraud, was in London at the time, trying to secure for himself a grant of the whole of Long Island. He must have had this title page printed specially for insertion into presentation copies; these were no doubt distributed among those whom he wished to impress with both his knowledge and his godliness.

Pierson's *Some Helps* was the only Indian translation printed during Eliot's lifetime in which he took no part. In fact it was a monument to the Commissioners' failure to find anyone who could rival Eliot's translations. Eliot, of course, dominated the whole policy of publication as he dominated other policies, and so his cherished ambition of an Indian Bible was to be realized. By the autumn of 1655, Genesis had been printed as a trial issue and a start had been made upon Matthew, as a further trial. *The First Book of Moses called Genesis*, as the first of these trial pieces was entitled, had an interlinear English version for the first nineteen chapters after which only the Indian text appeared. The parallel texts must have had advantages for those unfamiliar with the language, but the cost of production rendered the practice uneconomical and it was largely abandoned in later enterprises during Eliot's lifetime. This particular issue was obviously meant for English eyes as well as Indian and the final half page read: 'Such English as may have occasion to look upon this Impression, are intreated to consider That some defects there be in the work which could not be helped for want of letters or tipes, wherewith the press cannot suddainly be furnished. Which hath put us upon the using of some unsuitable Characters, though we endeavoured to fit them in the best manner we could. . . .' Either Samuel Green the printer, or Eliot himself, had foreseen the typographical difficulties of printing in Indian, and Eliot had requested the Society to send type designed to meet special needs. In particular founts were needed containing large supplies of O and K, both of which letters occur very frequently in Algonquian.[1] The first request was made in 1653; it was repeated officially by the Commissioners in the following year and twenty pounds worth of type and paper for the work arrived at Cambridge, Mass., during 1655.[2] Further trial was made by printing a few metrical

[1] The first and last pages of *The First Book of Moses* are reproduced in facsimile in *C.S.M.*, XXXIV (1943), 12.

[2] *Acts*, II, 118, 123, 139.

psalms at some time before 1657, but as with so much of the early production of the Cambridge press, no copy survives either of this psalter or of the Gospel according to St. Matthew.

By 1658 Eliot had completed his translation of the whole Bible. In a letter to the Society's Treasurer he announced this news, at the same time pointing out that his skill in translation had been upheld before the Commissioners in September of the previous year. On this occasion 'sundry of the Elders' petitioned the Commissioners for printing the Bible in the Indian language. Eliot wrote: 'And God so guided (without mans contrivance) that I was there when it came in. They moved this doubt whether the Translation I had made was generally understood? to which I answered, that upon my knowledge it was understood as farre as *Conecticot* . . . they further questioned whether I had expressed the Translation in true language? I answered that I feared after times will find many infirmities in it, all humane works are subject to infirmity, yet those pieces that were printed, *viz. Genesis* and *Matthew*, I had sent to such as I thought had best skill in the language, and intreated their animadversions, but I heard not of any faults they found.' Eliot had repaired to Governor Endicott after the meeting of the Commissioners and had persuaded him to write to the Society expressing the need for 'some honest young man, who hath skill to compose (and the more skill in other parts of the work, the better)' to be sent to New England at the Society's expense, together with a supply of paper.[1]

Governor Endicott was as good as his word and wrote to the Society on the same day, 28 December 1658. He proposed the printing of the whole Bible and pointed out the need for type, paper and a journeyman printer to help Green. '*Mr. Eliot*', he wrote, 'will be ready at all times to correct the sheets as fast as they are Printed, and desireth nothing for his paines.'[2] Eliot's was not the only request for type for the Cambridge press; on 5 June 1658, Samuel Green, in a petition, had explained that the College's press stood in great need of new materials, especially of type, and had suggested that the Society should be asked for assistance.[3]

[1] J. Eliot, *A further Accompt of the Progresse of the Gospel* (1659), 2–3.
[2] *Ibid.*, 4–5.
[3] M.H.S. *Proceedings, 2nd series*, XI (1897), 250.

At a court held on 26 February 1658/9 the Society resolved that the Bible should be printed, but that the New Testament should go through the press first. Three weeks later the resolution was reiterated 'consideringe the difficulty & Charge' of the undertaking. At the same time it was ordered that application should be made to exempt the Society from customs and excise duty on the paper for printing the Bible.[1] The Society wrote to the Commissioners on 7 May 1659 informing them of its decision and asking how many copies should be printed, how much paper would be required (a sheet was to be sent to the Society so that it could be matched), what materials were needed and what kind of printer was required — 'a Composer or letter printer.'[2] On 7 September 1659 the Commissioners informed the Society that they would order work to begin on the New Testament 'being Incurraged by youer selves and pressed by Mr. Elliatts affectionate zeale which hee hath constantly held forth for this worke.' They intended to have a thousand copies printed. They also explained that Mr. Usher had undertaken to supply the printer's needs.[3] Usher did supply more than eighty pounds worth of type and at about the same time the college printer received from the Society another press. This was placed with the College's press in the Indian College, the workshop of the Cambridge press, where most of the books for the Indians were printed.

The Society had much with which to occupy itself at a time when its future existence must have seemed in the balance. On 17 March 1659/60, Ashurst, Babington, Clarke and Molines were 'desired to repaire unto Mr. Calamy &c to consult his advice & intreate his assistance that ye Provinciall Assembly of London at Sion College would contrybute their Endeavours towards ye printing of the Bible in the Indian tongue.'[4] Two days later the matter was considered by the Provincial Assembly: 'There was then propounded by some of ye corporation for New England that Our helpe should bee administred for ye printing of ye Bible in ye Indian language. It was then ordered that ye designe propounded was Eminently acceptable And that ye Ministers would Engage that they would promote this designe to their utmost capacity. And that Dr. Reignolds bee desired to call ye Ministers of ye citty together for ye

[1] Minutes (M.H.S. Ms.).
[2] *Acts*, II, 216.
[3] *Acts*, II, 217.
[4] Minutes (M.H.S. Ms.).

carrying on of this grand affaire.'[1] On 10 April 1660 another committee was appointed by the Company 'to repare to Mr. Ashe ye Ministers howse to treate with the Committee of Ministers appoynted by Sion Colledge in order to the printinge of the Bible. . . .'[2] But the time was unripe for eliciting further contributions from Londoners' pockets and so the Bible was paid for out of the Society's current income.

An extremely pressing matter was the choice of a suitable journeyman printer to assist in the work. In April 1660 a young man named Marmaduke Johnson was found who was willing to go to New England under contract for a period of three years, or longer should the Society desire it, to assist in printing the Indian Bible. Johnson was allowed forty pounds per annum as salary together with 'Dyett, lodginge & washing.'[3] At the same time one hundred reams of paper were purchased to be sent with him to America. Marmaduke Johnson set sail from Gravesend aboard the *Prudent Mary* on 14 May 1660. Thomas Bell, who saw him on his way, paid £5 for his passage and eighteen shillings 'for a Sea bed, Boulster, Rugg, & Blanquett.'[4] The Society asked the Commissioners in a letter of 28 April: 'att the earnest request of Mr. Johnson the Printer and for his Incurragement in this undertakeing of printing the bible in the Indian language his name may bee mencioned with others as a printer and person that hath bine Instrumentall therin.' In the same letter the Society acknowledged the trial sheet of the New Testament and recommended that fifteen hundred, instead of a thousand copies, should be printed. To make this possible 104 reams of paper had been purchased at a cost of five shillings and eight pence per ream. The Society hoped that the Old Testament would also be printed in the same number of copies 'knowing that the foundation of true religion is from the bible the ould and new Testament and that the furtherance therof is of principle Consernment.'[5]

Johnson must have arrived at Cambridge at about the end of July

[1] Sion College, London Provincial Assembly Record Book, 1648–1660, f. 254.

[2] Minutes (M.H.S. Ms.).

[3] *Ibid.*, 21, 25 April 1660. The articles of agreement between M. Johnson and the Society are printed in *Acts*, II, 447–9.

[4] Ms. 7944/1, 18 Sept. 1660; Minutes (M.H.S. Ms.), 22 May 1660,

[5] *Acts*, II, 239–41; Ms. 7944/1, 11 Sept. 1660.

1660 when at least the first six sheets of the New Testament were completed. The Commissioners reported in September 1660 that Eliot, Usher, Green and Johnson had decided that both Old and New Testaments should be printed together and that this could be done at the rate of one sheet a week.[1] Considering the difficulty of the work and how much easier it is to make a schedule than keep to one it is surprising that this speed was more or less maintained during the two and a half years which followed.

The first thirty-two sheets which made up the New Testament were completed by the spring of 1661. The Society's clerk wrote in May 1661 with the news that the Society had ceased to exist but, while urging economy upon the Commissioners, desired 'that the printing of the bible may not bee retaurded.' The Commissioners, meeting at Plymouth in September, decided to dedicate the New Testament to Charles II 'as the first fruits and accomplishment of the Pious Design of your Royal Ancestors'. They informed His Majesty: 'The Old Testament is now under the Press, wanting and craving your Royal Favour and Assistance for the perfecting thereof.' This dedication was duly printed and inserted into twenty copies of the New Testament which were sent to England. The Commissioners had given instructions that two copies should be specially bound, one for the King and the other for the Lord Chancellor, and that five other copies 'be presented to Docter Reynolds, Mr. Carrill, Mr. Baxter and the two vischancellers of the universities whoe wee understand have greatly Incurraged the worke.'[2] In the event, Samuel Thomson, stationer, received £3. 8s. for binding twenty-six copies presented to the King and several members of the Privy Council.[3] The Commissioners ordered Usher to take custody of the sheets of the New Testament and to have about two hundred bound ready for issue to the Indians. He was also told to 'take order for the printing of a thousand coppyes of mr Elliots Catichismes which wee understand are much wanting amongst the Indians.'[4] In fact 1,500 copies of this little book were completed by the following September, although none have survived.

The Bible was still unfinished in October 1661 when Marmaduke

[1] *Acts*, II, 243.
[2] *Acts*, II, 255, 257, 260.
[3] Ms. 7944/1, 8 March 1661/2.
[4] *Acts*, II, 265.

Johnson, who had left his wife in England, was charged with 'obtaining the affections' of Samuel Green's daughter. It was reported that through 'his flattering & allureing expressions shee was greatly insnared by him.' He was charged with threatening violence to anyone who proposed to her and also with having proposed to her himself. The case was not heard in the County Court of Middlesex, Massachusetts, until April 1662 when Johnson was fined five pounds for attempting 'to draw away the affections of the daughter of the said Samuel Green without his consent.' 'For his presumptuous and wicked attempt of marriage' it was ordered that 'he return with the first opportunity that he may to his wife, on penalty of twenty pounds.' What happened to cause a reconciliation between Johnson and Green is not known, but Johnson seems to have been allowed to return to work, and this in spite of the court's ruling.[1] The Commissioners reported in September 1662 that the Bible was about half done but that Johnson was proving very unsatisfactory. Not only was he lazy, but he had also been convicted in open court, although the sentence had not been put into execution 'peculiare favor haveing bine shewed him with respect to the Corporation that sent him over.'[2]

Johnson was fortunate not only in the Company's support, but also in having a brother, Thomas, who was an influential bookseller in London and who appealed to the Company on his behalf. In a letter written at intervals from February to April 1663, Thomas informed his brother of his wife's death, and implored him to reform his ways and make up his quarrel with Green. The Company was, he continued, prepared to reappoint him for one more year but its members would 'take any misdemeanor against . . . [Green] as done to themselves.' He continued: 'Mr Eliot's letter prevailed much on your behalf and Mr Boyle wished me to write you to return Mr Eliot humble thanks for his love, and for you to make good that character which he gave of you.'[3]

Boyle wrote in April 1663 expressing the hope that the Bible would soon be finished, informing the Commissioners of Johnson's reappoint-

[1] The records of the Middlesex, Mass., County Court are quoted by G. P. Winship, *The Cambridge Press*, 225–6.

[2] *Acts*, II, 276.

[3] Quoted by G. P. Winship, *The Cambridge Press*, 230

ment for a further year and ordering them to have printed the Psalms in metre.[1] As it was a common practice to issue the Bible with a metrical psalter bound in, the Company was, no doubt, quite ready to comply with Eliot's wishes in this respect, for clearly Eliot had prompted Boyle's order. The Commissioners replied in September 1663 that the metrical psalter was in the press.[2]

But they also had more important and long awaited news: the Bible was finished. As soon as an English title page and a dedication, once more to Charles II, were ready, twenty copies were sent to England, and were there bound and distributed according to Boyle's directions.[3] Eliot's wishes in distributing presentation copies were also observed; at his request copies were sent to his old college, Jesus, Cambridge, to his patron Lady Armine, to Sion College, and one to each of the universities.[4] By 21 April 1664 Boyle was able to take a presentation copy to the King. As it was an event of such importance in the Company's history he at once hastened to write to New England: 'I waited this day upon the King with your translation of the Bible which, I hope I need not tell you, he receved according to his custome very gratiously. But though he lookd a pretty while upon it, & shewd some things in it to those that had the honour to be about him in his bed-chamber, into which he carryd it, yet the unexpected comming in of an Extraordinary Envoyé from the Emperour hindred me from receveing that fuller expression of his grace towards the translators and Dedicators that might otherwise have been expected.'[5]

Neither Charles II, nor Boyle, nor the Commissioners were qualified to pass judgment upon this remarkable book. Not only was it the first Bible in Algonquian but it was also the first Bible printed in any language on the North American continent. If Eliot's contemporaries doubted his ability as a translator, it is as well to quote J. H. Trumbull,

[1] *Acts*, II, 292.

[2] The cost of printing thirteen sheets was £26 (Ms. 7946/2).

[3] *Acts*, II, 295. The cost of printing the preliminaries was £1 (Ms. 7946/2). Samuel Gellibrand received £10 in June 1664 for binding the Bibles (Ms. 7911/1).

[4] Minutes (M.H.S. Ms.), 7 March 1663/4.

[5] J. C. Pilling, *Bibliography*, 141.

a nineteenth-century expert, who considered that: 'On the whole, his version was probably as good as any *first* version that has been made, from his time to ours, in a previously unwritten and so-called "barbarous" language.'[1]

Financial difficulties after the Restoration prevented the Company from rewarding Eliot for his translation as generously as many wished to do. In the annual letter of 1664 to the Commissioners, Boyle wrote: 'wee can not but take notice of Mr Elliott's Great paines and labour amongst the poor Indians and the good Effect that hath followed therupon; and alsoe his care in translateing the bible into the Indian language and attending upon the Correcting of the presse whiles the said bible was printing . . . which althoe att present wee can not gratefully acknowlidge; yett when enabled therunto shall Indeavor to make a proportionable Requitall.'[2] At a meeting of the Company's Court on 17 May 1664 it was proposed to pay Eliot £100; another proposal was to pay £100 immediately and a further £50 the following year. But the actual sum finally voted was only £50.[3]

Two minor pieces were probably produced before or soon after the completion of the Bible. The first of these was a psalter, in nine sheets, printed in an edition of five hundred copies. This was quite distinct from the metrical psalter issued with the Bible, but it is hard to envisage the particular purpose for which it was intended. Furthermore, no copy of this psalter has yet been discovered.[4] The second was a single leaf entitled *A Christian Covenanting Confession*. Two distinct editions of this item exist and it has been assumed that the first edition was printed for the use of Eliot's Indians at Natick, who, it will be remembered, were preparing for church membership at this time. The leaf is printed on one side only in English and Indian.[5]

Eliot was not prepared to rest content with the completion of the Bible. On 6 July 1663 he wrote to Baxter: 'My Work about the

[1] J. H. Trumbull in *The Memorial History of Boston*, ed. Justin Winsor (Boston, Mass., 1882), I, 473.

[2] *Acts*, II, 313–14.

[3] Minutes (M.H.S. Ms.).

[4] The nine sheets were printed at a cost of £1 per sheet, as opposed to the metrical psalter where the cost was £2 per sheet (Ms. 7946/2).

[5] J. C. Pilling, *Bibliography*, 132.

Indian Bible being (by the good hand of the Lord, though not without difficulties) finished, I am meditating what to do next for these Sons of our Morning: they having no Books for their private use, of ministerial composing. For their help, though the Word of God be the best of Books, yet Humane Infirmity is, you know, not a little helped, by reading the holy Labours of the Ministers of Jesus Christ.' He then asked permission to translate Baxter's own *Call to the Unconverted*, believing that it would not be unacceptable to him to have his works read by the Indians. In fact, Eliot had already begun the translation and, finding it different from his other translations, he wrote: 'I am forced sometime to alter the Phrase, for the facilitating and fitting it to our Language, in which I am not so strict as I was in the Scripture. Some things which are fitted for *English* People, are not fit for them, and in such cases, I make bold to fit it for them. But I do little that way knowing how much beneath Wisdom it is, to shew a Man's self witty, in mending another Man's Work.' Baxter replied that he was only too willing to allow his works to be translated 'and wholly submit the Alteration and use of it to your Wisdom.'[1]

Eliot finished his translation of Baxter's *Call to the Unconverted* on 31 December 1663. On 7 March 1663/4 the Company's Court in London showed signs of uneasiness at the choice of this work and ordered Ashurst to write to Eliot desiring 'that the Practise of Piety bee first translated & printed into the Indian language.'[2] The reason for this uneasiness, Baxter explained, was 'the envy and distaste of the times' against him.[3] However, the Company's anxiety was to no avail; Eliot wrote to the Commissioners on 25 August 1664: 'Touching the Presse, I thank God & yourselves for the good successe of the work in it. Mr. Baxter's Call is printed and dispersed.'[4]

Towards the end of 1664 Marmaduke Johnson set sail for England. The Commissioners wrote to the Company in September 1664 reporting that they had 'Improved him as well as wee could for the yeare past

[1] M. Sylvester, ed., *Reliquiae Baxterianae*, lib. I, pt. II, 293, 296.

[2] Minutes (M.H.S. Ms.).

[3] M. Sylvester, ed., *Reliquiae Baxterianae*, lib. I, pt. I, 115.

[4] *Acts*, II, 385. The accounts recorded: 'To printing Mr Baxters call 8 sheets 50^{s} per sheet 20^{li}' (Ms. 7946/2).

by Imploying him with our owne printer to print such Indian Workes as could be prepared which hee was not able to doe alone, with such other English Treatises which did present.' At the same time the Commissioners asked for more type to be sent over which would enable them to obtain better terms from the printer for works printed in Indian.[1] From the Commissioners' point of view Johnson's appointment had never been very satisfactory. On the other hand Eliot was anxious to keep him, partly because he was now skilled in composing Indian texts and partly because he was ready to fall in with Eliot's wishes, the more so as Eliot had spoken on his behalf more than once. Johnson had another ally in Charles Chauncy, who wrote to the Company on 2 October 1664 recommending his reappointment and suggesting that he should be furnished with type. The result was that in May 1665, Johnson returned from England with a press and some type of his own together with additional type supplied by the Company.[2] From this time on there were two master printers' shops in Cambridge, although the first book printed by Johnson after his return, *The Practice of Piety*, was contracted out to both Johnson and Green.[3]

Eliot first referred to this tract in a letter to Baxter dated 6 July 1663 in which he stated his intention of translating it 'or some other such Book' after completing Baxter's *Call to the Unconverted*.[4] Lewis Bayly's *Practice of Piety* had long been acceptable in Puritan circles and had been printed in many English editions before 1665, when it was printed in Indian for the first time in a considerably abbreviated form. The Company, and in particular Boyle himself, considered the work quite inoffensive, coming as it did from the pen of the Bishop of Bangor, and certainly less liable to give offence than anything by either Baxter or Shepard. The Commissioners were not particularly exercised on that score, but were by no means happy about the steadily increasing list of Indian imprints, and they recorded their protest in a letter to the Com-

[1] *Acts*, II, 316.

[2] W. Kellaway, 'Marmaduke Johnson and a Bill for Type', *Harvard Library Bulletin*, VIII (1954), 224–7.

[3] The six sheets of which it consisted were printed at a cost of £12 (Ms. 7946/3).

[4] M. Sylvester, ed., *Reliquiae Baxterianae*, lib. I, pt. II, 293.

pany of 13 September 1665: 'Wee understand by Mr Elliot that your honours have ordered him to translate into ye Indian Language and cause to bee printed ye Practice of Piety & Some works of Mr. Shepherds which will cost nere 200^{li}: wee humbly conceive that those with what are alredy printed will be sufficient for ye Natives for many years, & had they ben lesser books or some abridgement of these, they would have ben altogether as useful for ye Indians, & ye disbursements for ye same farre lesse.'[1] This protest did not go altogether unheeded for the only other Indian work to be printed during the next four years was Eliot's *Indian Grammar.*

The *Indian Grammar* was primarily for the use of English readers. Eliot, not unnaturally, found its compilation a task far less congenial than making translations. It was, in fact, a work requiring great sweat of brow. He wrote to the Commissioners on 25 August 1664 mentioning that the Company had asked him to compile a grammar 'which my sonns and I have oft spoken of, but now I must, (if the Lord give life and strength) be doeing about it. But we are not able to doe much in it, because we know not the latituds and corners of the language: some general and useful collections, I hope the Lord will enable us to produce.'[2] Eliot also wrote to Boyle on the subject, promising as soon as the *Practice of Piety* was finished 'to set upon some essay & begining of reducing this languag unto rule; which, in the most common & usefull poynts, I doe see, is reducible; though there be corners & anomalities full of difficulty to be reduced under any stated rule, as your selfe know, better than I, it is in all languages. I have not so much either insight or judgment, as to dare to undertake any thing worthy the name of a Grammar. Only some preparitory collections, that way tending, which may be of no small use unto such as may be studious to learne this language.'[3]

Worthy or no, the work appeared under the title: *The Indian Grammar begun; or, An Essay to bring the Indian Language into Rules, For the Help of such as desire to Learn the same, for the furtherance of the Gospel among them. Cambridge: Printed by Marmaduke Johnson, 1666.* Eliot concluded this work by describing how he had learnt the language, and

[1] Ms. 7936, f. 6.
[2] *Acts*, II, 385.
[3] Royal Society, Boyle Letters, II, 153.

how he had 'diligently marked the difference of their Grammar from ours; When I found the way of them, I would pursue a Word, a Noun, a Verb, through all the variations I could think of. And thus I came at it. We must not sit still, and look for Miracles: Up, and be doing, and the Lord will be with thee. Prayer and Pains, through Faith in Christ Jesus, will do anything.'[1] There is no record of payment to Johnson for printing this book. But it is unlikely that Eliot paid for the printing himself as the stock was certainly in the Commissioners' hands and in 1667 they paid three shillings a hundred for having four hundred and fifty copies bound.[2] This probably consisted of no more than just stitching the quires together.

Charles Chauncy, the President of Harvard, was constantly on the look-out for any assistance which the Company might give to the College. In 1664 he wrote to the Company complaining that the College had received no allowance on books printed by the college printer, in particular on the Indian Bible: 'which losse I intreat you to consider, for it is not too late, besides other Indian books have bene printed without any advantage at all to the Colledge.' The Company expressed some surprise at this request and asked the Commissioners for advice. This was given in a letter of 13 September 1665; the Commissioners, after conferring with Chauncy, had found that the printer had formerly allowed the college ten shillings a sheet for the use of its equipment, but that this was no longer necessary as both press and type now belonged to the Company. 'Yet nevertheless', the Commissioners continued, torn between two loyalties, 'if you shall please to order any encourragement to the Colledge, on this or any other consideration wee shall thankfully embrace it.'[3] The respite in the production of books for the Indians, instead of silencing Chauncy's pleas, simply changed them. In November 1669 he and the Fellows of Harvard sent a letter in Latin to the Company asking for a free gift of the Company's press and type including the type in Johnson's possession as 'there is no more need to issue yet further books from the press for the use of the Indians.'[4] The

[1] *Op. cit.*, 66. [2] *Acts*, II, 330. [3] Ms. 7936, f. 4, 5, 6.

[4] Ms. 7936, f. 13. The original text of this passage, here translated, reads: 'vt nunc certiores nos faciamus pluribus Libris ex Praelo superadditis amplius non sit opus ad Indorum Vsum.'

Company was, in the end, sympathetic; on 31 March 1670 it agreed to lend its press and type.[1] The Commissioners heard of the loan in September 1670 and thanked the Company 'for their kinde respect to our poore Colledge in lending to them the printing utensills that belong to the Indian stock, allthough for our parts wee were ignorant of any motion in that kinde.'[2] The College took possession of the press and the types which were at the Indian College, but the type brought over by Johnson was not recovered before his death and whether it was recovered afterwards has not been finally established.

Although the Company had lent its press and types to the College they were still used for printing books for the Indians. The book most needed by the missionaries remained the Indian primer or catechism and it was this book which was printed next. By 1669 stocks of the 1661 edition were apparently exhausted, for the Commissioners wrote to the Company in September of that year reporting that they were 'informed by Mr. Eliot and Mr Bourne that the instruction of the Indians is greatly obstructed for want of a Small primer & Cattachisme in their Language, which being prepared by Mr Eliott wee have Ordered the printing thereof, And doe hope on ye Consideracions promissed it will not be displeasing to your selves.'[3] On 27 January 1669/70 the Company gave its formal consent to this publication, which was entitled: *The Indian Primer; or, The way of training up of our Indian Youth in the good knowledge of God, in the knowledge of the Scriptures, and in an ability to Reade. Composed by J. E. . . . Cambridge, Printed 1669*. The contents of this little book, the earliest edition of an Indian primer to have survived, consisted of a syllabus for the Indian schools: 'Wise doing to read Catechism. First read Primer. Next read Repentance Calling [i.e. Baxter's *Call*]. Then read Bible.' Then followed the Lord's Prayer with a series of questions and answers based upon it and 'the ancient Creed', also with questions and answers. Next came a section on Christian duties illustrated by Biblical texts, and finally there was the Westminster catechism in a shorter and a longer version.[4] The Commissioners' accounts for 1670 included an item for £22. 15s. 8d. 'To printing 2,000 Indian prymers paper binding of them & some other bookes as by Mr Ushers

[1] Minutes (M.H.S. Ms.).
[2] Ms. 7936, f. 14.
[3] Ms. 7936, f. 11.
[4] J. C. Pilling, *Bibliography*, 129.

bill of disbursements.'[1] Unfortunately Usher's itemized bill for 1670 has not survived.

However, Usher's bill for the following year, 1670–1, is extant and contains references to two more small works produced by the press at this time:

To printing y^e Indian Dialogues per Mr Eliot at	$5^{li}\ 0^{s}\ 0^{d}$
To stitching ditto at	1 0 0
To paper 7 Ream at	2 5 0
To printing y^e A.B.C at	3 0 0[2]

The first entry refers to *Indian dialogues, for their Instruction in the great Service of Christ, in calling home their Country-men to the Knowledge of God, and of themselves, and of Iesus Christ . . . Printed at Cambridge, 1671.* Unfortunately the bill makes no reference to the printer but, as Eliot was such a staunch supporter of Marmaduke Johnson, it is most likely that the work was entrusted to him. It was the first book entirely in English paid for by the Commissioners. No copy of the second work — the A B C — has been discovered, although it was referred to by Eliot on 4 August 1671 in a letter to the Commissioners: 'Further I doe present you with our Indians A B C & our Indian Dialogs with a request that you would pay the printer the accompt whereoff is upon Mr Ushers Booke, for which I stand charged. And besides the Printers work an ingenuous young schollar (Sr Foster) did cut, in wood, the scheame for which work I request that you would pay him. I think him worthy of 3 or 4 or 5^{li} but I leave it to your wisdoms.'[3] The Commissioners acceded to Eliot's request and the accounts for 1671 record a payment 'To Mr Foster for cutting ye Print for ye Indian A.B.C. by Mr Eliots advise 4^{li}.'[4] It can only be assumed that this Indian A B C was some kind of substitute for a hornbook, designed especially for Indian children. In a letter to Baxter, Eliot wrote: 'My difficult attempt to teach them the liberal Arts I have entered upon with an a.b.c. with some ocular demonstrations.'[5] The A B C was apparently the only illustrated book printed

[1] Ms. 7946/5.
[2] Ms. 7946/6.
[3] Ms. 7936, f. 16.
[4] Ms. 7946/6.
[5] Dr. Williams's Library, Baxter Letters, III, 264.

for the Indians, so perhaps John Usher had it in mind many years later when he wrote to Joseph Thompson, a member of the Company: 'As to Bookes they are mightily taken with picktures; & therefore [I] judge bookes with pictures may win much upon them.'[1] But his advice was not followed; indeed the Company feared that illustrated books would promote Popery.[2]

The last book printed by Marmaduke Johnson for the Commissioners was: *The Logic Primer. Some Logical Notions to initiate the Indians in the Knowledge of the Rule of Reason; and to know how to make use thereof. Especially for the Instruction of such as are Teachers among them . . . Composed by J. E. for the use of the Praying Indians. Printed by M. J. 1672.* Unlike the *Indian dialogues*, this work was in Indian except for the last seven pages which included an interlineal English translation. The Commissioners ordered Johnson to be paid £6 for his labours and the payment was duly made: 'To Marmaduke Johnson for printing, stitching & cutting of 1000 Indian Logick primers 6^{li} 00^{s} 00^{d}.' A further payment was made in about 1675, presumably after his death: 'To Mr Johnson for binding 2000 Primers for the Indians 20^{li}.'[3]

In 1675 Samuel Green complained to John Winthrop junior that the press and type brought over by Johnson should have gone to him but that it had fallen into the hands 'of a young man that had no skill of printing' and that this young man was being employed by the Commissioners to print for the Indians.[4] The young man was John Foster, who had prepared the blocks for the A B C. The Commissioners' accounts make little mention of him, however. In 1675 he received £10. 5s. 'for printing' while John Usher's bill shows that on 2 June he had been supplied with sixteen reams of paper, costing £5. 4s. and that three weeks later he had received a further three reams costing 19s. 6d. Unfortunately the purpose of these payments is not mentioned. The last appearance of John Foster in the Commissioners' accounts was in 1677 when he was paid 10s. for printing some unspecified work, pos-

[1] Ms. 7956, 9 June 1692, from Falmouth.
[2] Letter book (Univ. of Va. Ms.), 12.
[3] Ms. 7946/7, 10.
[4] M.H.S. *Collections, 5th series*, I, 422–4.

sibly the second edition of the *Christian Covenanting Confession*, which was only a single leaf.[1]

The next work to be printed for the Indians was also a second edition, but far from being a single leaf, it was in fact the whole Bible. After King Philip's war the stocks of the first edition were quite exhausted. Eliot made application to the Commissioners for a new edition, but they — 'haveing had some Debate about that matter' on 20 March 1678 — referred it to their next meeting.[2] On both sides of the Atlantic the advisability of such an undertaking was discussed with an eye to the growing contention that the Indians should really learn English rather than the missionaries Indian. In London the Company's Court reached a compromise on 13 August 1679, ordering that £250 be laid out in New England for printing the New Testament and a prose version of the Psalms in the Indian language, and that £100 sterling be devoted to the purchase of English Bibles to be sent out to New England for the Indians' use.[3] The Commissioners wrote to the Company on 26 December 1679: 'Wee fully concur with your advice as to their learning the English tongue.'[4]

Eliot, however, was hardly satisfied with this compromise and began to persuade Boyle that only the whole Bible, and that in Indian, would fully answer his needs. On 4 November 1680 he wrote: 'Our Praying Indians, both in the Ilands & on the maine, are (considered together) numerous; thousands of soules, of whom some true believers, some learners & some are still enfant & all of them, beg, cry intreat for bibles, having allready injoyed that blessing, but now are in great want.'[5]

The work on the New Testament was well under way by 8 July, when Eliot received a visit from two Dutch Labadist missionaries who were returning home from Manhattan. They recorded in their diary that, although Eliot spoke neither Dutch nor French, they managed to

[1] Ms. 7946/10, 12. Two further entries in the accounts remain unexplained: 14 Aug. 1679, 'To Samuel Greene printer 4^{ll}. 10^{s}.' and 'For printing 6^{ll}.' (Ms. 7946/14). One of these payments may have referred to *The Dying Speeches of several Indians* which Eliot had printed 'not so much for Publishment, as to save charge of writing out of copies for those that did disire them' (*John Dunton's Letters from New England*, Boston, Mass., Prince Society, 1867, 233–4).

[2] *Acts*, II, 366.

[3] Minutes (M.H.S. Ms.).

[4] Ms. 7936, f. 24.

[5] Royal Society, Boyle Letters, II, 159.

converse 'by means of Latin and English'. The diary continued: 'He said in the late Indian war, all the Bibles and Testaments were carried away, and burnt or destroyed, so that he had not been able to save any for himself; but a new edition was in press, which he hoped would be much better than the first one, though that was not to be despised.'[1]

The New Testament which bore the date 1680 on its title page was not completed until late in the following year. This was followed by the metrical psalms, as authorized by the Company. Eliot wrote to Boyle on 17 June 1681: 'Untill we have Bibles, we are not furnished to cary the Gospel unto them for we have no means to cary religion thither, saving by the Scriptures.' He again urged Boyle to persuade the Company to authorize the printing of the whole Bible, but also warned him 'that the charge doth somewhat surmount (by some accidental impediments) my expectation. But I beseech your honour let not that be so much as named to be an impediment of such a work.'[2] And Eliot did not confine his entreaties to Boyle. In a letter to Baxter, whom he knew to be extremely influential although not a member of the Company, he wrote: 'My request to your selfe is that you would please to stir up the honorable corporation to it.'[3] Baxter did not let Eliot down; he wrote to Boyle on 29 August 1682: 'I am desired by Mr Eliot to solicite you for your consent to the printing of his 2d Edition of the whole Bible: It seemes they want not money: I heare you are against it. I intreate you to consider that the question is not whether it be most profitable to the present generation, but whether it shall ever be done: ffor if the old man die first its a great doubt whether ever any will perform it: And when it is extant it may be usefull, in time to come. I hope you will not be against it longer without greater reasons than I can thinke of.'[4]

The Commissioners, who were now more ready to support the old man, wrote to the Company on 29 May 1682 explaining that the New Testament had already cost £249. 2s. 6d.: 'We went the best way to work wee could, Yet are perswaded that if you shalbe pleased to grant

[1] J. C. Pilling, *Bibliography*, 154, contains a translation of the portion of the diary relating to Eliot.

[2] Ms. 7936, f. 25.

[3] Dr. Williams's Library, Baxter Letters, V, 83.

[4] Royal Society, Boyle Letters, I, 35.

Mr Elliots motion & Expectation, for the printing of the Old Testament also, we may be able to do better, and contract with Workmen cheaper.' But in spite of this recommendation, Boyle wrote on 13 October 1682: 'wee are not yet fully sattisfied that it will answeare the end proposed.'[1]

Eliot was, as usual, master of the situation, as becomes quite clear in his letter to Boyle dated 15 March 1682/3:

> The great work that I travaile about is the printing the old testament, that they may have the whole bible . . . I desire to see it done afore I dye, and I am so deepe in years that I cannot expect to live long . . . For such reasons, so soone as I received the sum of neere 40^{li} for the bible work, I presently set the work on foote; and one tenth part (or neere) is done: we are in Leviticus. I have aded some part of my salary to keepe up the work, and many more things I might add, as reason of my urgency in this matter.[2]

Eliot's haste in starting the Old Testament without the Company's consent can hardly have surprised the Commissioners. They had seen him get his own way over most things during the last thirty years and now his strength of will weakened theirs. It was, they afterwards explained to the Company, Eliot's 'extreame urgency after he had wholly taken upon himselfe to begin the work of Printing' that prevailed with them to call in £70 from stock, Eliot 'engaging the payment thereof himselfe in case your allowance could not finally be obtained.'[3] But Eliot did not rest, for on 21 June he wrote once more to Boyle: 'Your hungry Aloones [Alumni] doe still cry unto your honour for the milke of the word in the whole booke of God. . . . my age makes me importunat. I shall depart joyfully, may I but leave the Bible among them, for it is the word of life, & there be some godly soules among them, that live thereby.'[4] Long before Boyle received this letter, in fact only six days after it was written, on 27 June 1683, the Company ordered that £400 should be drawn from stock in New England for printing the Old Testament.[5] On 27 November Eliot wrote to Boyle returning thanks for the Company's decision. He asked Boyle to forgive his haste in beginning the Old Testament without his fiat, on the grounds, once more,

[1] Ms. 7936, f. 26, 27.
[2] Royal Society, Boyle Letters, II, 161.
[3] Ms. 7936, f. 28.
[4] Royal Society, Boyle Letters, II, 167.
[5] Minutes (M.H.S. Ms.).

that he was old: 'if I doe not procure it printed while I live' he wrote, 'it is not within the prospect of humane reason, whether ever, or when, or how, it may be accomplished.' Then, with delightful simplicity he asked 'that you would please to draw a curtaine of love over all my failures, because love will cover a multitude of transgressions.'[1]

The Commissioners promised the Company, in a letter of March 1683/4, to 'hasten it and be frugall in the Expences of it as much as may be.'[2] In the accounts which accompanied their letter it was shown that £136. 16s. 9d. had been paid, while £147. 15s. 0d. remained in hand for carrying on the printing.[3] The Company was apparently unimpressed by the Commissioners' explanations and in its letter of 26 September 1684 enquired how far the Bible had progressed and requested twelve copies of the Pentateuch for the inspection of members in London.[4] Eliot, however, asked that they might be spared sending copies of the Pentateuch 'because so many as we send, so many Bibles are maimed & made incomplete.'[5] Instead, one copy only of all the sheets printed at this time was sent to England.

The second edition of the Bible appears to have been finished in the autumn of 1685. A brief dedicatory epistle addressed to the Governor and Company and signed by William Stoughton, Joseph Dudley, Peter Bulkeley and Thomas Hinckley at Boston on 23 October 1685 was placed in a few presentation copies. And so Eliot's wishes were fulfilled at a total cost of about £900. Early the next year Samuel Sewall, who was to become the Company's Secretary and Treasurer in New England, wrote to Stephen Dummer: 'The best News that I can think to speak of from America, is, that Mr. John Eliot, through the good hand of God upon him, hath procured a second Edition of the Bible in the Indian Language.'[6] John Dunton, the bookseller, visited Eliot the next summer and was presented with twelve copies of the Bible. The gift was no doubt acceptable, although it may be questioned whether

[1] Royal Society, Boyle Letters, II, 163.
[2] Ms. 7936, f. 28.
[3] Ms. 7946/17 (cf. Ms. 7946/16).
[4] Ms. 7936, f. 40.
[5] Royal Society, Boyle Letters, II, 165.
[6] M.H.S. *Collections, 6th series*, I, 22.

Dunton regarded its publication with an enthusiasm approaching that of Sewall.[1] Moreover, the gift suggests that the demand for Bibles was not as great as Eliot must have anticipated when he refused to send a dozen copies of the Pentateuch to the Company.

It has been argued that the revision of this edition of the Bible was the work of John Cotton rather than of Eliot. This argument is based partly upon a memorandum made by Thomas Prince some decades after the event, in which he records that John Cotton 'took this method — while a good Reader in his study read ye English Bible aloud, Mr Cotton silently look'd along in ye same Place in ye Indian Bible: & where He thot of Indian words which he judg'd could express ye sense better, There He substituted them & this 2nd Edition is according to Mr Cotton's correction.' In the Roxbury church records, Eliot himself refers to the changes made by Cotton: 'He read over the whole bible, & whatever doubts he had, he writ them downe in order, & gave them to me, to try them & file them over among our Indians.'[2] Eliot also acknowledged assistance in a letter to Cotton himself, written in April 1680, in which he thanked him for returning a corrected leaf of the Bible: 'This one leafe hath afforded me more helpe in that work of translation, then ever I had before from any English man.' Eliot informed Cotton that the first sheets of Matthew were already printed 'but in all that follow I hope I shall make due use of your observations.'[3] It appears, then, that the work of revision was shared between the two men and that Thomas Prince's statement that 'this 2nd Edition is according to Mr. Cotton's correction' is only half true.

After the completion of the second edition of the Bible, a second edition of Bayly's *Practice of Piety* was printed, at a cost to the Company of £20. A second edition of Baxter's *Call* came from the press in 1688 and in the following year appeared Eliot's last work — the Indian translation of Thomas Shepard's *Sincere Convert.* Although Eliot had almost completed the translation as early as 1664 it was not until 1688 that he took up the work again, writing to Boyle that in its revision only Cotton could help him. In the event, however, Grindal Rawson, the pastor

[1] J. Dunton, *The Life and Errors of John Dunton* (1818), I, 115.
[2] J. C. Pilling, *Bibliography*, 154, quotes both Prince and the Roxbury records.
[3] M.H.S. *Proceedings*, L (1917), 78–9.

at Mendon, assisted him and the work appeared in 1689 bearing both Eliot's and Rawson's names. Rawson received a gratuity of £11 for his pains.[1]

When the next Indian work appeared, John Eliot was dead. The translation was made by Grindal Rawson and the work chosen was John Cotton's *Spiritual Milk for Babes*. It appeared in 1691 bearing the names of both Samuel and Bartholomew Green in the imprint. How many titles were covered by the following extract from the accounts for 1692/3 is not known, but it may well have included Baxter's *Call to the Unconverted* as well as *The Sincere Convert* and *Spiritual Milk for Babes*: 'To paper for the presse & to Mr Green for printing practical bookes for ye Indians £58: 01: 10.'[2] It was certainly the last payment made for Indian books printed at Cambridge.

Eliot's death did not bring the printing of books for the Indians to an end. In fact, the number of books produced for the Indians during the next three decades showed no signs of diminishing although the books themselves tended to be less ambitious. Moreover, instead of one translator, the Commissioners now had three: Grindal Rawson, Eliot's collaborator, Samuel Danforth, minister of Taunton, and Experience Mayhew of Martha's Vineyard. In 1698 there appeared Samuel Danforth's translation of five of Increase Mather's sermons, with the title in Indian: *Greatest sinners called and encouraged to come to Christ.* This was followed by a translation by Grindal Rawson of the Confession of Faith adopted by the Synod of Boston in 1680, which appeared in 1699. It was probably this Confession of Faith to which Cotton Mather referred in his diary, describing how 'with as much Artifice and Contrivance as I could, I interwove into it, such Things, as I thought it of most Consequence, for young persons to have their Minds tinged withal, and such Things also, as were more peculiarly agreeable to the Conditions and the Temptations of the *Indians*.'[3] The Commissioners ordered on 8 April 1700 that Danforth should be allowed 'Six pounds as a gratuity for his Translating about Eight English Sermons of the Revd Mr Increase Mather into Indian for the edification of the Natives', and Rawson was allowed 'four pounds Mony as a gratuity for his Translating

[1] Ms. 7946/19, 20. [2] Ms. 7946/20.
[3] M.H.S. *Collections, 7th series*, VII, 328.

the Savoy Confeshion of faith.'[1] The cost 'of translating a Confession of Faith . . . & Some Sermons of Mr Mathers & for printing & binding the Same' amounted to £76.[2]

On 13 November 1699 the Commissioners ordered 'that Three Thousand of Indian Primer be printed, it being at this time out of print, & none to be had.' On 8 December 1701 the Commissioners further ordered 'that Mr Grindal Rawson be allowed five pounds in Consideration of his Extraordinary Labours in making the Indian primer: and that said Rawson be desired to send ye Copy of it in English to ye Commissioners for their perusall.'[3] Although no copy of this edition has been identified, it seems to have been printed since it is included in the inventory printed below and since the accounts show a number of charges for binding Indian primers from February 1704/5 onwards, at sixteen shillings per hundred.[4]

Grindal Rawson was also the translator of Cotton Mather's *An Epistle to the Christian Indians, Giving them a Short Account, of what the English Desire them to know and to do, in order to their Happiness*. . . (Boston, 1700). This little book was at great pains to present the English to the Indians in the guise of good Samaritans, asserting: 'It was the great compassion in the English, not only to offer you many comforts of this Life, but also to show you the *Way that leads to Everlasting Life*.'[5] The first edition must have been quickly distributed as on 1 July 1706 the Commissioners, of whom Cotton Mather was one, ordered: 'Whereas a Treatise Entituled an Epistle to the Christian Indians & alia printed in Englesh & Indian is all Ready out of Print and the Natives are Inquisitive After it, Ordered that It be immediately Reprinted about Eight hundred copies.' Three days later 'upon further Consideration' it was ordered that 1,000 should be printed.[6] Bartholomew Green printed the two sheets of which the book consisted for £2. 8s.[7]

On 15 October 1706 the Commissioners ordered that 'In as much as a Number of Christianised Indians are unhappily Leavend with the Error of the Saturday Sabbath and there is Danger Lest that Number increase It is Directed that Mr Experience Mayhew Translate into the Indian Language a Small Book Entituteled: The day which the Lord

[1] Ms. 7953/1. [2] Ms. 7946/25. [3] Ms. 7953/1. [4] Ms. 7946/27.
[5] *Op. cit.*, 2. [6] Ms. 7953/3. [7] Ms. 7946/28.

has Made and that Mr. Treasurer provide for it.'[1] This sermon, delivered by Cotton Mather at Boston in 1703, had been printed in English in that year. The Indian edition which appeared in 1707 had the English on one side of the page and the Indian on the other, the English title page reading: *The Day which the Lord hath made. A Discourse Concerning the Institution and Observation of the Lords-Day* . . . (Boston, 1707). The last three leaves contained: *Some part of the first Chapter of John*. The accounts show the following payments for 26 July 1707 and 3 October 1707 respectively:

To Bartholomew Green for Printing Magna sheet	£2. 6.	8: 16: 0
Lords day 5 sheets Mr Exp: Mayhew's Translation	6: 10	
To Thomas Short for folding & stiching in painted paper the Lords day & Iroquoes		5

The accounts also reveal that Experience Mayhew received £6 'for translating ye Sermon of ye Lords day & correcting ye press.'[2]

The other work referred to in these accounts: 'To Bartholomew Green for Printing Magna sheet' was the Company's only attempt at printing in the Iroquois language. It was entitled: *Another Tongue brought in, to Confess the Great Saviour of the World. Or, Some Communications of Christianity, Put into a Tongue used among the Iroquois Indians in America; And, Put into the Hands of the English and Dutch traders* . . . (Boston, B. Green, 1707). This little book of sixteen pages, consisting of a series of questions and answers in Indian, Latin, English and Dutch, is one of the most curious of all the works printed for the Indians' conversion. Addressed 'To the English and Dutch Traders Among the Iroquois Indians' an introduction explained to its readers: 'You are now earnestly Solicited, *That* you, who are Traders for *Bever-Skins*, would be as Instrumental as you can to Convey the *Garments* of *Righteousness* and *Salvation*, among the Naked Salvages.'[3] In fact it was a practical endeavour to employ the fur traders as missionaries — an idea familiar from the time of Hakluyt onwards. But what the Dutch and English traders who actually received copies of this little book may have thought of it can only be left to the imagination.

Soon after this work was completed, Samuel Sewall made a return

[1] Ms. 7953/3. [2] Ms. 7946/29, 30. [3] *Op. cit.*, 3.

to the Company in London, listing its property and possessions in New England. It is of particular interest as it shows the number of copies of each book in stock. The portion of this inventory of 25 February 1707/8 dealing with the Company's publications is printed here in full:[1]

One Indian Bible.
One Baxter Two more, three in all.
Five Duzen of Indian Catechises, without Date.
One Duz. Logick Primers, printed 1672. Ano
427. of the Practice of Piety bound, 1685.
292. Mr. Shepard's Sincere Convert — 1689.
265. Dr. Mathers Sermons on John, 6–37, mostly unbound } 1698
563. Confessions of Faith Eng & Ind 1699
688. Epistles Engl. & Indian — 1706.
1400. Indian Primers in Sheets / 176. ditto Bound } 1700
373. Sermons of the Lords' Day Engl. & Indian stitched in painted paper } 1707
35 Of an Essay for the Iroquois one sheet } 1707

It can be seen from this list that concern over the wisdom of printing in the Indian language had been dispelled. In fact, so long as the works undertaken were small, so that costs were correspondingly low, the question of whether it was advisable to print in the Indian language was ignored. But when it came to reprinting the entire Bible the question could be ignored no longer. The stock of the second edition must have been very low when, in April 1703, the Commissioners ordered payment to Captain Ephraim Savage for binding and printing title pages for twenty-four Indian Bibles that he had recovered 'out of ye Rubbish in Duncan Cambells Garret.' A third edition of the Bible was first mooted on 12 December 1705 at a meeting of the Commissioners where it was decided that 'The Consideration of printing the Indian bible againe is to be revived at every meeting.'[2] It was not until 5 May 1708

[1] Ms. 7962. Another copy in Sewall's hand is endorsed: 'N.B. This is a duplicate recd Augt *1708* & agrees with a former.'

[2] Ms. 7953/1, 2.

that the Company considered the proposal: 'Doctor Mathers Mr Mahew and Mr Sewalls Letters being read relating to the Reprinting of the Indian Bible, all the Impression being out, and this Court having considered the same, and Judging the work to be very necessary . . . do agree to the Commissioners Proposall, That the same be reprinted at Boston.' A committee was appointed to buy paper on the best terms possible and to send it by the next ship. But some underlying misgivings were perhaps reflected in another order made on the same day: 'that notwithstanding the order of this Court for Reprinting the Indian Bible that the Commissioners be desired to Continue to Encourage the Schools for Instructing the Indian Children in the English tongue, as being a very proper method towards Civilizing them and bringing them to the knowledge of the Christian Religion.'[1]

The committee appointed for the purchase of paper certainly had lavish ideas. It appears from an undated memorandum that they envisaged an edition of 2,000 copies of the Bible as well as 4,000 copies of Reading Psalms, New Testament and Metrical Psalms. They also sent extra 'in case of Damage by Sea.' This extra paper was to be genoa 'because that will serve for writing as well as Printing.' Although the point had already been made, another hand endorsed the memorandum: 'If you think the paper too much to be printed you may do as you think convenient.' The paper was purchased from Henry and John Hatley: 960 reams of fine paper at seven shillings a ream and 262 reams of foolscap at six shillings a ream. The complete consignment, which was loaded aboard the *New London* Brigantine on 30 June 1708, consisted of twenty bales. The export duty, amounting to £35. 15s. 6d., was recovered, and by vote of the Masschusetts House of Representatives the Company was subsequently exempted from import duty. However, freight still had to be paid, £36. 10s. in all: six shillings portage, ten shillings 'To Isaac Goose [for] sledding it home' while the greatest part went to John Mason, Captain of the *New London*.[2]

[1] Ms. 7952.

[2] Ms. 7950; Ms. 7911/2; original bill of lading (Ms. 7947); Ms. 7945, account of Henry and John Hatley, 20 May 1709; Ms. 7955/1, no. 7, 22 March 1708/9; Ms. 7946/31.

Sir William Ashurst wrote to the Commissioners in July 1708 informing them that the paper was on its way. 'I hope it will be with you in Good time,' he continued, 'so that the work may Imediately go on. We suppose you have taken care to provide a Printer that is a good Artist and one that has a good letter otherwise ye charge will be to little purpose, we desire also that the Commissioners will be very Carefull in the Choice of a Person that is to Correct ye Press, that he be a good Critick in the Language & one that will be very diligent in the work for any Mistake in ye Printer may be very fatall to the Undertaking.'[1] The Commissioners met at Boston on 3 January 1708/9 and formally read Sir William's letter. It provided an excellent pretext for demanding further supply of printing type and so it was ordered 'that a suitable Font of Letters be sent for, for Printing the Scriptures in the Indian Language.' At the same time, to show the Company that they were in earnest, the Commissioners ordered 'that the Psalter be immediately Revised and Printed in Indian & English, in two distinct Collumns answering each other.'[2]

Six weeks later, on 14 February 1708/9, it was decided that the Psalter and Gospel according to St. John should be printed together in English and Indian. A committee was appointed consisting of Cotton Mather, Nehemiah Walter and Samuel Sewall to deal with the matter. There may well have been some disagreement over the choice of translator for the work. Some years earlier, on 6 December 1703, the Commissioners had resolved to write to Grindal Rawson 'to know what his design is as to ye Translation of ye psalms; and that he send an account of it & of ye charge.' Whether the committee approached him again in 1709 is not known, but by 4 July they had still not decided whom to appoint, so when the Commissioners met they ordered the committee to 'entertain Mr Experience Mayhew now in Town, immediatly to set about that work; And that James Printer and John Neesnummin be sent for to Assist him the said Mayhew: or any other persons, as the Committee shall find Convenient.'[3] Sewall was able to report in his next letter, dated 17 August 1709, that the printing had begun 'and some sheets

[1] Letter book (Univ. of Va. Ms.), 87.
[2] Ms. 7953/5.
[3] Ms. 7953/1 and 5.

wrought off; which proves to the great Satisfaction of the Natives at the Vinyard, and on the Main. Mr Experience Mayhew, and John Neesnumin (like Bezaleel and Aholiab) labour in revising the former Translation, and correcting the Press. James Printer is chiefly taken up in Printing and gains a youthfull cheeriness in your Service.'[1] In November 1709 Mayhew was given ten pounds 'in consideration of his Continual Labour in Revising the Translation of the Psalter and Correcting the Press.'[2] A month later Sewall reported that ' the Printing of the Psalter goes forward: and the unusual mildness of the Weather much favours the Work.'[3]

Nevertheless, it was not until the end of 1710 that the Psalter was finished, although the imprint bore the date of the previous year. The English title page reads: *The Massachuset Psalter . . . Being an Introduction for Training up the Aboriginal Natives, In Reading and Understanding the Holy Scriptures . . . Boston, N.E. Printed by B. Green and J. Printer for the Honourable Company for the Propagation of the Gospel in New-England, &c. 1709*. The translation was, according to Trumbull, based upon Eliot's, but almost every verse was altered, with the result that the finished work in some respects surpassed Eliot's.[4] Sewall recorded in his diary on 1 January 1710/11: 'Mr Mayhew returns, having with great Patience staid the finishing that Excellent work. . . . He was abundantly Laborious in Skillfully revising the Translation; and Correcting the Press.'[5] By order of the Commissioners, on 27 December 1710, he was paid: 'One Hundred Pounds, in full for his Labours in Revising the Translation of the Psalms, and Gospel of John; and correcting the Press (that difficult Work being now finished, through the Goodness of God) and in full for his stated Salary to the 28th of October 1710. And that he be Allowed over & above, Twenty pounds for his Board, during his abode in Boston, to attend the aforesaid Work.' It was also ordered that three or four hundred copies of the work should be bound 'as the weather will permit.'[6]

In the meantime the Company had received the Commissioners' demand for type. A detailed memorandum of the Commissioners' re-

[1] Ms. 7955/1, no. 8.
[2] Ms. 7953/5.
[3] Ms. 7955/1, no. 10.
[4] J. C. Pilling, *Bibliography*, 350.
[5] M.H.S. *Collections, 5th series*, VI, 296.
[6] Ms. 7953/6.

quirements had been drawn up for them by Bartholomew Green and is here printed in full:[1]

> Memorandum.
> Printing leters for the Bible in the Indian Language (viz)
> Two Sheets of Brevere leter first compos'd from the English Bible, quarto two Columns Roman, with but a Small quantity of the Italic Capital & Lower case; after which distributed & put in Coffins as usual.
> A full faced leter clean.
> Beside the abovemenconed these sorts.
> To two pound of K & oo } Roman Lower Case.
> To one pound of q, u, sh }
> To four pound of two line Brevere Capitals
> To about two pound of all sorts of Accents on the Vowells.
> Also, q, *, †, [ ], and ( ) with all sorts of Points
> To about 30 pound of great Primmer Roman
> To about one pound of great Pica w, lower case
> pray be carefull that there be no imperfections.
> To 12 doz: good printing Ink { 6 doz: Strong / 6 doz: Weak.
> Boston N.E. Jan^{ry} 4th 1708/9 per Bartho. Green Printer

The Company was ready to supply the Commissioners' needs and on 21 April 1709 ordered 'that Mr Chiswell be desired to provide the Letters that are wanting in New England for reprinting the Indian Bible.'[2] Sir William Ashurst wrote to Sewall about ten days later regretting that the type had not been ordered at the same time as the paper 'that no time might have bin Lost in so necessary a work.' The type founders anticipated four or five months delay before they would be able to deliver the type and Sir William added: 'One of the members of our Corporacion who is extraordinarily well skilled in printing assures us ye Large Letters which your Printer ordered are not proper for this work, but ye small ones being the same which were made use of the last impression, as we find by Comparing them together, And the Printer must be confined to ye Smaller Letters or ye Book will swell to

[1] Letter book (Univ. of Va. Ms.), 89–90. Another copy of this memorandum with only minor differences, is endorsed 'Concerning Printing Letters to be sent to New England. 21st April 1709' (Ms. 7952).

[2] Ms. 7952.

too great a Bulk, ye Last Bible being already full Large enough.'[1]

The type was paid for on 17 November 1709, the accounts recording: 'For £46: 17 paid James Roberts for printing Letters Ink &c.'[2] But it was not sent until February of the following year. Sir William Ashurst explained: 'we directed the Letters to be set for 20 capters in Genesis which was Judged sufficient to try whether the number were enough for the work; you have a Specimen of a Chapter or two struck off and by it you will perceive the character to be very clear and fair.'[3] The type and ink, in two casks and two boxes, were shipped on board the *Lusitania* on 16 February 1709/10, the invoice reading:[4]

212 pounds of Small Brevier Letters at 3^{s}	31	16	0
41 pounds great Primmer ditto at 12^{d}	2	1	0
To Porteridge for bringing the Letters in	0	2	6
To Composing 2 sheets in q^{to} for ye Indian Bible	2		
To 2 Strong Boxes for the Letters		5	
Porteridge for sending the Letters to Warehouse		2	6
12 doz Printing Ink at 12/-	7	4	0
2 Casks for the Ink		6	
Commission to a Printer for providing ye Letters	3		
Custome	2	1	1
Charges Entring at Custome house		5	
To Searchers Wharfage and Wateridge		4	6
Cart and primage		3	
	£49	10	7

This was the third and last occasion on which the Company sent a supply of type to New England. As soon as it arrived the Commissioners appointed a committee to treat with Bartholomew Green about its sale. On 6 June the committee agreed to sell the type and the ink to him for the sum of £99 and two days later the Commissioners confirmed this arrangement. Eight days later, Samuel Sewall wrote to the Company telling of the type's safe arrival, which was particularly satisfactory as: 'The Printer was even just out of Ink, and is using that now sent, to go on with printing the Psalter.'[5]

[1] Letter book (Univ. of Va. Ms.), 91.
[2] Ms. 7911/3.
[3] Letter book (Univ. of Va. Ms.), 96.
[4] *Ibid.*, 97.
[5] Ms. 7953/6; Ms. 7955/1, no. 12.

Although the Company supplied paper and type for reprinting the Bible and although the Psalter was being printed as a preliminary measure, the Commissioners were still divided on the whole question of providing books for the Indians. Sewall more than any other Commissioner was a devotee of the Indian Library and had the reprinting of the Bible very close to his heart. During February 1708/9 he mentioned it in letters to his friends and relations and asked them to pray for it. Two months later he confided to a friend: 'I think most of the Commissioners here are against it, though I am confident they of the Commissioners that are for it have most Cogent Arguments on their side. Pray that we may have Light and Peace from GOD in an affair of that moment.' In his letter to Sir William Ashurst of August 1709 he reported: 'The Revd Mr Cotton Mather, Mr Nehemiah Walter and my self were appointed to take order about it. I am confident if your Honor and the Honourable Company were conversant with them as I am you would without any Ifs or Ands go on in printing the whole Bible in Indian.'[1]

The fullest and most cogent arguments against reprinting the Bible expressed at the time, were contained in a letter from some of the Commissioners to the Company, although there is reason to believe that it never reached its destination. It was drafted by Cotton Mather before November 1710. The version known to us[2] was copied by Samuel Sewall into his letter book, with a note to the effect that he had — 'accidentally heard Mr. Sergeant and Foster talking upon it, ask'd it of them, and Copied it out.' The fact that Sewall knew nothing about it until then lends added point to the letter's stated intention of laying before the Company 'the Sentiments which your Commissioners here generally have of the matter.' Not only would the Bible take a long time to print, if it were to be corrected as the Psalter had been, but the most competent ministers would be kept from their flocks while it was in the press. The amount of money and time it would take to print the Bible 'would go very far towards bringing [the Indians] to a sort of *English Generation*. Is it very sure, the best thing we can do for our Indians is to Anglicise them in all agreeable Instances; and in that of Language, as

[1] Ms. 7955/1, no. 8; M.H.S. *Collections, 6th series*, I, 379, 382.

[2] M.H.S. *Collections, 6th series*, I, 400–3.

well as others. They can scarce retain their Language, without a Tincture of other Salvage Inclinations, which do but ill suit, either with the Honor, or with the design of Christianity.' It was pointed out that religious ideas brought to the Indians in their own language 'unavoidably arrive in Terms that are scarcely more intelligible to them than if they were entirely English.' The letter continued optimistically: 'And it is hoped, That by good English Schools among the Indians, and some other fit methods, the grand intention of Anglicising them would be soon accomplished.' A particular objection to ambitious printing schemes put forward by Mather, was the difficulty of choosing one out of many dialects: 'The former Editions of the Bible were in the *Natick* Dialect. But if it be done in the *Noop* Dialect, which would best suit the most valuable body of our surviving Indians: those on the *Main*, and at *Nantucket* would not understand it so well as they should. The Books written by two eminent Preachers in their Tongue, the Indians complain of a Difference in them that is considerable.' Cotton Mather then quoted 'a discreet person whom we lately employed in a visitation of the Indian Villages . . . : "There are many words of Mr Elliott's forming which they never understood . . . and there seems to be as much difficulty to bring them unto a competent knowledge of the Scriptures, as it would be to get a sensible acquaintance with the English Tongue." ' The letter concluded by pointing out that the signatories (who included no ministers, as they did not wish to commit themselves) had not known that 'certain particular Gentlemen' had recommended a new edition of the Bible to the Company.

The Company was bewildered by the Commissioners' lack of unanimity, the more so because they had begun selling the supply of paper for the Bible as soon as it arrived. In fact the Company had authorized the sale of any surplus paper but the Commissioners considered that no time should be lost in disposing of it wholesale and Sewall was entrusted with its sale. In a letter to Sir William Ashurst of 22 March 1708/9 he reported: 'The Commissioners held the paper so high at first that very little of it is sold. The Booksellers have bought some to print the Psalter at 16^{s} per Ream; by which it is seen that the Genoa Paper makes excellent good work.' Five months later sales totalled 150 reams at sixteen shillings and Sewall explained: 'To encourage the sale of it, I after awhile sold a single Ream to any that offerd ready Money for it.'[1]

Sir William Ashurst expressed his surprise at the sale of so much Genoa paper and reminded the Commissioners of the difficulty with which it had been purchased. 'As to what ye Printer & Booksellers tell you of the Holland paper being properer for this business,' he wrote, 'It is altogether a mistake, for those here who understand that matter very well have fully convinced us that ye Genoa paper is ye more proper, & will do much better than the other; besides the Last impression being on the same sort of paper.' In February 1709/10 Ashurst was even more surprised by Sewall's demands that the Company should have the whole Bible printed 'being we have expressed so great a desire for it, and been wanting in nothing to promote it, by sending Paper and now providing Letters for the work.' He also recorded his disapproval of the sale of paper 'till you see what you shall have occasion for in Reprinting the Bible.'[2]

Almost exactly a year later, in February 1710/11, Ashurst enquired why the Bible had not been started, but to this question he received no satisfactory answer. No definite reference to a change of policy occurs in the Commissioners' minutes, but on 30 October 1711 the Commissioners considered it 'for the Company's Interest to Sell the Genoa Paper now; the Indian Affairs calling for it.' A proviso was added that they would replace it by paper of equal quality should the Company order them to do so.[3] But in fact the sale of the paper was tantamount to the abandonment of the third edition of the Indian Bible. Sir William Ashurst was 'mightily surprized' at this news as he had been expecting to hear of the Bible's progress and once again demanded an explanation. If an explanation was ever forthcoming it has not survived. Cotton Mather apparently suggested that the Bible might be printed in London but Sir William pointed out in July 1713: 'I am afraid it will be impracticable to have it done here, in regard nobody amongst us is master of the Language and capable of Correcting the Press, besides so tedious a piece of work as you represent it will require a great deal more money then our present Circumstances will afford.' When an account of the

[1] Ms. 7955/1, nos. 7, 8.

[2] Letter book (Univ. of Va. Ms.), 91, 95.

[3] Ms. 7953/7.

Indians of Martha's Vineyard by Experience Mayhew appeared some years later mentioning the Indians' desire for Bibles, Governor Robert Ashurst wrote to Sewall on 14 February 1722 remarking that paper and type had formerly been sent for reprinting the Bible 'butt was putt of[f] for Some reasons. I desire that you will give me the Commissioners thoughts of itt and whether itt be practicable, and if it is what will be wanting.' But the third edition of the Indian Bible was never printed. This did not bring an abrupt end to printing for the Indians; it simply meant that the Indians were supplied with a number of works entirely in English as well as several small books in Indian.[1]

Even before the reprint of the Bible was finally abandoned the Commissioners decided to use the printed English word as a weapon against drunkenness, the Indians' 'epidemical Disease' as Sewall called it.[2] In July 1708 the Commissioners ordered that 'a suitable number of the Rever'd Mr. Cotton Mather's Essays against the abuse of Rum, be sent to the Indian plantations.'[3] This was Mather's *Sober Considerations, on a growing Flood of Iniquity* . . . (Boston, 1708). It was not written specifically for the Indians nor was it printed at the Commissioners' expense. Nevertheless they purchased a substantial number of copies and in so doing somewhat misjudged the Indians' requirements: sixteen years later there was still a bundle which had not been distributed.

On 14 November 1709 the Commissioners ordered that 'the Reverend Mr Samuel Danforth be desired to transcribe his Sermon preach'd at Bristol, October 12th, 1709 being the day of the Execution of Josias & Joseph Indians for murder: that it may be ready for the Press'. It was decided on 12 December to print five hundred copies of this work entitled:[4] *The woful effects of Drunkenness. A sermon preached at Bristol, Octob. 12, 1709. When two Indians, Josias and Joseph, were executed for murther, occasioned by the drunkenness both of the Murthering & Murthered parties* . . . (Boston, 1710). It was in English, but concluded with a short passage in the Indian language addressed to the two condemned men. Unhappily, the printed word was not mighty enough to save the Indian from his worst enemy.

[1] Letter book (Univ. of Va. Ms.), 116, 125, 178.
[2] M.H.S. *Collections, 6th series*, I, 376.
[3] Ms. 7953/4.
[4] Ms. 7953/5.

Two other books in 'the Indian Library' were not primarily intended for the Indians at all, but the Commissioners supplied the paper to the printer and received a number of copies in return. On 20 January 1714/15 the Commissioners resolved: 'It is advisable that now the English Primer is in the Press; the Treasurer supply paper for the Printing of Five hundred Copies to ly in readiness for the Companies use.'[1] The accounts for 1715 show that on 9 December a ream of paper was delivered to the printer 'for ye primer now printing.' This was probably only the final consignment of paper for this English Primer. The paper for the other book was mentioned in the accounts on 13 February 1715/16: 'Delivered two Reams of paper to print the well instructed servant.'[2] This may have referred to Cotton Mather's *Servants of Abraham, with Motives for the Instruction of Servants* (Boston, 1716).[3]

Cotton Mather, while opposed to reprinting the Indian Bible, was not opposed to the Commissioners printing his own works in Indian translations. Early in 1713 he noted in his diary his intention to 'promote a short Essay, to be written and printed in the Indian tongue, to excite and assist the Worship of God in their Families.' In July of the same year, he further noted his intention of laying several proposals before the Commissioners: 'Particularly, the publication of an Instrument, for the Maintaining of houshold Piety among the Indians.' In December he resolved to 'accelerate the Publication.'[4] On 4 February 1713/14 the Commissioners ordered 'that a Treatise of the Revd Mr Rowland Cotton in English and Indian Entituled Family Religion Excited and assisted be Printed, Six hundred Copies for the use and encouragement of the Natives.'[5] The book was, in fact, written by Cotton Mather, but the translation was by Roland Cotton. The work appeared in 1714 with the text in both English and Indian and Sewall was able to send a dozen copies to Sir William Ashurst with his letter of 31 August 1714.[6]

In June 1716 Cotton Mather entered in his diary the following 'Good

[1] Ms. 7953/9.
[2] Ms. 7946/36.
[3] No copy of this tract has been located. The title is taken from T. J. Holmes, *Cotton Mather: a bibliography* (Cambridge, Mass., 1940), III, 969.
[4] M.H.S. *Collections, 7th series*, VIII, 180, 218, 274.
[5] Ms. 7953/9.
[6] Ms. 7955/1, no. 30.

Devised': 'Among the Commissioners for the Indian-Affairs, there are several Things to be prosecuted. Especially, a translated, *Monitor for Communicants*.'[1] The Commissioners' minutes for 6 July 1716 ordered: 'that a Sheet prepared by Dr Cotton Mather as a Monitor for Communicants at the Lords Supper, in English and Indian be printed five hundred Copies.'[2] Early in the New Year three reams and five quires of paper were delivered to the printer for this purpose.[3] The English title page of the tract read: *A Monitor for Communicants, An Essay to Excite and Assist Religious Approaches to the Table of the Lord* ... (Boston, N.E. Printed by B. Green. 1716).[4]

The next mention of a book by Cotton Mather printed at the Company's expense occurs in his diary on 18 December 1718. Here he asked himself whether the Commissioners should not 'keep a Day of Prayer together, and I on the Day entertain them with a Sermon suited unto the Occasion, and then publish the Sermon accompanied with some other Things to serve the Cause of Religion in the world?' He was able to answer his question on 28 February 1720/21: the sermon had been given and the Commissioners had approved its publication.[5] Accordingly it appeared in 1721 under the title: *India Christiana. A discourse delivered unto the Commissioners for the Propagation of the Gospel among the American Indians.* Bartholomew Green, the printer, received £10. 14s. for 'printing India Christiana 8 sheets.'[6] It was mainly in English but contained 'a taste of the language' which must have been included in order to impress Robert Ashurst and the other members of the Company in London to whom the book was dedicated. On 14 March 1721/22 Sewall wrote to Robert Ashurst telling him that he had sent 'a Box of India Christiana near Six Dozen; as many as it would hold; Superscribed to your Honour; of which pray Acceptance.'[7] Mather himself was not unpleased with the production, as he too sent copies 'into several Parts of *Europe* with Designs to serve the Kingdome of GOD.'[8]

[1] M.H.S. *Collections, 7th series*, VIII, 355.
[2] Ms. 7953/10.
[3] Ms. 7946/36.
[4] A copy of this very rare item is to be found in the Bodleian.
[5] M.H.S. *Collections, 7th series*, VIII, 576, 604.
[6] Ms. 7946/39.
[7] Ms. 7955/1, no. 64.
[8] M.H.S. *Collections, 7th series*, VIII, 619.

According to his own account, Cotton Mather could write in seven languages, but it seems that Algonquian was not one of these. J. H. Trumbull, the nineteenth-century scholar, considered that 'he had not mastered the rudiments of the grammar, and could not construct an Indian sentence idiomatically.' Trumbull went further and suggested that the translations may not have been his at all.[1] In fact the Commissioners' minutes and accounts show that Trumbull's view was correct: the translations were Roland Cotton's. On 9 November 1722 the Commissioners ordered payment of £7. 10s. to Roland Cotton 'for Translating Several Treatises into Indian which is printed with ye English, Column against Column.'[2] The accounts fortunately specify that the 'several treatises' were 'Family Religion, Monitor & a piece in India Christiana.'[3]

Similar to *India Christiana* in being intended for English rather than Indian eyes was Solomon Stoddard's tract entitled: *Question Whether God is not Angry with the Country for doing so little towards the Conversion of the Indians?* The cost of producing it is shown in the accounts for 26 October 1723: 'To Mr Bartholomew Green for paper, printing & stitching 1000 of ye Revd Mr Solomon Stoddard's discourse on Gospellizing ye Indians £7. 2. 0'.[4] Sewall was not without hope that the Indians might find it edifying and accordingly dispatched a dozen or so copies to each of the English missionaries for distribution among their flocks.

The last of the main series of Indian titles published at the Company's expense was, like the first, a primer. On 19 March 1718/19 the Commissioners had ordered that 'a few Sheets of the most Necessary texts of Scripture be printed in the Indian tongue, with a Column of English over against them: the Indian bible being now out of Print.' This was the last time that the Commissioners considered providing the Indians with the Scriptures in their own language and it appears that no action was taken. It was no doubt agreed that a primer would serve the Indians' needs quite adequately: on 23 July 1717 the Commissioners had ordered: 'the Indian primer being near out of print . . . that a new Impression be made, and that it be Translated into the English Language;

[1] J. Winsor, ed., *The Memorial History of Boston*, I, 479–80.
[2] Ms. 7953/15. [3] Ms. 7946/40. [4] Ms. 7946/41.

so that the English and Indian be printed in Severall Columns Over against each other. Two thousand to be printed.' By 24 November of the following year the Commissioners ordered: 'Let John Neesnumun be employed in Translating & printing the Indian primer as before ordered.'[1] John Neesnumun, who was the Indian preacher at Natick, did not live to carry out this particular task. Samuel Sewall wrote to Sir William Ashurst on 17 February 1719/20 explaining: 'I waited long, hoping to have had it translated by John Neesnumun: but being supris'd with his death, I sent to Mr Samuel Danforth of Taunton, who took it in hand and speedily finish'd it.'[2] Danforth received £5 for his translation, so a former attribution of this work to Experience Mayhew is shown to have been wrong. On 9 November 1719 the Commissioners had repeated their order for printing, while questioning how many copies should be printed.[3] On 26 December 1719 they paid £39. 2s. 'To Mr Samuel Phillips . . . for 46 ream of paper to print the Primer Indian and English.' Bartholomew Green received £10 on 24 May 1720 and a further £4. 12s. 2d. on 18 October 1720.[4] The work must have been finished by 26 July as Sewall had by this time dispatched two copies to Robert Ashurst.[5] Presumably the second payment to Green was for stitching and possibly for binding some copies. Its English title page read: *The Indian Primer or The First Book By which Children may know truely to read the Indian Language. And Milk for Babes* (Boston, 1720), but it is often referred to by its Indian title: *Indiane Primer Asuh Negonneyeuuk*.

To Sewall's enthusiasm must be attributed the initiative for many of the Indian titles which had appeared during the first two decades of the eighteenth century. With his retirement the list of Indian titles virtually came to an end. In one of his last letters to the Company written on 28 October 1723 he reported that he had in his possession, amongst other things, 'Two Boxes of Printing Letters, sent to print the Bible in Indian. A good Stock of Psalters with the Gosple of John, some bound & some in sheets, English & Indian. A good Stock of Primers, Indian & English, and of the Confession of Faith. Practice of Piety are almost spent. There

[1] Ms. 7953/10–12. [2] Ms. 7955/1, no. 55.
[3] Ms. 7953/14, 17 March 1720/21; Ms. 7953/12.
[4] Ms. 7946/37, 38. [5] Ms. 7955/1, no. 58.

are some stich'd Books as a Sermon on the Lords Day, English & Indian. Monitor to Communicants &c.'[1] In the following year on 1st May, Adam Winthrop, Sewall's successor as treasurer, signed an inventory of the bonds and stationery wares of which he took receipt.[2] The list of books is of great interest, showing as it does the state of the stocks at this time. After listing the bonds, the inventory continued:

Receiv'd also
One Iron Chest empty &
Two Boxes of printing Letters
Stationary Ware recd

English Primers	331
New Primmers Engl: & Indian	894
India Christiana	133
Sincere Converts	48
Danforth agst Drunkeness	91
Iroquois Latin English Dutch	207
Stoddard propagating Gospell	152
Monitors for Communicants	187
Family Religion Engl & Indian	27
Dr Mather against Rum 1 bundle . . .	
Psalters with Evangelist John	324
Practice of Piety printed 1685	45
Confessions of Faith Eng: & Indian	408
Epistles English & Indian	64

Unfortunately, not many accounts of the stationery wares distributed have survived, but such as are still extant for this period show that this stock was not likely to be quickly exhausted.

No further printing for the Indians was undertaken by the Commissioners during the American colonial period.[3] This was partly because the Indians were learning English, partly because it was a difficult and costly business and partly because no one came forward to champion

[1] Ms. 7955/1, no. 67.
[2] Ms. 7946/43a.
[3] It is possible that a further edition of the *Indian Primer* of 1720 and two tracts by John Sergeant entitled *Morning Prayer* and *A Prayer before Sermon* were paid for either wholly or in part by the Company, but no reference to them occurs in the Company's records.

the printed Indian word as Eliot and Sewall had done. Nor were the Commissioners tempted to print books in English specially for the Indians; instead they bought English Bibles and primers from the local booksellers. The question of whether the Indians understood these more readily than they had understood Eliot's translations must remain a matter for doubt. But the 'Indian Library' contained some noteworthy and curious books and was, perhaps, the Company's most remarkable achievement.[1]

[1] One other title might be mentioned as forming part of the Indian Library, namely Cotton Mather's, *The Hatchets, to hew down the Tree of Sin, which bears the Fruit of Death. Or, the Laws, by which the Magistrates are to punish Offences, among the Indians, as well as among the English.* (Boston, Mass., B. Green, 1705.) See J. C. Pilling, *Bibliography*, 223, and M.H.S. *Collections, 7th series*, VII, 511–12. However, there is no positive evidence that this item was printed at the Company's expense.

7

The Company, 1692–1776

BOYLE had resigned from the post of Governor in 1689, but it was not until after his death in 1691 that the Company set about electing his successor. Boyle had outlined the requirements and virtues which should be looked for in a governor: he should be 'vigorous, active, versd in letting, setting, & other Œconomical Affairs'; and he should be one 'who, especially if he be a single man, may further your Pious Endeavours, and contribute to the Wellfare of your Society, not only by his Counsell & Direction, but with his Purse.'[1] Candidates were nominated by the Treasurer and on 25 March 1692 Major Robert Thompson was elected unanimously.[2] He had been elected a member without opposition in 1668, and had been constantly active on the Company's behalf during the intervening years. As a merchant trading with New England, he had often conveyed part of the Company's annual revenue to the Commissioners by means of bills of exchange, thus performing a service advantageous both to himself and to the Company. However, Thompson made little or no effect upon the Company's prosperity and with his death in 1695 a new Governor was once more needed. This time the choice fell upon Sir William Ashurst.

Membership of the Company tended to run in families, a son taking the place of a father and the same names recurring again and again, but none provided as many, or such able members as the Ashurst family. Henry Ashurst, as Treasurer both to the Society and then to the Company, had been one of its mainstays during the seventeenth century. He had two sons who were members of the Company, the eldest of whom, Henry, was elected in 1681: he was created baronet in 1688 and served

[1] Ms. 7956, Boyle to the Company, 22 Aug. 1689.

[2] Ms. 8010, memorandum.

as Member of Parliament for Truro and then for Wilton. The second, Sir William himself, had four sons who were members: Henry, Town Clerk of London (1700–1705/6) was elected in 1698, as was Robert who was to succeed his father as Governor; William of Lincoln's Inn, Controller of the Stamp Office, and Samuel, a woollen draper and a member of the Court of Common Council, were both elected to the Company at some time before 1720. Robert in his turn had two sons who became members: William in 1722 and Thomas in 1733.[1]

His father apart, Sir William Ashurst did more for the Company than any other member of the family, and more than most members of the Company. On 14 October 1681, the day of his election to membership, he had also been elected Treasurer, in order that he might continue where his father had left off. There is some evidence to show that he had, before this date, assisted his father unofficially on several occasions. Sir William, although brought up a staunch dissenter like his father, was allowed by his conscience to become an alderman of the City of London in 1687. He was knighted in the same year and served his term as sheriff in 1691–2 and as Lord Mayor in 1693–4. During most of the period 1689–1710 he was a Member of Parliament for London and from 1697 to 1714, with only four short intervals, he was a director of the Bank of England.[2] Furthermore, his business connections with New England and his knowledge of many of the leading men there made him particularly suited to the direction of the Company's affairs. He was well regarded in New England: in 1709 he was sent a commission to act as agent for the province of Massachusetts-Bay, but this he refused.[3] Jeremiah Dummer, who was appointed agent instead of him, wrote of him eleven years later: 'He was a hearty lover of our civil and religious liberties, and stood faithful to all our interests in the various changes of court and ministry here . . . though he had an extreme aversion to a court, and the tedious ceremonies of attendance there, yet he always went with alacrity when there was a prospect of doing us

[1] F. C. Cass, *East Barnet* (Westminster, 1885), 68 pedigree; J. & J. B. Burke, *Extinct and Dormant Baronetcies* (1884), 17–18.

[2] A. B. Beaven, *The Aldermen of the City of London*, II, 114.

[3] Ms. 8010, instructions sent with commission to act as agent, 10 Feb. 1709.

service.'[1] Like most of the active members of the Company at this period, he was engaged in trade with New England and usually had a share in the bills of exchange issued by the Company for conveying the annual allowance to the Commissioners. But, as the years went by, he spent more and more time at Bath, which made it increasingly difficult for him to lavish on the Company's affairs the care which Boyle had devoted to them. Nor does he seem to have taken the deeply personal interest in the Indians' conversion which Boyle had always shown.

On 10 February 1719/20 Robert Ashurst was elected Governor in his father's place. Less notable than his father as a man of affairs, he had nevertheless amassed considerable wealth as a sugar refiner and merchant, more than enough to purchase Hedingham Castle in Essex. He had found a wife amongst the daughters of fellow members (a common enough occurrence in the history of the Company) his choice falling upon Elizabeth Gunston, daughter of the Company's Treasurer. When he became Governor he had the advantage of being known to many in New England as his father's son, and during his six years in office he seems never to have neglected the Company's business.[2]

Robert Ashurst died on 25 February 1726, but the family's connection with the Governorship of the Company did not come to an immediate end; his successor, William Thompson, grandson of Major Robert Thompson, had married Judith, the daughter of Sir William Ashurst. A lawyer by training, William Thompson had made his money as a London merchant. He owned property both in London and at East Barnet in Hertfordshire. He was a director of the Bank of England from 1714 and its Governor during the years 1725–7. His governorship of the Company was of short duration; in fact it lasted only two years, as he died in June 1728.[3]

If his term of office was short, that of his successor, Sir Nathaniel Gould, was shorter still — he was the Company's Governor from 19 July 1728, the day of his election, until his death two days later on 21 July. The Company's choice had fallen upon a London merchant who had been M.P. for Shoreham from the beginning of the century until

[1] M.H.S. *Collections, 3rd series*, I, 146.

[2] P. Morant, *The History ... of Essex* (1768), II, 296; Ms. 7952.

[3] F. C. Cass, *East Barnet*, 68 pedigree; *Notes and Queries*, **179** (1940), 80.

the year before his death, a director of the Bank of England from 1697 and its governor for the years 1711 to 1713. He was, too, the supposed author of *An Essay on the Publick Debts of this Kingdom* (1726).[1]

The Company met on 9 August 1728 and unanimously elected Sir Robert Clarke to take his place. Sir Robert's father, Samuel Clarke, had become a member of the Company in 1681 and was created baronet of Snailwell, Cambridgeshire, in 1698. Robert had been admitted to Gray's Inn on 23 June 1701 and was elected a member of the Company in 1713. He was M.P. for Cambridgeshire from 1717 to 1722 and on his father's death in 1719 succeeded to the baronetcy. In fact Sir Robert spent most of his time in the country and only occasionally made the journey to London; in his absence the Company's affairs were dealt with by the Treasurer, Joseph Williams.[2]

When Sir Robert Clarke died in November 1746 the Company turned once more to the Clarke family and elected Sir Samuel, the third baronet, to the post of Governor, in his father's place. Like both his father and his grandfather, Sir Samuel had received his legal training at Gray's Inn. In 1753–4 he served as sheriff for the counties of Cambridge and Huntingdon and died four years later, unmarried, at the age of forty-three. His brother, Robert, also a member of the Company, succeeded him as baronet but not as Governor of the Company.[3]

When the Company met on 19 January 1759, it elected James Lambe of Lincoln's Inn Fields to fill the vacancy. Unlike the Clarkes, Lambe was not merely a sympathizer with nonconformity but was himself a dissenter. Indeed the Company was to make no further attempts to conceal its strong dissenting character by the election of moderate Anglican Governors as it had usually done in the past. In future the Company's Governors were to be prominent nonconformists; Lambe himself had been one of Dr. Williams's Trustees since 1751 and a member of the Presbyterian Board to which he left £100 in his will. His

[1] *Notes and Queries*, **179**, 57–8; Ms. 7952.

[2] G. E. Cokayne, *Complete Baronetage*, IV (Exeter, 1904), 174; Ms. 7952; Ms. 8010, memorandum.

[3] G. E. Cokayne, *Complete Baronetage*, IV, 174.

term as Governor lasted little more than two years; he died on 21 February 1761.[1]

His place was taken, on 13 March 1761, by Dr. Benjamin Avery, one of the Company's most distinguished Governors during the eighteenth century. Avery had received the degree of LL.D. at Edinburgh University in 1711. He became a Presbyterian minister but quitted the ministry in 1720 as a result of the Salters' Hall Conference which was at least nominally concerned with religious liberty versus subscription. He subsequently became a physician and ministered to bodies instead of souls. He was elected one of the governors of Guy's Hospital in 1729 and was, according to the Hospital's latest historian: 'quite the most active among them.' In 1742 he was appointed the Hospital's Treasurer, a post which he held until his death in 1764. He was also one of Dr. Williams's Trustees from 1728 until his death. His prestige as a leader of English dissent was such that his name was well known in New England; in fact the General Assembly of Connecticut had unanimously chosen him agent for the colony in 1749, a post which he had wisely declined. It was the Company's misfortune that he served as Governor for only three years.[2]

His successor was his friend and close associate for many years, Jasper Mauduit, who was elected on 8 March 1765. He was descended from a family of French Protestants who had settled at Exeter about a century and a half earlier. His father, Israel Mauduit, had been the first dissenting minister at the Chapel of St. John's, Bermondsey. By trade he was a woollen draper, sharing a business with his brother Israel, afterwards also to be a Governor of the Company, and Thomas Wright, for many years its Treasurer. Thomas Wright had married Jasper's only child from his first marriage. Jasper had become a member of the Company in 1745 and three years later he took over the work of Treasurer from Joseph Williams. Like Avery, he was a prominent dissenter, one of Dr. Williams's Trustees (1753–72) and Treasurer of the Presbyterian Board

[1] W. D. Jeremy, *The Presbyterian Fund and Dr. Daniel Williams's Trust* (1885), 140; Ms. 7952.

[2] *Dictionary of National Biography*, II, 274–5; H. C. Cameron, *Mr. Guy's Hospital* (1954), 97–8; W. D. Jeremy, *The Presbyterian Fund*, 130; *Conn. H. S.*, XV, 340, 366; Ms. 7952.

(1756–58), to which he left a bequest amounting to £40 a year for nearly thirty years. But unlike Avery he had accepted the position of colonial agent. In the 1760s, when feeling against episcopacy was rising in Massachusetts, he was appointed agent in place of William Bollan, who had been dismissed largely because of his adherence to the Church of England. A few days after his election as Governor, Jasper Mauduit told Andrew Oliver in a letter that he did not expect to live much longer. He had, he wrote, been obliged 'to Accept of the appointment as Governor In the room of That Great and worthy Man Dr. Avery contrary to my will; and to make it Easy to me the Company have appointed my Son-in-law Thomas Wright their Treasurer in my stead.' In spite of his gloomy prediction, he lived to govern the Company for seven years with considerable ability and vigour.[1]

The last Governor of the New England Company during the American colonial period was William Bowden, elected on 31 March 1772. He too was a prominent dissenter, a trustee of Dr. Williams's charity (1761–80) and a member of the Presbyterian Board (1772–80). He was also Treasurer of St. Thomas's Hospital and a director of the Bank of England from 1763 until his death in 1780. It was left to Bowden and his successor, Richard Jackson, the famous lawyer and politician, to bring to an end the Company's work in New England.[2]

Even before Boyle's death there had been a slackening in the Company's activities. Administration of the Company's affairs required far less time than formerly and two meetings a year were found sufficient for most contingencies. This meant that members were less constantly in touch with what was going on across the Atlantic, and few, if any, of the missionaries corresponded with the Company as Eliot had done. The Company's main concern was that it should be able to produce adequate accounts showing how the funds had been disposed in New England; details of distribution were left to the Commissioners. When the Company did hold court it was rarely in the houses of private mem-

[1] *Dictionary of National Biography*, XXXVII, 82, article on Israel Mauduit; W. D. Jeremy, *The Presbyterian Fund*, 142; M.H.S. *Collections*, LXXIV, 37–8; Ms. 7952; Ms. 7927, f. 9.

[2] *Notes and Queries*, **179**, 116; W. D. Jeremy, *The Presbyterian Fund*, 153; Ms. 7920/1, p. 11.

bers, as it had been during Boyle's governorship, but usually in coffee houses; the Virginia Coffee House in Bell Alley, Cornhill, was very often chosen for this purpose. Meanwhile people willing to become members were as difficult to find as ever: and the people had to be the right people, that is to say, dissenting London merchants. At one time there seems to have been a deliberate policy to choose bachelors whenever possible, although Jeremiah Dummer was certainly exaggerating when he recommended the Governor of Connecticut to cultivate the friendship of members because they 'are all very wealthy men, and most of them batchellours (being chosen on purpose for their having no domestick obligations).'[1] Whereas during the seventeenth century the Company had many non-dissenting members in its ranks, in the eighteenth century their number dwindled. With the death of Boyle a strongly moderating hand was removed from the Company's elections and as the high court judges and the sprinkling of lords originally added to satisfy the Privy Council died off, they were replaced by dissenting commoners. The founding of the professedly Anglican Society for the Propagation of the Gospel in Foreign Parts in 1702 only served to emphasize the New England Company's nonconformist character. Membership was not confined to any one denomination but was, as Mauduit explained to Samuel Davies, an ardent Presbyterian, 'a Mixture of all ye protestant denomination here (except Quakers).' They were, nevertheless, able to 'transact this business with great Ease to themselves & much honor to ye Company.'[2] It is therefore not surprising to find the closest ties between the Company and the Deputies of the Protestant Dissenters.

This body, which began to meet in 1732, consisted of two deputies from every congregation of the three principal denominations of Protestant Dissenters — Presbyterians, Independents and Baptists — within ten miles of London. Their earliest meetings had been to make application for repeal of the Corporation and Test Acts, but they quickly saw that the system of deputies would serve admirably for the consideration of many matters of common interest. Two men in particular served to link the Company with the Deputies — Benjamin Avery and Jasper Mauduit; both were intimately connected with the affairs of the Pro-

[1] *Conn. H. S.*, IV, 63.

[2] Letter book (Univ. of Va. Ms.), 297.

testant Dissenters. In fact, Avery was Chairman of the Deputies from 1735 until his death in 1764 and also held the post of Treasurer from 1738 until 1748. He was succeeded as both Governor of the Company and Chairman of the Deputies by Jasper Mauduit. These two men must have been responsible for persuading many of the Deputies to become members of the Company; for throughout the eighteenth century the Company numbered many Deputies amongst its members. And a number of them were very prominent: Thomas Lucas, William Bowden, Nathaniel Polhill, George Brough and Edward Jeffries all served as Chairmen, while Nathaniel Carpenter, Michael Dean and James Boyle French held the office of Treasurer. Thus, the Company contained in its ranks some of the most politically active dissenters of the period.[1]

The work which the administration of the Company's property required of members changed very little with the years. New means of raising funds were never considered; the annual revenue changed only when occasional bequests were received. One of the most important of these was that of Robert Bogle. By his will of 18 July 1691 and a number of codicils, Boyle directed that the residue of his estates after the payment of debts and legacies should be disposed of by his executors for charitable purposes, but in particular he recommended the laying out of 'the greatest part of the same for the advance or propagation of the Christian religion amongst infidels.'[2] The only gift made specifically to the Company was a legacy of £100, but the executors, of whom Sir Henry Ashurst was one, naturally thought of the Company when it dealt with the residue of the estate. In 1695 they purchased from Sir Samuel Gerrard the manor of Brafferton, in the county of York, for the sum of £5,400 and granted to the Company a rent charge of £90 per annum arising from it.[3] Half of this sum was to be given to two ministers as their salary for instructing the natives 'in or near his Majesty's colonies in New England in the Christian knowledge.' The other half was to be transmitted by the Company to the President and Fellows of Harvard, who in their turn were to bestow it upon two ministers as their salary for teaching Indians in or near the College. The residue of

[1] B. L. Manning, *The Protestant Dissenting Deputies* (Cambridge, 1952), 481–2.

[2] *The Works of . . . Robert Boyle*, I, clxiii.

[3] Ms. 8002, indenture tripartite, 30 Aug. 1695.

the rents was to be laid out for the advancement of the Christian religion in Virginia, to be disposed of according to the orders of the Earl of Burlington and the Bishop of London. The rent charge was signed and sealed on 13 August 1695. The Earl of Burlington and the Bishop of London agreed upon a set of rules governing the charity and these were confirmed, with only one minor alteration, by an order of the Lord Chancellor on 9 June 1698. Under these rules the residue of the rents was to be paid to William and Mary College in Virginia for the care and education of Indian children. At the same time Micajah Perry, merchant, later Alderman and Lord Mayor of London, was chosen as receiver of rents from the trust estate.[1]

The Brafferton rent charge proved a regular and reliable source of income except in the 1740s when, with Alderman Perry's bankruptcy, three years' annuity were lost and when, ten years later, the cattle on the Brafferton estate died and the Company allowed the tenants about £30 by way of relief. However, Harvard College did not receive its share of the rent charge with the same regularity. In July 1710 the Company received a letter from the President and Fellows enquiring after their share. The Company recorded its intention of paying them the £45 per annum which was due in future, but hoped that they would not insist upon payment of arrears as the money had, in fact, been spent by the Commissioners on ministers' salaries.[2] Sir William Ashurst addressed a letter to the President and Fellows admitting that, although the Commissioners had been ordered in 1697 to make annual payments to the College, this had never been done. He also asked the President and Fellows to settle the matter of arrears with the Commissioners.[3] On 28 November 1710 the President, the Treasurer and one of the Fellows met the Commissioners to discuss terms: the Commissioners offered to pay £90 per annum for the next six years and then £45 per annum at the current rate of exchange,[4] and the Harvard committee 'condescended to the desires of the said Commissioners.'[5]

[1] *Rules and Orders respecting the Charity Left by the will of the Hon. Robert Boyle* [*c.* 1750?]. (Several copies of this small pamphlet are contained in the Company's archives. e.g. Ms. 7933 & Ms. 7966.)

[2] Ms. 7952, 11 July 1710.

[3] *C.S.M.*, XV, 394. [4] Ms. 7953/6. [5] *C.S.M.*, XV, 393.

However, the rightful application of Harvard College's share of Boyle's charity always remained a matter of some delicacy. It was summed up by Increase Mather in a letter to Sir William Ashurst dated 10 January 1710/11: 'Some pretend that the young scholars who shall have the benefit of this charity for their education, must ingage to devote themselves wholly and soly to the service of the Indians.' He recommended that the ministers should be engaged to preach to Indians and English as Eliot, Danforth and Rawson had done, and that then — 'the design of this charity will be truly complied with.'[1]

Although the Company was not responsible for making payments to William and Mary College under the rules of Boyle's charity, 'the President, Master or Professors of the College' were, in July 1772, represented at a meeting of the Company's Court by the College's agent, Osgood Hanbury, a merchant of Tower Street, London. His request was that timber at Brafferton manor should be cut down for the benefit of the College.[2] In November the Court approved this suggestion but, presumably because it was not ultimately responsible for the administration of Brafferton manor, it did not actually give permission. As the College considered that it was not receiving the residual rents to which it was entitled, it instituted legal proceedings against the Company and others, but did not secure what it considered to be its rights.[3]

The other large bequest which the Company received during the eighteenth century was that of Dr. Daniel Williams. Daniel Williams was born in about 1643 and was probably of Welsh peasant or yeoman stock. At the age of twenty-four he became one of the ministers of Wood Street Presbyterian Congregation in Dublin. In his thirty-second year he married a wealthy widow who was sister of the Countess of Montrath. This lady, who was seven years his senior, died in 1698. Three years later Williams married again, this time Jane Barkstead, the widow of a wealthy silk mercer, thus further consolidating his personal fortune.[4]

[1] Ms. 8010 (A modern transcript).

[2] Ms. 7920/1, p. 13–14.

[3] H. L. Ganter, 'Some notes on "The Charity of the Honourable Robert Boyle Esq., of the City of London, deceased." ', *William and Mary College Quarterly Historical Magazine, 2nd series*, **15** (1935), 1–39, 207–28, 346–84.

[4] Stephen Kay Jones, *Dr. Williams and his Library* (Cambridge, 1948), 4–5.

His last will and testament is a document of some complexity. However, in the clause which concerned the Company, he bequeathed to it the estate called Tolleshunt, Beckenham manor, after the death of Mrs. Hannah Fox, alias Bradley, from whom he had bought it. This reversionary interest was to be administered by the New England Company 'for the good of what Pagans and Blacks lie neglected there.' More specifically, the rent was to yield £60 to be paid to two well-qualified persons acting as itinerant preachers to the Indians; they were to be nominated by the trustees appointed under the will. The residue of the rents was to be paid to Harvard College, and was also to be used for 'the blessed work of converting the poor Indians there.' The most famous bequest in Dr. Williams's will was that founding the library in London which still bears his name.[1]

Dr. Daniel Williams died in 1716, but thirty years passed before the death of Mrs. Hannah Fox, alias Bradley, so that his death made no immediate difference to the Company's revenue. Jeremiah Dummer, who was at this time colonial agent for Connecticut as well as Massachusetts, wrote to Timothy Woodbridge, pastor of the First Church at Hartford, on 21 February 1716/17 to inform him of the terms of Dr. Williams's charity. He was, naturally enough, on the look-out for any pickings which he could find for Connecticut, even at Massachusetts' expense, and it seemed to him that the annuity of £60 should be appropriated to Connecticut because the Indians of that province 'have bin hitherto wholly neglected, & there is a word in the demise that seems to fix it there, for it is said the *neglected pagans*, which cannot be the Massachusett Indians after so much pains have been taken with them.' The Governor of Connecticut had written to the Company asking that his colony might be remembered in the distribution of funds. Dummer informed his correspondent that he had handed this letter to the Company and added: 'I think I have interest enough with them to carry it so' but pointed out that there was no hurry because of 'a life upon the Estate.'[2]

Dummer proved right for it was not until July 1746, after Mrs. Hannah Bradley's death, that the Company formally resolved to accept

[1] P.C.C. 218 Fox; *N.E.H.G.R.*, XLVI (1892), 436–9; S. K. Jones, *Dr. Williams and his Library*, 8–9.

[2] *C.S.M.*, VI (1904), 179–82.

the trusts placed upon it under the terms of Dr. Williams's will.[1] The trust was to administer the farm called Tolleshunt, Beckenham Hall, near Malden, Essex, which had fallen into very bad repair during the life of Mrs. Hannah Bradley. It was for this reason that the Company requested Harvard College to allow money to be spent on its repair. The College gave the Company *carte blanche* in the matter, asking it to do whatever was necessary.[2] By the time these repairs had been carried out the annual rents were about £135 per annum, of which £60 was appropriated for the salaries of two itinerant preachers and the remainder was ordered to be paid to Harvard College.

So difficult was it to find missionaries that the Company decided to raise the salaries offered from £30 to £45 per annum and in order to do this, in 1769, appropriated the interest from £1,200 invested in South Sea stock. In fact, this yielded £42 per annum so that the salaries offered were now £51.[3] Jasper Mauduit wrote to Andrew Oliver, the Commissioners' Secretary and Treasurer, in March 1768 informing him of this plan and asking him to send the names of two missionaries for the approval of Dr. Williams's Trustees.[4]

The Company found it difficult enough to apply the rents arising from the Tolleshunt estate for the ends intended under Dr. Williams's will, but the President and Fellows of Harvard College found it even more difficult. In fact, both Boyle's and Williams's bequests provided the President and Fellows with an embarrassing problem: they would have had no difficulty in spending the money for the good of the College, but to find missionaries was not an easy matter. It was upon this subject that they wrote to Jasper Mauduit on 30 November 1769: they had neglected no opportunity of improving the donation and had 'not scrupled to improve it in the general service of the College.' However, separate accounts had been kept and at no point had they departed from

[1] Ms. 7952; Dr. Williams's Trustees were notified of the death of Mrs. Bradley on 14 Oct. 1745. On 9 April 1746 they ordered all papers relating to the Essex estate to be handed to the New England Company. (Dr. Williams's Library, Trustees' Minutes, 1742–8, No. 12, pp. 50, 54.)

[2] *C.S.M.*, XVI (1925), 780.

[3] Ms. 7912/2, f. 24. Mauduit reported to Dr. Williams's Trustees on 29 March 1769. (Dr. Williams's Library, Trustees' Minutes, 1755–86, p. 171.)

[4] Ms. 7927, f. 15.

the spirit of Dr. Williams's will. It was, they argued, no longer possible to pay a salary to a minister who converted the Indians as a part-time occupation, because the Commissioners already supported those ministers who had any claim to this kind of assistance.[1] To educate the Indians themselves had been proved, time and again, an undertaking fraught with difficulties, while to use the money for the education of missionaries was hazardous, as students were likely to change their minds upon graduating.

In May 1770 Mauduit wrote to Nathaniel Appleton, the senior Fellow of Harvard, and informed him that, though he had reported to Dr. Williams's Trustees the difficulties of finding missionaries, the trustees had resolved that Dr. Williams's wishes must be observed and considered that two missionaries should be sent to some part of America where the French influence did not prevail.[2] Accordingly the College undertook to make up the salaries of the two missionaries appointed by the Company from the surplus which had accumulated since the first payments from the charity had been made. Dr. Williams's Trustees were informed of this in March 1771 and were presented with an account of the application of the funds by the College. The Trustees declared themselves 'greatly pleased' and entirely agreed with the College's intention of making up the salaries of the Company's missionaries.[3] In April 1771 Mauduit wrote to Andrew Oliver informing him that the Company had sent £750 for Samuel Kirkland's mission and that in future Harvard would be able to support this mission, as the College had £1,000 of Dr. Williams's money in hand.[4]

Apart from the money left by Robert Boyle and Daniel Williams, the Company received a number of smaller bequests. During the last decade of the seventeenth century, Benjamin Williams gave £70 in five payments. Roger Lock, an extremely active member of the Company, gave £100 in 1698 and a further £30 at his death in 1703. The next bequest was an Exchequer annuity of £25 made in 1715 by the execu-

[1] M.H.S. Ms.

[2] Ms. 7927, f. 24; cf. Dr. Williams's Library, Trustees' Minutes, 1755–86, p. 182.

[3] Dr. Williams's Library, Trustees' Minutes, 1755–86, p. 193.

[4] Ms. 7927, f. 26.

tors of Edward Barton of Hackney, a member of the Company. In February 1717/18 the Company received £160 from the widow of the Rev. Matthew Henry. Henry had been a nonconformist minister at Chester for many years, but two years before his death had moved to Mare Street, Hackney. Sir Henry Ashurst had left £800 to Henry to dispose of 'as he should think would be most for the Glory of God.' Three years later, in 1720, the Company received £500 from Joshua Brice, executor of James Hulbert, who had been elected a member of the Company in 1704. This was the largest cash bequest received by the Company during the eighteenth century. Other gifts and bequests were: Ursula Yale's £20 in 1730; Samuel Sheafe's £50 in the following year; Samuel Palmer's £300 in 1734; Henry Palmer's £100 in 1741; ten guineas from Josiah Chitty, a member of the Company, in 1742; Samuel Harris' £100 in 1746; Nathaniel Carpenter's £50 in 1752 and in the same year the same amount from Joseph Williams, who had served the Company as Treasurer from about 1729 until 1748. In 1756 John Howard paid £100, the legacy of Mrs. Mary Howard, to the Company: 'to be applyd solely to preaching ye Gospell amongst ye Indians & not for ye schools.' This was unusual, for donors seldom specified the way in which they wanted their money to be spent. John Howard accepted a consequent invitation to become a member of the Company. In 1750 Joan Collibee of Bath gave £100 and left a further £200 in her will, which the Company received in 1758. The accounts show one other bequest of £100 made in 1757 by Harding Tomkins and Joshua Lock.[1]

These gifts came the Company's way without any effort on its part. A few gifts were also made in New England: Governor Dudley gave £20 in February 1708/9.[2] Mrs. Hezekiah Usher junior in her will of 1723 left £400 for charitable purposes, of which the Company received one quarter;[3] Benjamin Marston bequeathed the rent of Misery Island in Salem Harbour, after the death of his wife;[4] Richard Martin, a Boston shopkeeper, by his will of 1761 bequeathed one third of his estate to 'the Society in New England for propagating the Gospel among the Indians

[1] Ms. 7911/2, f. 4; Ms. 7911/3, f. 3, 7; Ms. 7912/1, f. 23.

[2] Ms. 7953/5.

[3] M.H.S. *Collections, 6th series*, II, 217 *et seq.*

[4] Sibley, VI, 96.

in America' but the Company's claim to this bequest was contested in several quarters.[1]

The Company's estates occupied most of the attention of members at their meetings. But apart from the property left the Company by Dr. Williams, the landed property in the Company's care remained much the same as it had been in the seventeenth century and yielded about the same amount of rent. In the 1760s the rents from the manor of Eriswell amounted to £182, Chamberlains to £135, Plumstead farm in Kent brought in £80, and London properties in Trinity Lane, Bucklersbury and Poultry yielded about £229 per annum.[2] The most important additions to the Company's property were several purchases of land adjoining Eriswell and Chamberlains, made between 1767 and 1778 at a total cost of £1430.[3] There remained, of course, the endless problems of arrears of rent and of demands for abatement of rent on various grounds. For example one tenant had replaced old buildings which had fallen about his ears with new ones, another had lost his farm-house, stables and barn by fire, while a third wrote to Sir William Ashurst in 1708 pleading: 'Sir, I beleive you are not ignorant what seasons and prizes we have had ever since I have been concerned in the farm, all ye summers (but this) haveing been very dry, and our hot sands produced but very little corn; and Rey and sheep (on which the proffitts of the farm cheifly consist) so cheap as they have not been (so long together) in the life of man.'[4] One of the Trinity Lane tenants demanded abatement because the sugar baking house was in need of extensive repair, adding: 'I am told many New Sugar houses have of late yeares been built near the River side which are much more convenient, & indeed the Town is overstock'd with Sugar houses.'[5] In addition to its rents, the Company had, by 1764, £5,000 invested in South Sea stock which yielded about £175 per annum.[6]

[1] Ms. 7927, f. 5, 6; Ms. 7952, 6 April 1764; Register House, S.S.P.C.K. Minutes, V, 62–3.

[2] Ms. 7913/1, f. 1–2.

[3] Ms. 7912/2, f. 41.

[4] Ms. 7956, John Cocksedge to Sir William Ashurst, 26 July 1708.

[5] *Ibid.*, Robert Stamper to John Gunston, 27 July 1725.

[6] Ms. 7912/2, f. 5.

The Company was not always fortunate in its choice of servants. In 1709 John Bellamy, the current Secretary, sustained heavy financial losses in his private business. He was declared bankrupt, the Company recovering only £2. 18s. of the £116 which he owed it. A memorandum in an account recorded unhappily: 'They say there will be a Distribution of 14 Pence & no more though once there was an Expectation of somewhat more.'[1] In 1725 John Carter, who had been responsible for collecting rents at Eriswell, died, owing the Company £240 which it was unable to recover.[2] Nearly forty years later the accounts still carried entries for these debts, no doubt serving as a reminder of the hazards of administering trust funds.

Bills of exchange were still normally used for conveying these funds to the Commissioners in New England. But sometimes other arrangements were made, as when Increase Mather was in London in 1691–2; on this occasion the Company paid his expenses in England, amounting to £400, while the Massachusetts government, on whose behalf he was acting, undertook to repay the Commissioners at the rate of 28 per cent interest. The Commissioners wrote to the Governor, Robert Thompson, in February 1692/3: 'The Government here are very thankfull to your Honour for Supplying Mr Mather with that Summe to be Expended in their Service: and they pray that you would please to shew ye Like kindness in Supplying Sir Henry Ashurst & Mr Constantine Phips as they shall have occasion for disbursements in behalf of ye Country, which will bee accepted as a great favour by this Government: & their bills will without fail wee trust bee answered as you shall appoint.'[3]

Sending goods to New England for sale or distribution amongst the Indians was no longer practised in the eighteenth century, with one notable exception. In October 1705, and then on and off for the next seventy years, the Company sent two bales of duffel or blankets for distribution amongst the Indians. The first consignment of 'Mazarine Blew Duffills' costing £50 was purchased from Sir Edward Wills, a woollen draper and a member of the Company.[4] The duffel was a great success with the Indians; Sewall explained that he tried to delay its distribution

[1] Ms. 7911/3, f. 6; Ms. 7913/1, f. 3.
[2] Ms. 7913/1, f. 3.
[3] Ms. 7955/1, no. 2a.
[4] Ms. 7911/2, f. 32.

amongst them until October or November, but 'when that time comes there's no delaying them Longer: the pinching Cold also makes them deaf to denial: And being out, I was fain to buy a Bale of Duffal to furnish them.'[1] The Commissioners, too, were pleased with the duffel and ordered: 'For the encouragement of good government among the Indians in their several Hamlets . . . that every Indian Justice have a Coat of Duffal made them.'[2]

One other commodity the Company sent to New England: books, not for the Indians, but for Harvard College Library. In 1724 Thomas Hollis, a Company member who was one of Harvard's chief patrons, founder of chairs in Divinity, Mathematics and Natural Philosophy, proposed that, as Harvard Library lacked 'numbers of useful books fitting for such a library', £100 should be voted for this purpose. He justified his proposal: 'You send books to the Indians, you pay masters and ministers to instruct them, you send out orders to seek out Indian youth fitting to send to College at the Corporation's expense. I argue, How shall youth be instructed, if such books as are necessary are wanting in the library?'[3] The Company, however, was at first unconvinced by these arguments, and so Thomas Hollis made bequests himself. But when the disastrous fire of 1764 destroyed the whole Library the Company decided to lend its assistance. On 6 April Jasper Mauduit reported the catastrophe to the Company's Court; the donation of money towards rebuilding the Library was considered, but 'the Court having taken into Consideration the Intention of the Charter — And that the said Colledge had heretofore and still continued to be of great Service in educating and instructing Young men who have afterwards become & probably may be useful Missionaries among the Heathen Indians — And Whereas the Works of pious and learned Authors are among the most necessary means of Education and Instruction — do Resolve that the Treasurer do apply a sum of money not exceeding £200 towards purchasing such Books as he shall think most usefull for the said Purpose.'[4]

[1] Ms. 7955/1, no. 6. [2] Ms. 7953/6, 17 Oct. 1710.

[3] J. Quincy, *The History of Harvard University* (Cambridge, Mass., 1840), I, 431.

[4] Ms. 7952. Mauduit notified Andrew Oliver of this decision in a letter of 10 April 1764 (Ms. 7927, f. 6).

Thomas Hollis, grand-nephew of Harvard's great benefactor, and inheritor of his fortune, gave £200 for the purchase of scientific apparatus, which donation was entrusted to the Company;[1] he also presented a large number of books directly to the Library. A convinced republican, he spent several hundred pounds a year on gifts to libraries — books, medals and prints, calculated to foster his political views, and the Harvard fire proved an ideal opportunity for his generosity.

Jasper Mauduit wrote to the Overseers of Harvard on 12 April 1764 informing them of the Company's gift and at the same time asking for 'a list of such as were destroy'd by the late fire and will be useful.' In August of the same year he wrote again announcing that the Archbishop of York had contributed and that many smaller sums might be expected. Dr. Avery, who had died earlier in the year, had unfortunately given away many of his books six months before, but his executors had promised the College any of those books which remained and would be of use, and in fact the Company purchased about fifteen pounds' worth from this source.[2]

Four cases of books costing £150 were purchased from James Buckland, a London bookseller who specialized in theological works.[3] It was no doubt partly for this reason that Mauduit dealt with him, but also because he was himself an eminent dissenter, 'respected for simplicity of manners, and irreproachable integrity.'[4] On 8 March 1765 the Company received a vote of thanks from the Overseers for the assistance it had given, whereupon the Court voted that a further £100 be devoted to the purchase of books.[5] Mauduit wrote to the Rev. Edward Holyoke on 19 March 1765 informing him of this further gift and asking what books were still required by the Library, taking into account books which had been received from other sources.[6] Meanwhile some well-wishers sent

[1] Francis Blackburne, *Memoirs of Thomas Hollis* (1780), 217; Ms. 7927, f. 7.

[2] Ms. 7927, f. 7.

[3] Ms. 7912/1, f. 92.

[4] C. H. Timperley, *A Dictionary of Printers* (1839), 765.

[5] Ms. 7952. This further gift was the subject of a renewed vote of thanks by the Overseers, a copy of which dated 1 Oct. 1765 is contained in Ms. 7961.

[6] Ms. 7927, f. 9. A copy of the list sent over is contained in the Company's archives (Ms. 7960) and virtually constitutes a catalogue of the Library at this time.

their donations to the Company to be forwarded to the College: amongst these were the Rev. William Harris of Honiton, Devonshire; Dr. Nathaniel Lardner, the famous biblical scholar; Nathaniel Neal, brother-in-law of Lardner and son of Daniel Neal, the historian; and Daniel Neal's son-in-law, Joseph Jennings, son of the distinguished nonconformist minister, Dr. David Jennings.[1] Mauduit wrote again to Holyoke on 10 October 1766 to say that a case had been dispatched containing the remainder of the books purchased by Dr. Chandler, 'a quantity of pamphlets' from Dr. Avery's library given by the executors when Mauduit paid for the other books, six 'books of the Reformd pastor' the gift of Samuel Palmer, minister of the Independent congregation at Mare Street, Hackney, and some pamphlets from his own library.[2] In the list of bequests to the Library the Company's contribution appears as '1101 vols. and £300', while it was put on record: 'Catalogues were sent to Jasper Mauduit, Esq., by whose care this money was laid out to such advantage that the books completely fill an alcove, over which is this inscription, "Societas de Propag. Evang. in Nov. Anglia et Partibus Adjacent" 1101 Vols.'[3]

In June 1766, the second vote for books — £100 — had been paid to Israel Mauduit, Jasper's brother, and in December of the same year the balance of the original grant of £200, amounting to just over £27, was also paid to him. The College had presumably entrusted him with the purchase of more books.[4] It was not until 1769 that Mauduit found an opportunity of spending part of the £200 earmarked by Thomas Hollis for apparatus for the College. In that year he paid £147 to Dr. Benjamin Franklin who purchased 'a large reflecting tellescope' for one hundred guineas and 'an equal altitude Instrument' for forty guineas.[5]

There was another occasion during the eighteenth century when the Company helped the College. In 1709 it began the long legal proceedings which resulted in the recovery of a legacy under the will of Edward Hopkins. Hopkins had died in 1657 leaving a reversionary bequest of

[1] Ms. 7961.

[2] Ms. 7927, f. 10–11.

[3] J. Quincy, *The History of Harvard University*, II, 493, 495.

[4] Ms. 7912/2, f. 40.

[5] Ms. 7927, f. 21, J. Mauduit to Rev. A. Eliot, 13 Sept. 1769.

£500 to be spent on educating 'hopeful youths in a way of learning, both at the grammar school and college.' At the time of his death the Society had inspected his will hoping to find a bequest from its deceased member, but found that Hopkins had made no gift specifically to the Society, so the matter was dropped. More than half a century later Matthew Evans, of Clement's Inn, advised the Company that it should try to recover this bequest,[1] and two years later the Lord Chancellor was asked to place the £500 (with interest) in the hands of the Company and its Commissioners to be administered by them. It suggested that not more than half should go to Harvard and the the rest should go to a grammar school. This solution was not acceptable and in November 1712 Henry Newman, Harvard's agent in London, and Jeremiah Dummer, agent for Massachusetts, suggested that one quarter should go to educating five boys at Cambridge grammar school and the other three quarters should be devoted to educating four students of divinity at Harvard. The Company approved this arrangement but the Lord Chancellor was not prepared to make an order for the recovery of the money unless a purchase was made with it.[2] The Commissioners conferred with Harvard's Fellows to decide upon a suitable purchase for an investment.[3] The Company received the money, amounting to £869. 14s. 1d., on 31 March 1715.[4] It was transferred to New England and acknowledged by Sewall in a letter of September 1715.[5] A few weeks earlier he had written to the Company explaining that the General Court had given licence to purchase a considerable tract of land 'that I hope will give Satisfaction to those in England who have been Instrumental in Conveying this charity to us.' He was able to report in September that he had seen this land, which was about twenty miles west of Boston, and was called Magunkog. But he continued: 'The

[1] Ms. 7956, letter to John Bellamy, 10 March 1708.

[2] Ms. 7952, 11 July 1710, 6 Nov. 1712, 25 Sept. 1713.

[3] Ms. 7953/8, 17 July 1712.

[4] Ms. 7911/3, f. 2.

[5] Ms. 7955/1, no. 34. In July 1722 Henry Newman asked the President of Harvard for a copy of the deed of purchase under the college seal to show the Lord Chancellor 'and be at ye same time enabled to take up a Bond which Sir William Ashurst, Mr Dummer & I gave for its being duly executed.' Society for Promoting Christian Knowledge, New England Letter book, 1721–3, f. 19 (CN3/1).

Indians, at present, shew some Indisposition to part with it. This arises as I conjecture, from the Influence of English-men, who hanker after it themselves. But I hope that Difficulty will be surmounted, when the Natives shall be perswaded to consider that the Purchase-Money is to be husbanded by the Commissioners, for the benefit of the Indians, especially the Inhabitants of Natick.' In March 1716/17 Sewall informed Sir William Ashurst that the Massachusetts General Court had given five or six thousand acres of land adjoining Hopkinton, as it was now called, as an addition to the town. But the administration of Hopkinton was placed in the hands of trustees. It was, therefore, purely as a matter of interest that Sewall reported in June 1718 that extravagant grants at Hopkinton had caused the trustees much work 'to reduce them to their just Measures.'[1]

Whereas, during the seventeenth century, the New England Company was the only body in the British Isles which promoted missionary endeavours in New England, in the eighteenth century it was by no means alone in the field. One of the bodies with which it came into contact was the Society in Scotland for Propagating Christian Knowledge. In 1701 a small number of Edinburgh citizens formed a society for the reformation of manners, having as its principal object the combating of Popery in the Highlands. It obtained a charter in 1709 and less than twenty years later it was financing more than seventy Scottish schools. The work of setting up and maintaining these schools fully occupied its members and absorbed its annual revenue.[2] In fact, the Society in Scotland entered the field of foreign missions quite fortuitously and against the better judgment of some of its members. It would almost certainly have continued to devote itself exclusively to its activities in the Highlands and Islands had not Dr. Daniel Williams included it in his will. During his lifetime he had made the Scottish Society a gift of nearly £128 without any conditions as to how it should be spent.[3]

[1] Ms. 7955/1, nos. 33, 34, 43, 45; Letter book (Univ. of Va. Ms.), 92–141 *passim.*

[2] H. Hunter, *A Brief History of the Society in Scotland for Propagating Christian Knowledge* (1795), 6–16.

[3] Register House, S.S.P.C.K., Minutes, I, 115–16, 204; Committee minutes, I, 195; General ledger, 1709–79, 27.

But in his will be bequeathed his estates at Catworth, Huntingdonshire, to the Society on condition that it first send three qualified missionaries into 'foreign Infidel countries' for a year at its own expense, and thereafter spend the rents arising from the estate on financing foreign missions. The Society's members did their utmost to persuade Dr. Williams's Trustees to modify the terms of the bequest 'with regard to the smalness of their stock and the Great Ignorance that prevails amongst the poor people in the vast and desolate bounds of the Highlands and Islands of Scotland which necessarily requires a greater number of schools than they have been yet able to support upon their yearly revenue.' They continued to plead that they 'were discouraged from looking after the forsaid Legacie, because the Condition adjected to the Donors Grant seemed to them Impracticable.'[1] Impracticable or no, Dr. Williams's trustees refused to modify in any way the conditions set out in the will. It was thus that the Society entered the missionary field in New England, appointing in 1730 a board of Correspondents to see to its interests there. Three missionaries were duly appointed: Joseph Seccomb at Fort George, George's River, Ebenezer Hinsdale at Fort Dummer on Connecticut River and Stephen Parker at Fort Richmond, each at a salary of £20 sterling. Although the Massachusetts government paid them an additional salary of £100 each for their services as chaplains to the forces stationed at these forts, by 1737 the Boston Correspondents were so dissatisfied with the three ministers that they were dismissed. However these attempts proved sufficient to satisfy Dr. Williams's Trustees that the conditions specified in the will had been complied with. The Catworth estate was, therefore, duly transferred to the Society, at which time its annual value after the deduction of taxes amounted to about £56.[2]

It was not until 1756 that the Company and the Scottish Society began to co-operate. This was brought about by the Rev. Samuel Davies, who was to become President of the College of New Jersey. Davies, when in England, had been an intimate acquaintance of Jasper Mauduit, and it was to Mauduit that he had first expounded his plan for sending a schoolmaster and a missionary to the Catawba Indians. Upon further

[1] Register House, S.S.P.C.K., Committee minutes, III, 148–9.

[2] H. Hunter, *A Brief History of the Society in Scotland*, 30–31.

consideration he had decided that the Cherokee nation was larger and of more importance than the Catawba. Accordingly he wrote to Mauduit suggesting that if the Company did not have sufficient funds to send missions to both of these tribes, it would be more profitable to concentrate upon the Cherokee. But he proposed that two missionaries and two schoolmasters should be sent to keep each other company.[1]

In 1705, when the matter of sending missionaries as far as Virginia had been mooted in the Company's Court, there were members who thought that the charter prevented it from going so far afield, and for this reason it was decided to seek counsel's opinion. In October 1709, when Sir Edmund Harrison reported that he had several letters from ministers in New England asking that missionaries might be sent further south, the court ruled that it had insufficient funds and that in any case it was 'without the Limits of their Charity.'[2] But on this occasion the question of the territorial limitations of the charter does not seem to have been raised. In October 1756 the Company appointed a committee to confer with Adam Anderson, the Scottish Society's secretary in London, about Davies's suggestion. The Company proposed that it should send one minister and one schoolmaster to the Cherokee on condition that the Scottish Society do the same. The Society's general meeting was advised by its committee to accept the proposal, as the Company had formerly given £90 to two of the Scottish Society's missionaries, Azariah Horton and one of the Brainerd brothers, and had also paid the salary of William Tennent, who visited an Indian congregation under John Brainerd's care. The proposal was thereupon accepted and £60 per annum was voted for the purpose. It was originally arranged that the Scottish Society's contribution should be paid to the Company, which would then convey it to Commissioners to be appointed in Virginia. However, the Scottish Society decided, after the initial payment, to act independently, although the Company remained ignorant of the fact until 1760 when it demanded payment of the Society's share. The fact remains that Davies's suggestion had borne fruit, although he had asked for £240 and had received only half that

[1] *Memoir of the Rev. Samuel Davies* (Boston, Massachusetts Sabbath School Society, 1832), 115–17.

[2] Ms. 7952.

amount; the Company warned him that he must be as frugal as possible.[1]

But the problem was still the same — that of finding suitable missionaries, especially when frugality was the order of the day. In February 1758 the Company heard from Davies that John Martin had gone as a missionary to the Cherokee at a salary of £30 per annum.[2] His place was taken by W. Richardson, at the same salary, but not for long; Richardson himself related: 'In *October* 1758, I undertook a mission to the *Cherokees*; hearing from Mr *Martin*, my predecessor, their desire to be instructed in the Christian faith; but by the time I got to that nation they were much of another opinion, several of their people having been killed by the *Virginians*. . . . This enraged them so much, that after I had stayed near three months among them I could not prevail on them to give me a public hearing, except in one small town.'[3] Nor were his successors any more successful: in 1760 a Mr. Holt received £40 and John Tod £14. 11s. for their missionary labours. But by 1763 this mission, like so many others, had to be abandoned: in this instance the Indians joined in the hostilities with the French against Great Britain. The last payment made was to Martin in June 1763.[4]

Though relations between the Company and the Scottish Society had been cordial they were not improved by the Society's support of Wheelock's plans for collecting funds in England and Scotland. Eleazar Wheelock, a leading New Light in the Great Awakening, had been violently attacked by the Boston clergy, and twenty years later was still regarded with suspicion in Boston. During the 1750s he had started a school for Indian children, afterwards known as Moor's Indian Charity School, which aimed to remove native children from the influence of their parents and their tribe and to bring them up with English children. From 1756 the Company had supported his endeavours,[5] but when he

[1] Register House, S.S.P.C.K., Minutes, IV, 596; Ms. 7952.

[2] Ms. 7952.

[3] *Letters from the Rev. Samuel Davies and others: shewing the State of Religion in Virginia* . . . (1761), 20.

[4] Ms. 7912/1, f. 81; H. Hunter, *A Brief History*, 33.

[5] J. D. McCallum, ed., *The Letters of Eleazar Wheelock's Indians* (Hanover, N.H., 1932), 301. Total payments by the Company to Wheelock amounted to £164. 10s.

started raising funds in England it not only withdrew its support but severed all connections with him. The story of this rupture reflects little credit upon either of the parties concerned.

In 1765 the Connecticut Board of the Scottish Society decided, at Wheelock's suggestion, to send Nathaniel Whitaker and Samson Occom to England to collect funds for the Indian school. Occom, an Indian minister, was to be the show piece. He had first turned to religion when the Great Awakening swept over New England and had then been brought up by Wheelock, who was subsidized by the Commissioners. In 1751 Occom had been allowed £15 for his services at Montauk on the eastern extremity of Long Island. Five years later the Commissioners recommended that he should be ordained, but when Wheelock and several other New Light ministers examined him the Commissioners changed their minds. It was not until 1759 that he was ordained by the Long Island presbytery. By this time he had run into debt, the Commissioners offering assistance to the extent of £20. The Scottish Society employed him to preach to the Oneida tribe and in 1764 the Commissioners sent him as a missionary to the Niantics. However, the newly formed Connecticut Board then took him into its employ with the consent of the Boston Commissioners.[1]

Thus, it was only human that the Commissioners should feel irritated when Wheelock asked them to support Occom's and Whitaker's mission to England. They were, in any case, distrustful of Wheelock for the part he had played in the Great Awakening, and resentful of his sending out missionaries on his own authority without first consulting them. They may also have anticipated adverse comparison of their efforts with his.[2] It was in this frame of mind that they wrote, on 2 October 1765, warning the Company of the forthcoming visit of Occom and Whitaker and giving an account of Occom, the most damaging part of which read:

> How Mr Occom hath been employed since he left us we know not excepting that he hath been preaching in the principal Towns of this & the neighbour-

[1] W. de L. Love, *Samson Occom and the Christian Indians of New England* (Boston, Mass., 1899); Harold Blodgett, *Samson Occom* (Hanover, N.H., 1935).

[2] E. Wheelock, *A plain and faithful Narrative* (Boston, 1763), 20, 23.

ing Governments among the white People, & by some Means or other *where ever he came*, a report prevailed that he was a Mohawk lately emergent out of gross Paganism, & fitted in a very little Time by Mr Wheelock to be what he is — The Report of an Indian so lately brought from Heathenism, & fitted in such a short Time to fill a christian Pulpit, so affected People *where ever he came*, as to be a Means of procuring large Contributions for Mr Wheelock.[1]

The point was taken by the Company and Mauduit wrote in March 1766 thanking them for their 'candid account of Samson Occom.'[2] Whitaker heard of the letter soon after his arrival in London and was very apprehensive of the damage it might do to his cause. When, at his own request, he was actually shown the letter by Mauduit his anger knew no bounds. It was, he declared, 'a wicked devilish thing'. Whitaker asked Mauduit for a copy and was refused one, while Wheelock wrote to Andrew Oliver (who had actually signed the letter in the name of the Commissioners) asking for a copy, but he too was refused. Whitaker, who enjoyed nothing so well as strife, wrote to his mentor in New England: 'Mauduit is not 6d better than Oliver, but really worse' and added darkly, 'If the affair comes to an open debate, I Suspect it will devide between the two orders of Calvinists & Armenians thro' the Kingdom & tho' I would do nothing to Set these in opposition, yet it may be that God Sees it for the good of his Church here.'[3] Needless to say the Company contributed nothing to Whitaker's and Occom's collection and only one member, Thomas Hollis, made an individual contribution.[4] Nevertheless, they succeeded in collecting over £12,000.

The Company made no secret of its disapproval of Wheelock and on 31 March 1767 ordered the Commissioners to discontinue the payment of £20 per annum to his school, 'having been credibly Informd & beleiving that he by his Agents has collected great Sums of Money in England for the use of the said School.'[5] Relations between the Com-

[1] From a copy made from memory by Whitaker. L. B. Richardson, *An Indian Preacher in England* (Hanover, N. H., 1933), 137.

[2] Ms. 7927, f. 9.

[3] L. B. Richardson, *An Indian Preacher in England*, 161, 166.

[4] E. Wheelock, *A Continuation of the Narrative* (1769), 85–91.

[5] Ms. 7952.

missioners and Wheelock reached a climax in November 1767. Wheelock had charged them with 'Falshoods even gross Falshoods, and scarce anything but Falsehoods.' To this Andrew Oliver, on the Commissioners' behalf, answered that it was 'a Charge so illiberal, that we shall henceforward be obliged to forbear any further correspondence with you.'[1] Nor did the feeling against Wheelock subside when it became generally known that he wanted to devote the money collected to founding a college primarily for English students: Mauduit wrote to Nathaniel Appleton, Senior Fellow of Harvard, on 12 May 1770, reporting that the trustees of Dr. Williams's charity had 'expressed their dislike of Dr Wheelock's Intent of founding another English College' and that the New England Company would have expressed itself in the same way had the matter come before its Court. Mauduit promised to do his best to dissuade Dr. Wheelock's Trustees from allowing the money to be spent on a new college 'as changing if not perverting the profest design of the Donors.'[2] In 1771 resolutions of disapproval were passed by Dr. Williams's Trustees and by the Company but they were of no avail in preventing the foundation of Dartmouth College.[3]

The Society for the Propagation of the Gospel in Foreign Parts, which was chartered in 1701, was never closely associated with the Company, indeed there was often unveiled antipathy between them. In March 1703/4 Sir William Ashurst wrote to Sewall urging the Commissioners to send some missionaries among the Five Nations bordering on New York — 'to which not only our duty but reputacion does oblidge us, since there is now Erecting a new Corporacion for the same purpose amongst the Bishops and others of the church of England, who (by the accounts they have printed) have put their project into a very good posture for success.' The S.P.G., according to Ashurst in a letter of August 1704, had intimated that there were no ministers in several parts of New England where the Company had its ministers. 'I suppose they mean they are not ministers because not episcopal,' he added. At the

[1] Letter dated 11 Nov. 1767 (M.H.S. Ms.).

[2] Ms. 7927, f. 24.

[3] Ms. 7956, J. Mauduit to the Commissioners' Treasurer, 10 April 1771; Ms. 7927, f. 26–27; L. B. Richardson, *History of Dartmouth College* (Hanover, N.H., 1932), I, 13–90.

same time he asked for details of any of the Company's successes 'that we may have something to answer these gentlemen who seem so forward to lessen what has been done by this Company that they may gain the greater reputacion to their own.'[1]

Early in 1714, 'that cursed Vermin called high Church',[2] as Sir William Ashurst immoderately described it, threatened to investigate the Company's affairs in New England. Whether these threats were in any way prompted by the S.P.G. can only be surmised but they were sufficiently serious to throw Samuel Sewall into a flurry. One evening Sir Charles Hobby, Lieutenant Governor of Massachusetts, and a High Churchman, called at Sewall's house and asked to see the Company's commission. Afterwards Sewall wrote: 'I readily fetch'd it to him, and he took what time he pleased to read it by my Fire. Then he asked to carry it home with him; I told him I could not do that, and would not: the Corporation had committed it to me and it behov'd me to keep it. He grew pretty warm; at last desired a copy of it.' This too the ever cautious Sewall refused. He also warned the Company: 'General Nicholson took occasion once in Council to say that he must shortly call the Commissioners to an Account. . . . My opinion is, and of the Commissioners so far as I can Learn that if an Account be demanded, General Nicholson be refer'd to the Governour & Company at Home.'[3] Sir William Ashurst replied that this news 'would have given us some uneasyness if we were not conscious of our having faithfully discharged the trust invested in us by our Charter.' But the Company would not submit to any 'indifferent authority' which General Nicholson's was judged to be and in any case the Providence of God had brought what authority he had to an end.[4]

In 1727 the S.P.G. received a petition from Charles Augustus Ninagret, sachem of the Narragansett. He asked that a missionary might be sent to his people and promised in return to give a tract of land on which to build a church and as a glebe for the minister. The S.P.G., being vaguely aware that the New England Company existed for

[1] Letter book (Univ. of Va. Ms.), 60, 64.
[2] *Ibid.*, 162.
[3] Ms. 7955/1, no. 26.
[4] Letter book (Univ. of Va. Ms.), 140.

exactly this kind of purpose, sent on the petition to the Company's Governor. He, in due course, sent it on to the Commissioners but regarded it with the gravest suspicion because of its origin.[1]

The next occasion on which the Company came into contact with the S.P.G. was happier. In 1742 Thomas Wilson, son of the Bishop of Sodor and Man, offered to the Company a stock of his father's little book: *The Knowledge and Practice of Christianity Made Easy To the Meanest Capacities: or, an Essay Towards an Instruction for the Indians* (1742). Dedicated to the Archbishop of Canterbury, the Society for the Propagation of the Gospel in Foreign Parts and the Society for Promoting Christian Knowledge, it was the product of a High Churchman and as such was hardly the kind of work which would be welcomed in New England. Nevertheless the Company accepted the gift and in due course Andrew Oliver acknowledged the receipt of one hundred copies, promising that they would be distributed to the Indians.[2]

In New England it was generally believed that the S.P.G. was more concerned with the conversion of Congregationalists and Presbyterians to Anglicanism than with the conversion of Indians to Christianity. This view became most widespread in the 1760s, when Jonathan Mayhew published his *Observations on the Charter and Conduct of the Society for the Propagation of the Gospel in Foreign Parts* (Boston, New England, 1763). It was at this time that the Massachusetts General Assembly passed an act to incorporate a Society for Propagating Christian Knowledge among the Indians in North America.[3] Although this act required the royal assent before it could come into force, the Bostonians who promoted it met on 6 May 1762 and appointed James Bowdoin their President, the Rev. Joseph Sewall Vice-President, James Pitts Treasurer and Samuel Cooper Secretary. A few days later, on 13 May, they decided to ask Mauduit to obtain royal confirmation for the act.[4] They also succeeded in collecting about £2,000 towards sending a mission to

[1] *Ibid.*, 203; S.P.G. Journal, V, 146.

[1] Ms. 7955/2, no. 144. Wilson's book appeared in several editions: either the 2nd (1741) or the 3rd (1742) was sent to New England.

[3] *Acts and Resolves . . . of the Province of the Massachusetts Bay*, IV (Boston, Mass., 1890), 562–3.

[4] Ms. 7956, Copy proceedings.

Canada.[1] On 16 May the Company resolved that it would contribute to the new Society when it had heard its plans. Mauduit wrote to Oliver on 27 April 1762 reiterating the Company's readiness to contribute, but adding: 'how far we shall incorporate with them must be prudently Considered.' The Commissioners, on the other hand, wholeheartedly supported the new Society so that in October the Company's Court expressed surprise that the Commissioners should have contributed without consulting it or even explaining the plans of the new Society.[2]

Meanwhile the Rev. Jonathan Mayhew asked Thomas Hollis to use his influence on behalf of the new Society and to oppose the scheme for colonial bishops which was on foot. Hollis declined to take any part in either of these affairs but remarked that he considered the latter had long been talked of and was unlikely to come to anything. Nevertheless he recommended Jasper Mauduit as 'the properest person . . . to manage an opposition' to the scheme for colonial bishops because, since Dr. Avery's decline, he had become 'a leader among the dissenters, and in connection with People in Power.'[3] Mauduit did undertake the task of trying to obtain the royal assent for the act. He also did what he could to obtain the backing of members of the Company. 'But,' he wrote to Harrison Gray, 'you will yourself, Sir, easily see the impropriety of my solliciting Subscriptions to it, when I am myself not only a member, but Treasurer of another more antient Society.'[4] On 30 September 1762 he wrote to Andrew Oliver explaining that he could not proceed with obtaining the royal confirmation of the act as the Governor of the Company, Dr. Avery, was out of London and other members not available. He promised to place the matter before them in November. In April 1763 he wrote again to Oliver: 'We cannot have a Stronger Test by which to Judge of the Zeal of the Gentlemen at Boston . . . than their Voluntary subscribing to a Society of the same sort [as our own]; we would wish therefore to have Mr Bowdoin, Mr

[1] M.H.S. *Collections*, LXXIV, 75; Ms. 7955/2, no. 150, James Bowdoin to J. Mauduit, 13 May 1762.

[2] Ms. 7927, f. 1; Ms. 7952.

[3] M.H.S. *Proceedings*, LXIX (1956), 127–32.

[4] M.H.S. *Collections*, LXXIV, 75.

Harrison Gray & Dr Mahew appointed for the next Vacancies as our Commissioners.'[1]

The Church of England regarded the act of the Massachusetts Assembly as a direct blow aimed at the Society for the Propagation of the Gospel in Foreign Parts. The Archbishop of Canterbury was anxious, however, that the S.P.G. should not appear to oppose the new Society, as 'the answer would be that they have done little in this way themselves, & ought not to hinder others.'[2] But he did not abide by his own warning: both he and the S.P.G. spoke forcefully against the act, and, indeed, it was more by his efforts than by any other factor that the act was quashed. William Smith formulated the official Anglican attitude in a letter of 22 November 1762: the act would encroach upon the rights of other provinces, it would tend to upset royal plans for the management of Indian affairs, and it would create a society free from all civil control and responsible to no one. In a covering note to the Archbishop of Canterbury he pointed out that the real ground of opposition was that the royal confirmation of the act would be a blow to the S.P.G.[3] In May 1763 the Privy Council rejected the act on the grounds suggested to the Archbishop of Canterbury by William Smith.[4] Bostonians rightly interpreted the Privy Council's decision as the work of the Archbishop and the S.P.G., and even before he heard the news of the decision Andrew Oliver wrote to Mauduit: 'It is strange that Gentlemen who profess Christianity will not send the Gospel to the Heathen themselves nor permit it to be sent by others.'[5]

But in the following year the S.P.G. found itself bound to co-operate with the Company. This was unintentionally brought about by 'a worthy tho' plain Gentleman', Cornelius Bennet. Aged fifty and wish-

[1] Ms. 7927, f. 2, 5.

[2] W. S. Perry, ed., *Historical Collections relating to the American Colonial Church*, III (Hartford, 1873), 475.

[3] *Ibid.*, III, 477–81. The Bishop of London's copy endorsed 'Remarks on an Act lately passed in the Massachusetts Government received from the Archbishop of Canterbury, 1763' is in Lambeth Palace Library, Fulham Papers, Box 6, no. 179.

[4] *Acts of the Privy Council Colonial*, IV, 559–60; M.H.S. *Collections, 6th series*, IX, 14–16, gives Mauduit's report on the matter.

[5] M.H.S. *Collections*, LXXIV, 119.

ing to teach the Mohawks, but feeling himself too old to be ordained, he approached Dr. Samuel Johnson, the S.P.G.'s treasurer in America, for financial assistance. Johnson recommended him to the S.P.G. as a catechist in 1761 and again in 1762, but no assistance was immediately forthcoming. Meanwhile Bennet became impatient and obtained introductions to the Company's Commissioners at Boston. On 22 July 1763 they decided to allow him £20 and ordered that a letter be written to Dr. Johnson to assure him that they had not 'officiously engaged in this Affair', but that it had been suggested to them by his Excellency the Governor and by East Apthorp, the Anglican minister at Cambridge, Mass. In August 1763 Dr. Johnson wrote to the S.P.G. 'expressing his concern that the Society could not employ Mr Bennet as by that means the Dissenters are before hand with us', and reported that the Commissioners were 'so catholick' that they had allowed Bennet £20 'without obliging him to vary in the least from the Church of England.'[1] The S.P.G. in consequence agreed to supplement his salary. Meanwhile the Company was suitably gratified by the Commissioners' action and Mauduit wrote to Andrew Oliver on 10 April 1764 declaring that it did 'honour to our Commissioners, as making the first step in promoting that Charity which our common Lord has peremtory injoind on all his Disciples, notwithstanding, all have a Right to retain their different Sentiments in non Essentials. I think this may tend to quicken the same laudable Disposition in the Society for propagateing the Gospell in foreign parts.'[2]

The Commissioners continued to pay part of Bennet's salary for another year, during which he left the Mohawks on account of a smallpox epidemic and made a short visit to the Narragansett tribe in Rhode Island. But in September 1765 he wrote to the S.P.G. from Boston explaining that he was ill, and indeed soon afterwards he was dead. The co-operation between the S.P.G. and the New England Company was thus short-lived.[3]

The only other occasion on which the Company had dealings with

[1] S.P.G. Journal, XV, 190–91, 296; XVI, 5–6.

[2] Ms. 7927, f. 6.

[3] S.P.G. Journal, XVI, 329–30, 469; S.P.G. New England Letters B22 no. 73. Mrs. Ruth Bennet to the S.P.G.

the S.P.G. was in 1769 when the steward of Eriswell died; Dr. Daniel Burton, Secretary of the S.P.G., promptly sent a man to act as steward in his place, on behalf of his Society. The S.P.G.'s steward took possession of the books and papers relating to the estate and had even held a Court Leet and a Court Baron before the Company heard of what had happened. However, when the Company's clerk attended a meeting of the S.P.G. the mistake was admitted and the books and papers returned to their rightful owners.[1]

The Company's failure to secure the co-operation of the missionary societies which entered the field during the eighteenth century was regrettable rather than surprising. Such were the religious prejudices current at the time that each society tended to view with suspicion, and sometimes even with open hostility, the activities of other societies. It is thus far more significant that the Company did, on at least two occasions, attempt to co-operate, than that these attempts were failures.

[1] Ms. 7952, 19 July, 4 Aug. 1769; S.P.G. Journal, XVIII, 178.

8

The Commissioners for Indian Affairs, 1685–1776

THE Commissioners of the United Colonies held their last meeting in 1684. The Company was empowered by its charter to appoint commissioners of its own choosing to distribute the funds in New England, but this had been unnecessary until now. And even now the Company felt that none were more suitable than the men who already had experience of this work, so five Commissioners were asked to carry on as before — Simon Bradstreet, William Stoughton, Joseph Dudley, Peter Bulkeley and Thomas Hinckley.[1] They became known as the Commissioners for Indian Affairs, or Commissioners for Propagation of the Gospel.

During the 1680s both the Commissioners and the Company came in for some very severe criticism from Edward Randolph, who had already made some adverse comments upon the Company's work. He was at pains to draw attention to the Company and to suggest that its accounts might be thrown open for examination; he assured the recipients of his numerous reports and letters that such an examination would be worth while. In about 1684 he wrote: 'the money is bestowed upon some in ye Magistracy others in ye Ministry, rather as pension then, other publick good works proceeding from that charge, Christians becoming heathens, whilst endeavours are pretended to convert ye Infidels.'[2] On this occasion Randolph suggested that two able clergymen, recommended by the Bishop of London, should be sent over and should each be paid £100 per annum out of the Company's stock. Randolph wrote often on this subject to various people, including Dr. William Sancroft, Archbishop of Canterbury, and Henry Compton, Bishop of London. In a letter to the former dated 2 August 1686, he remarked: 'Its a great

[1] Minutes (M.H.S. Ms.), 30 Sept. 1685.

[2] R. N. Toppan, ed., *Edward Randolph*, III, 287.

pitty that there should be a Considerable stock in this Country (but how imployed I know not) & wee want 7 or 800 £ to build us a church.'[1] A few months earlier, he had written to Sir Edmund Andros asking him to procure a commission to see in whose hands the money lay, so that it could be used to build an Anglican church and maintain Anglican ministers.[2] A letter to the Archbishop of Canterbury dated 27 October 1686 contained one of his most damning attacks on the Company and its servants: 'I have taken care to informe myselfe,' he wrote,

> how the money sent over hither for the company . . . is disposed of here. Here are 7 persons, called Commissioners or trustees, who have the sole manage of it; the chief of which are Mr. Dudley, our president, a man of a base, servile and antimonarchicall principle, Mr. Stoughton, of the old leaven, Mr. Richards, a man not to be trusted in publique business, Mr. Hinkley, governor of New Plimouth collony, a rigid independant, and others like to these. The poor Indians (those who are called ministers) come and complaine to Mr. Ratclieffe, our minister, that they have nothing allowed them: We have spoken to the commissioners to have some allowance for them; all we can gett is the promise of a coarse coat against winter and [they] would not suffer Aaron, an Indian teacher, to have a bible with the common prayer in it, but took it away from him.

Randolph also charged the Commissioners with spending the income sent over on themselves and faking their accounts to show that it had been spent on the Indians.[3]

Two years later, in 29 March 1688, he wrote to Sir Nicholas Butler, who was a recent convert to Catholicism, and one of the Lords of Trade. Having furnished him with his usual accusations against the Company, Randolph claimed that: 'The natives are mightily inclined to the Romish Religion this the ffrench our neighbours well know, and take care they shall not want priests . . . by this meanes the ffrench dayly gaine upon them: and have engrosd all the Beaver trade.' He asked, as usual, that a commission should be set up to examine the Commis-

[1] *Ibid.*, IV, 106.

[2] A. T. S. Goodrick, ed., *Edward Randolph*, VI (Boston, Mass., Prince Society, 1909), 193.

[3] R. N. Toppan, ed., *Edward Randolph*, IV, 131–2.

sioners' doings and that some English priests should be sent over to convert the Indians to Catholicism. He continued his letter by promising Butler that 'upon my coming to England I shall discover to your Honour lands enough to maintain a small convent without any charge to the Crown.' He warned Butler that Increase Mather was coming to England 'either to gett their accounts shuffled up and passd by the Governor and Company . . . or to pray his Majestie to confirm their proceedings at the Colledge.' He also 'conjectured' that the Commissioners were returning stock to England for safety. He concluded his long and acrimonious letter by asking Sir Nicholas Butler that it might 'be received with all privacy as from my selfe.'[1]

However private the matter, four days later, on 2nd April 1688, Randolph wrote once more on the subject, this time to his patron, William Blathwayt. 'It's a meer cheat as now managed,' he wrote, 'twere better wee had some preists here who would fall heartily upon the worke of Conversions with the Natives and will bring them to us now dayly drawn away by the french preists: and by that meanes we loose our Beaver trade.'[2] But Randolph's papist recommendations came to an end with the Revolution of 1688, as did his career in New England.

On one other occasion, only two years later, an accusation which smacks strongly of Randolph's views was given currency by the author of *New England's Faction Discovered* (London, 1690), who signed himself C.D. He held up the labours of the Jesuits as an example to the English and asserted that, in spite of money collected by the Company for the Indians — 'a very small progress hath been hitherto made therein; and now scarce any Endeavours or proper Means used at all for their Conversion, the large Sums of Money are annually sent over and disposed of amongst the Brotherhood on that pretence.'[3]

Such criticisms carried little, if any, truth, and did neither the Company nor the Commissioners any harm. More moderate criticism might have been more telling, but such methods were not Randolph's. It is true that in the 1680s and 1690s the Commissioners seem to have taken

[1] A. T. S. Goodrick, ed., *Edward Randolph*, VI, 242–7.
[2] *Ibid.*, VI, 251.
[3] R. N. Toppan, ed., *Edward Randolph*, V, 67.

little interest in their duties, with the exception of William Stoughton, who kept such accounts as he deemed necessary and from time to time wrote to the Company in London to inform them of the state of the Indian missions in New England. A graduate of Harvard in 1650, Stoughton had taken a degree at Oxford three years later and become a Fellow of New College, Oxford. Ejected from his fellowship at the Restoration he had returned to Massachusetts colony in 1662 and become a prominent figure in its government; an assistant from 1671 until 1686, a Commissioner of the United Colonies from 1674, Lieutenant Governor under Sir William Phips in 1692 and acting Governor until his death in 1701, except when Bellomont was in Boston.[1] He was officially appointed Treasurer to the Commissioners on 27 March 1690.[2] On 14 April 1693 he wrote a letter to Robert Thompson, the Company's Governor, in which he admitted that 'it hath been too long a tyme before the accounts of the Indian worke were sent but my excuse is that Mr Bradstreet never accepting to act any thing I have all this while till now, been wholy left alone, without any body to joyn in the making up of accounts & attesting them & have also been under many discouragements during the late uncomfortable revolutions & confusions here.'[3]

He therefore welcomed the appointment of new Commissioners: Sir William Phips, Charles Morton, John Richards and Wait Winthrop; he himself, of course, was reappointed, but the most renowned of the new Commissioners was Increase Mather. Some members of the Company had met Mather when he was in London in 1688 and all must have had drawn to their attention his letter to John Leusden even if they had not actually read it. It was entitled *De Successu Evangelij apud Indos in Novâ-Angliâ* (1688) and was published in many editions and several languages. Leusden, professor of Hebrew at Utrecht and one of the most distinguished Hebraists of his day, was delighted with the letter[4] and dedicated to Mather his Latin and Hebrew edition of the Psalms, printed at Utrecht in 1688; and the same year he dedicated his English and Hebrew edition, printed in London, to John Eliot: '*As also* To the Reverend and pious *the* Twenty Four American Ministers, *Lately Gen-*

[1] *D.A.B.*, XVIII, 113–14.
[2] Ms. 8010, memorandum.
[3] Ms. 7936, f. 30.
[4] M.H.S. *Collections, 4th series*, VIII, 679.

tiles, but now converted to the Christian Religion (by the Grace of God, and Labour of the Reverend John Eliot *and other Ministers).*'

The Commissioners for Indian Affairs who actually attended to the Company's business were very few indeed. The quorum for most purposes was three, and there were rarely more than six present. In January 1697/8 Increase Mather wrote to Sir William Ashurst reporting that several of the Commissioners were dead, and that 'Mr. Morton is quite done. Infirmities of age have rendred him unserviceable these many moneths.' The only Commissioners left, apart from Increase Mather himself, were Stoughton and Major General Winthrop, and he recommended that the Company should appoint John Foster.[1] But the Commissioners' general lack of enthusiasm at this time was well matched by the Company's slackness in attending to its affairs. Slowness in appointing Commissioners was one instance of apathy amongst several which riled Stoughton in his duties as Treasurer. On 12 May 1698, he wrote to Sir William Ashurst complaining of the Company's slowness in issuing bills of exchange: 'This long disapoyntment of mony is a trouble to us, & to the prejudice of those that should receave it.' He then asked Ashurst to 'answer my particular desire, eyther yourselves to appoynt, or to leave it to the Gentlemen here to appoint one in my place, to doe that service which I can not well longer attend as to this Indian worke.'[2] Ashurst in his annual letter to the Commissioners begged them to persuade Stoughton to carry on as Treasurer, adding: 'I often think how much that good man Mr Elliot added to ye weight of his Crown in dying an Indifaticable Labourer in ye work of ye Gospell amongst ye poor Indians. I do not question but Mr Stoughton has frequent reflections of ye same nature.'[3] Such moral pressure apparently proved too much for Stoughton, who remained in office. In the same letter Ashurst named six new Commissioners; amongst these were Samuel Sewall and Cotton Mather, whose appointment inaugurated a more vigorous period in the Commissioners' affairs. If neither man possessed the passionate purpose with which John Eliot had goaded the Commissioners, they were nevertheless strong advocates of his cause.

[1] Ms. 7936, f. 31. [2] Ms. 7955/1, no. 3.
[3] Letter book (Univ. of Va. Ms.), 26.

Samuel Sewall was, like most of the Commissioners, a prominent Boston citizen but, unlike them, had a genuine personal interest in the Indians' conversion. By marrying Hannah Hull, the daughter of a wealthy and successful merchant, he had made a good match which gave him the entrée into the world of commerce. But he never seemed to be entirely at home in this world although he became a member of the Governor's Council and a judge holding court at Plymouth, Salem, Bristol and Springfield. He had been brought up with the ministry in view, but had never become a pastor, although he was always an extremely active church member and an avid hearer of sermons.[1] He had been acquainted with the Eliot family for many years and must have heard from Eliot of the New England Company; he was certainly entirely familiar with the attempts that had been made to convert the Indians. The acquaintanceship with Eliot certainly influenced Sewall's first published work entitled: *Phænomena quædam Apocalyptica ad aspectum Novi Orbis configurata. Or, some few Lines towards a description of the New Heaven as it makes to those who stand upon the New Earth* . . . (Boston, 1697). In the dedication to Sir William Ashurst and the Company he pointed out that 'the *English* Nation, in shewing Kindness to the Aboriginal Natives of *America*, may possibly, shew Kindness to *Israelites* unawares,' and referred to Downham, Thorowgood and Eliot in support of this view.

If Sewall intended to show the Company that he was deeply interested in the Indians' conversion, he was rewarded by his appointment as a Commissioner; he entered in his diary on 14 October 1699: 'I meet with the Governour, Lt Governour, Mr I Mather, &c. about the Indian Affair, which is the first time, The Lord make me faithfull and usefull in it.'[2] Useful and faithful he certainly was: indeed, the Company never had a Commissioner more sincerely devoted to the work of converting the Indians. In 1700 he consented to become the Commissioners' Secretary, and on 31 October 1701 the Company's Court in London resolved, that he should also take the place of Treasurer, left vacant by Stoughton's death in July 1701.[3] At no other time in its history had the Company

[1] G. P. Winship, 'Samuel Sewall and the New England Company', M.H.S. *Proceedings*, LXVII (1945), 65.

[2] M.H.S. *Collections, 5th series*, V, 502.

[3] Ms. 7952.

been kept so well informed of its affairs and interests in New England as it was by the new Secretary and Treasurer to the Commissioners. Sewall sent annually a transcript of the proceedings of the Commissioners and a copy of the year's accounts. The former caused him no difficulty; in fact he occasionally added a little local news, usually of someone's death. But the accounts, as he explained in a letter to Sir William Ashurst, were a burden: 'I had sent my Accounts by this Ship; but the way lately entred into of Borrowing & Discounting brings me into a Sorrowful Perplexity. I have not been bred to keep Accounts: Tis an Armour I have not proved, and know not well how to wear; and I pray the Honorable Corporation to take it off from me.'[1] This the Company was by no means willing to do: it was many years before Sewall managed to rid himself of the burden of Treasurership. In March 1707/8 he recorded in his diary that he had called a meeting of the Commissioners to approve his accounts, adding with obvious satisfaction: 'Not one error discern'd. *Laus Deo Adjutori.*'[2] Ashurst wrote consolingly on 25 January 1713/14 that the Company was concerned at his finding book-keeping so difficult: but 'we cannot upon that account think of trusting that affair in any other hands than your own, of whose ability and Integrity we have had so great Experience.'[3]

Sewall's letters have a charm seldom found in official records. An anecdote typifying the way in which he wrote is furnished by the following extract: 'Upon the 13th of July [1709], about two hours after Midnight, my House was in great danger of being burnt to the ground. The intolerable Smoke alarmed my Wife & me. I leap'd out of my Bed, and run about the House to find the cause of the Smoke: and found every place free but my own Bed-Chamber. At last I unlock'd my Closet, and there saw a lively fire in a Box of Wafers about 18 inches over; which by God's Help I quickly quench'd with a few Buckets of Water.' He went on to discuss whether the fire could have been carried into his closet by a burning mouse and concluded the anecdote: 'But however it came there I know your Honor will congratulat my being made Master of it, and that my Habitation is still left to me: Especially

[1] Ms. 7955/1, no. 23.
[2] M.H.S. *Collections, 5th series*, VI, 218–19.
[3] Letter book (Univ. of Va. Ms.), 132.

considering that the Company's Paper, and other Effects, are by the indulgent Goodness of God sav'd in it.'[1]

Sewall produced in 1713 another small book dealing with the Indians' conversion, this time entitled *Proposals Touching the Accomplishment of Prophesies Humbly Offered* . . . (Boston, 1713). Sewall, of course, sent copies to Sir William Ashurst, and in a letter of 31 August 1714 noted: 'Notwithstanding their Meanness, I could not forbear giving your Honor a Sight of the Proposals; the Dissertation being an Appendix to the Phaenomena, Your Honor may Supress them if you think they may be Offensive, or unacceptable.'[2] When sending a copy to Cotton Mather he wrote: 'I offer to your view a small Indian Basket of Summer Fruit. It has been long a-gathering by a weak and unskillfull hand.'[3] In this little book he suggested that America might well prove to be a particularly suitable place for the conversion of all peoples and all nations. At the end of the tract he filled a blank page with a poem, one verse of which read:

> Give the poor Indians Eyes to see
> The Light of Life: and set them free;
> That they Religion may profess.
> Denying all Ungodliness.

If this was not of a very high order poetically, it faithfully expressed Sewall's sentiments on the Indians' conversion — sentiments which were by no means common in New England.

In fact passions still ran high on the subject of the Indians. For example the Rev. Solomon Stoddard wrote to Governor Dudley in 1703 suggesting that the English might 'be put into a way to Hunt the Indians with dogs . . . as they doe Bears.' He continued: 'If the Indians were as other people are, & did manage their warr fairly after the manner of other nations, it might be looked upon as inhumane to pursue them in such a manner. But they are to be looked upon as theives & murderers, they doe acts of hostility, without proclaiming war. they don't appear

[1] Ms. 7955/1, no. 8.

[2] Ms. 7955/1, no. 30.

[3] M.H.S. *Collections, 6th series*, II, 22. Cotton Mather had just published *A Present of Summer-Fruit. A very brief Essay to Offer Some Instructions of Piety* (Boston, Mass., 1713).

openly in the field to bid us battle, they use those cruelly that fall into their hands. they act like wolves & are to be dealt withall as wolves.'[1]

Nearly twenty years later Stoddard had published a series of *Questions and Answers* one of which touched upon the conversion of the Indians. It was entitled: *Question: Whether God is not Angry with the Country for doing so little towards the Conversion of the Indians?* (1723). He, like Cotton Mather, praised missions sent to the East Indies by the Germans and the Danes, while ignoring the efforts made in New England by the New England Company. It was left to Sewall to protest: he wrote to Governor Saltonstall on the subject: 'Although the Missionaries of Denmark and the Company for the propagation of the Gospel in forein parts, make a great Noise; and much Honour is done them by Princes and great Men. . . .' yet Sewall trusted that God would own the conversions made by the New England Company, adding optimistically: 'These First-Fruits will be followed by a plentifull Harvest.' In July 1722 he explained to Saltonstall that he had 'ventur'd to expostulat a little' with Stoddard. 'And', he added, 'I hope my being Attorney to the Honorable Company . . . will bear me out in so doing.' Sewall also took up the cudgels with William Burnet, Governor of New York, on the subject of the Indians. In September 1723 he wrote to him attacking the notion that the Jews, after their conversion, should merge with other nations as being 'highly improbable, and altogether unnecessary.' Similarly, he argued, the national interests of the Indians should remain the same after conversion as they had been before.[2]

Although Sewall had by far the greatest share of the Commissioners' work by virtue of his position as Secretary and Treasurer, Cotton Mather was also extremely active. No ministers had served as Commissioners of the United Colonies, and although the Company had often expressed its wish that ministers might be consulted this was seldom done. When, however, the Company appointed its own Commissioners, it was quite free to appoint any minister willing to serve. The first to be appointed was Increase Mather, but he did not take more than a passing interest in the Company's work. His son, on the con-

[1] M.H.S. *Collections, 4th series*, II, 235–7.

[2] *Ibid., 6th series*, II, 140–41, 155–6.

trary, devoted much time and thought to his duties as Commissioner, as well as producing several works for the edification of the Indians.

Apart from the annual salary paid to the Treasurer, the Commissioners were not as a rule paid for their services. However, Cotton Mather was an exception: on 21 April 1709 the Company's Court ordered that he should be paid £25 'In Consideration of his great Services in promoting the great work . . . by his writings and other ways.'[1] Mather wrote to Sir William Ashurst on 30 January 1709/10 thanking the Company for 'a very kind present' and explaining that he had not expected any reward, but that the Commissioners had compelled him to receive it.[2] Less than nine months later he wrote again, asking Sir William to accept a copy of *Bonifacius. An Essay upon the Good, that is to be devised and designed by those who desire to answer the great end of life* (Boston, 1710), dedicated to him and to his brother-in-law, Joseph Thompson, the Company's Treasurer. The work contained an appendix on the Indians which had been added, according to its author, not only for the satisfaction of Sir William but also as the 'Vindication from an envious passage in a Sermon of the Bishop of *Chichesters*. . . . It seems,' Mather continued, 'No Good must ever be own'd to be done, but what is done under ye Influence of the *Mitre*. Lett the Gentlemen of the New *Society* [for the Propagation of the Gospel in Foreign Parts] then be prevailed withal, to send a Missionary or two for the Christianizing of the *Iroquois* Indians. . . .' This he said would free the Commissioners from one of their 'most uneasy Sollicitudes.'[3]

Like Sewall, Cotton Mather kept a diary which sheds some light upon the doings of the Commissioners, although it differs from Sewall's in that it was largely devoted to resolutions of 'GOOD DEVISED'. For example in March 1710/11 he resolved: 'I would procure a strict Enquiry, about the late way of Admission into the particular Church-State, practised among our Christian Indians; lest it should (which I hear) degenerate into a very lax Proceedure.' Less than two months later he resolved 'not only to promote Prayer for the Success of the Gospel among the Indians, every Time we hold a Meeting, but also more than ever to make it an Article of Prayer in the public Assemblies of Zion, my Omis-

[1] Ms. 7952. [2] Ms. 7936, f. 33. [3] Ms. 7936, f. 34.

sion of it has been blameable.'[1] Accordingly in October the Commissioners requested ministers 'to make the Conversion of the aboriginal Natives a more Constant Article in their Publick Prayers.'[2] In December 1711 Mather was still concerned with the same subject, and asked whether it would not be a good thing to write to all the English missionaries engaged in missionary work encouraging them to convene and discuss: 'the Mischiefs which most threaten the Christian Indians, and the Methods of preventing those Mischiefs; and be more in earnest than ever to advance the Kingdome of God and of His Christ among them: and with a true evangelical Spirit give Demonstration, that the little Pension received by them, is the least Thing they aim at?'[3]

Sewall seldom recorded the motions made by Mather in the votes of the Commissioners' proceedings, but on 10 February 1712/13 he recorded: 'A circular Letter presented by Dr Cotton Mather was Voted to be sent to the several Ministers employ'd in Gospellizing the Indians, to encourage and Quicken them in their Work.' This may well have been instead of the conference of ministers which he had suggested earlier, but no copy of this circular has been traced. The idea of a circular letter seems to have proved a success, for the Commissioners asked Cotton Mather to write another in the following year to the English ministers 'to Direct and quicken them in Services expected of them.' This letter was duly approved by the Commissioners who ordered copies to be made and sent out to the ministers.[4] In November 1718 he resolved to write yet another circular letter to the ministers employed by the Commissioners.[5]

Mather's writings seem indeed to have found favour with the Commissioners. He himself was present at a meeting of the Commissioners on 27 October 1713 when Captain Ebenezer Billings set forth the cost he had been to 'in supporting an Indian Woman in her sickness and burying her decently when dead.' The Commissioners voted that he should be presented with a copy of Mather's *Magnalia* as a gratuity. The records do not reveal at whose suggestion this gift was made.[6]

Although Mather was generally sufficiently in agreement with Sewall

[1] M.H.S. *Collections, 7th series*, VIII, 48, 69.
[2] Ms. 7953/7.
[3] M.H.S. *Collections, 7th series*, VIII, 143.
[4] Ms. 7953/8, 9.
[5] M.H.S. *Collections, 7th series*, VIII, 570.
[6] Ms. 7953/9.

and the other Commissioners to enable their meetings to proceed without undue heat, there is evidence to suggest that he did not always find his colleagues congenial or co-operative. As early as 1701 Sewall and Mather had quarrelled, although not on issues concerning the Commissioners.[1] But it was when the question of reprinting the Bible for the third time became a current item on the Commissioners' agenda that relations between them became tense. Although Mather's view prevailed, — that to reprint the Bible would be extravagant and unwise — he never seems to have been on really easy terms with his fellow Commissioners again. At about this time he resorted to what became one of his favourite devices — offering his resignation, safe in the knowledge that it would not be accepted. He noted in his diary in November 1713 that the Company had refused to dismiss him and he therefore resolved to 'more than ever sett myself to serve them.' Three years later, in April 1716, he confided to his diary: 'I would move it among the Commissioners of the Indian-affairs, who have a strange Dullness upon all their Managements, that they would appoint two or three of their Numbers, persons of a singular Activity and Capacity, to receive Proposals, for the good proceeding of our Affairs, and to prepare and offer what they think proper for the Board.' In July of the same year he resolved to 'concert, with two Gentlemen, for a better Proceedure of all Things among the Indian Commissioners.' But in spite of his good resolutions and plans for 'GOOD DEVISED' Cotton Mather found himself unable to get his own way at the Commissioners' meetings. In April 1721 he wrote to the Company explaining that he was 'so discouraged by some occurences, as to apprehend it most proper for me, to propose a Secession from the Board of your Commissioners.' He enclosed a copy of a letter, no longer extant — presumably explaining the 'occurences' — which he had sent to the Commissioners and they had ignored. But as on previous occasions, the Company did not accept his resignation and little more than three years later he proposed resigning again: 'being dissatisfied and discouraged with their Conduct; yett I would continue my Cares for the Indians.' But once more, the specific reasons for his resignation are far from clear.[2]

[1] M.H.S. *Collections, 5th series*, VI, 43–4.
[2] *Ibid., 7th series*, VIII, 252, 345–6, 361, 682, 709.

As the Governor of the Massachusetts colony usually acted as head of the Commission, Mather made a point of trying to gain his favour in order that his plans for the Indians might go forward. In October 1716 the new Governor, Samuel Shute, arrived in Boston bringing with him a new commission from the Company. Mather determined to be on good terms with him 'for all the good Purposes imaginable.' In August 1724 he wrote to a later Governor, Gurdon Saltonstall, expressing satisfaction at his appointment and at the same time hoping that 'it will not only procure something more Effectual than what has yett been done for your *Monhegins*, but also inspire a New Vigour into all our Motions.' In March 1724/5, when Saltonstall had been replaced by William Dummer, as head of the Commissioners, he at once wrote to congratulate him and to ask his support in persuading the Commissioners to appoint a visitor to the Indians. This had been a notion very dear to Mather for many years. He also asked Dummer to 'procure needful meetings of the commissioners, and Lett the Languishing State of many things be Enquired into.' In the same letter he pointed out that there were now no Commissioners who were also ministers of religion and that this should be rectified: 'And if a Minister or two should come into the Nomination, perhaps there might be some Advantage in it, as well as Decency for the Commissioners do not Look upon the Business of the Board, as if it were meerly or mainly to save money or manage a Discrete and Frugal Merchandise; but principally and perpetually to Invent and pursue the best Methods of serving the Interest of pure and undefiled Religion among the Indians.'[1]

When Mather was thus agitating for the election of ministers Sewall had already handed over the duties of Treasurer. On 21 February 1723/4 he asked the Commissioners to allow him to resign the position in which he had served 'for more than three times seven years; and now by reason of his Great Age and Increase of the Business, he finds the Work too heavy and Intricate for him, not having been bred to keeping Accounts; and therefore prays that he may be dismissed from that service; and that some younger person and more versed in accounts may be Employed . . .'[2] This time the 'armour' of account keeping,

[1] *Ibid., 7th series*, VIII, 375, 803, 808–9.
[2] Ms. 7953/16.

which had oppressed him now for twenty-two years, was lifted from him, though with reluctance.

The Company, in a letter of 9 April 1724, while begging him to continue in office, took the precaution of naming a possible successor: Edward Hutchinson, Treasurer of Harvard College.[1] Meanwhile, the Commissioners, meeting on 24 April 1724, heard from Adam Winthrop that he would accept the post of Treasurer.[2] Sewall wrote to Robert Ashurst on 9 May 1724 explaining that he was 'shock'd with a Fever the last March' that he was determined to resign, and that Winthrop had already been elected in his place: 'The choice was very unanimous. Nine were at the Meeting, and Eight Votes Written in papers were for him; every one but his own.' But in June the Commissioners had received Ashurst's letter asking them to appoint Edward Hutchinson. Thereupon Sewall and Thomas Fitch wrote back explaining that the Commissioners had had to act quickly as the election of Treasurer would admit of no delay. It was decided, as Winthrop had already been elected, that he should temporarily carry out the Treasurer's duties until his election was confirmed by the Company.[3]

Winthrop, a Harvard graduate (class of 1694) had been to England in 1699, where he probably met some members of the Company. He carried with him on that occasion a letter of introduction from Wait Winthrop to Sir Henry Ashurst recommending: 'my neer kinsman . . . who has taken his degreese at our colledg and has since betaken himselfe to merchandising.' But he soon returned home, and in 1714 was elected to the Massachusetts House of Representatives; two years later he became a Councillor for the Province of Maine. His 'merchandising' was never carried out on a very large scale, but he has been described as 'one of the great colonizers and land speculators of his generation.' He was also an active and faithful member of the Mathers' church.[4]

The Commissioners suggested him to the Company as one suitable to make up their numbers in July 1712, and by November 1713 he was acting as a Commissioner although the Company did not actually approve the appointment until 25 March 1714.[5] At this time he did much

[1] M.H.S. *Collections, 6th series*, II, 169.
[2] Ms. 7953/17–18.
[3] Ms. 7955/2, nos. 70, 72.
[4] Sibley, IV, 209–14.
[5] Ms. 7953/8–9; Ms. 7952.

to recover debts owing to the Commissioners. In fact, he had exerted himself to such an extent that the Commissioners asked the Company 'that Bills of Exchange drawn for the Companys use here in New England May be drawn upon the said Winthrop.'[1] He offered the Company the usual rate of interest but, in spite of the Commissioners' recommendation, he never received a very large share of the annual remittance. This was not for want of asking; he requested a share with monotonous regularity and when his request was heeded he asked that in future it might be more considerable. His election to the post of Treasurer gave him hopes of receiving a reasonable share of the annual bills of exchange. In writing of his election to Robert Ashurst on 16 May 1724 he said: 'Sir, I desire and hope the Station I at present Sustain till your further Order will be no Bar, but rather the contrary to my being interested in the Annuall Remittances, as I have sometimes been.'[2]

But by March 1724/25 he still had not heard from the Company whether his election had been approved. He wrote to Robert Ashurst at this time and made his usual request for a large part of the annual remittances. He also asked that his salary might be paid in sterling, a proposal already agreed to by the Commissioners on account of the precarious value of the province bills in which the Treasurer was normally paid.[3] The Company, however, while finally confirming his appointment, refused to pay him in sterling. The Commissioners continued to sympathize with Winthrop who was, after all, their man, and decided that he should receive £60 per annum in New England currency instead of his previous £30. William Thompson wrote to Winthrop on 6 October 1726 warning the Commissioners that, although on this occasion his salary had been allowed, it must not be regarded as a precedent for acting against the Company's wishes. He added: 'It ought to be remembred that the Corporation had Pitch'd upon an unexceptionable Person to discharge the Function you now do, and that such Person would have been content with noe better a reward then the Corporation directed to be allow'd you.'[4]

Repeatedly throughout the twenties Winthrop asked for a share in the remittances, writing often to both the Governor and the Treasurer

[1] Ms. 7953/10, 9 Sept. 1715.
[2] Ms. 7955/2, no. 71.
[3] Ms. 7955/2, no. 74.
[4] Letter book (Univ. of Va. Ms.), 198.

in England. In May 1735, he wrote to the Treasurer, Joseph Williams: 'I am sorry to find that I could not obtain any part of the Remittance, but you have been pleas'd to give me the reason of it, because several of the Gentlemen who are Members of the Corporation inclin'd to divide it among themselves, apprehending they have the best Right to it.' This was in fact a heavy blow to him as his own affairs were not in a very satisfactory state. In December he wrote again with the pathetic promise that — 'if the Court will now be pleased to gratify me, as I am their officer here, with a share, I will endeavour not to give them the trouble of any further applications of this nature.' But even this offer brought no bill in his name, so that in July 1736 he faced the bitter fact that 'the Gentlemen that trade this way have agreed to share it amongst themselves.'[1]

The Company had never been entirely satisfied with the appointment of Winthrop instead of Edward Hutchinson as the Commissioners' Treasurer. By 1741 it was so dissatisfied that his dismissal was mooted. On 15 October of that year Winthrop wrote to Joseph Williams acknowledging a letter, the contents of which 'struck me with concern and trouble inexpressible. Since you there intimate, "That you had hopes at the last Meeting of the Company to have put this office into a better & more able hand".' He regretted the delay in sending his accounts and claimed this was through no fault of his own. But events proved the Company's doubts about Winthrop to have been fully justified: it seemed that one who knew too little about book-keeping had been replaced by one who knew too much. On 8 December 1741 Winthrop wrote to the Commissioners explaining to them that he had suffered many losses by land and sea, thus falling into debt '& having in my hands money belonging to the Honourable Company', he continued, 'I did under my streights from time to time unwarily yeild to the temptation of making use of it, but with a full intention seasonably to repay it, & beginning with smaller sums, which I once & again refunded, but afterwards, again took out for various Occasions, but especially for discharging what I owed the Province. . . .' He was surprised that he should be 'so long under such unaccountable delusion &

[1] Ms. 7955/2, no. 105, 107a, 112.

infatuation & not be awake to see it, but I was bolstered up with vain hopes of selling in season & of successes which I never found, but on the contrary losses. . . .' He had placed all his property in trust under the care of Edward Hutchinson to be sold to repay the debt, and he would try to sell his own house. He concluded by asking to be treated with compassion.[1]

The Commissioners dismissed Winthrop and appointed Andrew Oliver in his place, who took over the little cash which remained. Winthrop himself wrote to the Company informing them of his misdemeanour: 'I have drawn out my sad & disgracefull accompt & likewise deliver'd to Mr. Oliver duplicates of it.' Having mismanaged his own and the Company's affairs he had acknowledged his offence: 'in the first place to God, then to the Commissioners here, and I now do it to the Honourable Company, in hopes of obtaining forgiveness from all.'[2] The Company wrote to the Commissioners admitting: 'We heartily pity him now in his declining years to meet with such a humbling providence, tho' not without blaming him for the abuse of so pious a Charity.' But part of the blame lay with the Commissioners who should have ensured that the accounts were settled annually and should have been aware of Winthrop's financial difficulties. The Company reasonably observed that as these difficulties had been 'not unexpected' by merchants in the City, they should have been easily discernible in Boston.[3]

Forgiveness could not be had cheaply. Winthrop's indebtedness amounted to £5,781 in N.E. currency. His mansion-house and land in Boston valued at about £2,000, together with 2,300 acres of uncultivated land in the towns of Rutland and Holden valued at £1,400, were placed in the hands of Edward Hutchinson. As well as this, about £100 a year, deriving from Governor's Island in the Harbour of Boston, was settled on the Company during his lifetime.[4] In March 1741/2 he wrote to Joseph Williams promising that, as the winter was over, he would apply himself to selling his estate. At the same time he asked that his place among the Commissioners might be 'lookt upon as vacant.'[5] But

[1] Ms. 7955/2, no. 138a, 139.
[2] Ms. 7955/2, no. 140.
[3] Letter book (Univ. of Va. Ms.), 237.
[4] Ms. 7912/1, f. 42.
[5] Ms. 7955/2, no. 141.

Winthrop died before the debt was repaid. The rent from Governor's Island had yielded only only £212. 10s. while the Boston mansion-house sold for £1,324. The land was sold gradually over the years until 1761, when the total receipts from Winthrop's assets amounted to only £2,586: but three years later the loss in sterling was estimated, at the current rate of £1,050 New England per £100 sterling, to be only £304. The debt was not finally written off until 1801.[1]

Winthrop's successor, Andrew Oliver, was a safe if uninspiring choice. He was at least as distinguished in colonial affairs as any who had held the office before him. He was the brother-in-law of Governor Hutchinson, and later the Governor's Lieutenant, and was generally identified with the British cause. It was often said that he was both avaricious and greedy for office, but the Treasurership was not a coveted office, especially as the Company now demanded security from its officer. Oliver himself admitted that 'the late unhappy failure naturally suggest[s] the expediancy of such a thing.' But he confided to a friend that he would not have accepted the post had he not 'so far engag'd in the affair & were it not for my Respect to the Gentlemen at home & regard to the Interest concern'd.'[2] Although he had already served as a Commissioner for nearly seven years, there is no evidence that he took any particular interest in the Indians' conversion. He nevertheless performed his duties to the Company's satisfaction and when he asked to retire after nearly twenty years service Mauduit begged him not to do so. And so it was not until his death in 1774 that the office once more fell vacant. William Phillips, one of the Commissioners, performed the Treasurer's duties until 1775 when the Company chose Isaac Smith its last New England Treasurer.

One problem neither Treasurer nor Commissioners in New England could long avoid — that of the Indians' title to land. The idea of setting aside land for the Indians' exclusive use was not new — in fact, by the beginning of the eighteenth century it seemed an outdated utopian dream. Wherever land had been set aside for the Indians' use the English had in time encroached upon it, and generally speaking the Indian had no practical means of redress. The problem was most succinctly ex-

[1] Ms. 7912/1, f. 42–3; Ms. 7912/2, f. 2. [2] Ms. 7955/2, no. 142.

pressed by Sewall in a letter to Sir William Ashurst dated 3 May 1700: here he advocated the allocation of tracts of land having 'plain and Natural Boundaries, as much as may be; as Lakes, Rivers, Mountains, Rocks — upon which for any English-man to encroach, should be accounted a Crime. Except this be done, I fear their own Jealousies, and the French Friers, will persuade them that the English, as they increase, and think they want more room, will never leave till they have crowded them quite out of all their Lands. And it will be a vain Attempt for us to offer Heaven to them, if they take up prejudices against us, as if we did grudge them a Living upon their own Earth.'[1] The idea of Indian reserves with natural boundaries was one which very much appealed to Sewall and one to which he adhered for the rest of his life. In a letter to the Rev. John Higginson, he reiterated the suggestion and argued 'that the lying of those Lands unoccupied and undesired by the English, may be a valid and lasting Evidence, that we desire the Conversion and Wellfare of the Natives, and would by no means extirpat them as the Spaniards did.'[2]

The Company welcomed Sewall's idea and agreed that, if it were carried out, the prejudice against the English in the Indians' minds might be removed. In 1701 the Company asked the Commissioners to raise the matter with the government in New England, so that it could approach the King to secure his approval. The Company considered the matter again in 1702 and yet again in 1720, suggesting that the English government should be approached in order to secure for the Indians some degree of protection from encroachment.[3] The Commissioners themselves frequently attempted to interest colonial governments in the problem: for example, in December 1712, they tried to encourage the Governor of Massachusetts to take 'some more Effectual Order . . . for preserving the Indian Plantations Entire according to the true intent of their Grants; and that Encroachments may not be made upon them.'[4] On 3 August 1704 the Company's Court approved a memorial presented to the Massachusetts House of Representatives by the Commissioners concerning 'the pretended purchasers of that Tract of Land

[1] Ms. 7955/1, no. 4.

[2] M.H.S. *Collections, 6th series*, I, 326.

[3] Ms. 7952.

[4] Ms. 7953/8.

called Nashâbo' formerly set out for the Indians at the order of the General Court on the petition of John Eliot. The Company, while very concerned at the 'horrible massacre' of the English which had taken place near Casco Bay, considered that it would not only be a 'warning to them against the like surprizes but against the many unjust Incroachments they have made upon those poor Savages.'[1]

To take legal proceedings against encroachers was not only expensive, but often ineffective. There was, too, the question of whether the Company's funds should be spent on protecting Indian rights. In 1698 the Commissioners had successfully defended the title of some Indians to their land at Martha's Vineyard at a cost of about £18.[2] But in 1703, when the Governor of Massachusetts proposed John Leverett as an Inspector of the Indians, the Commissioners declined to appoint him on the grounds that his duties would be purely civil. However, two years later they must have changed their minds, for in April 1705 they appointed Thomas Swift 'to prosecute the English that take leases of the Indians Land at Punhapoinge contrary to law', allowing him forty shillings per annum for his trouble, as well as paying all legal expenses. A few months later they did appoint John Leverett to look after the Indians' interests at a salary of £20 per annum. After a year, the Commissioners asked Leverett and Swift to give their views on how the English leases on Indian reserves could best be prevented, but neither of these gentlemen was able to offer satisfactory advice on a problem which defied solution. They were not reappointed, and the Company ordered that no supervisor of the Indians was in future to receive a salary unless both the Company and the Commissioners approved the appointment.[3]

By far the most ambitious attempt on the part of the Commissioners to secure reserves for the Indians was the purchase of land at Martha's Vineyard. The Mayhews' title to Martha's Vineyard was confirmed by a deed dated 8 July 1671 under the hand and seal of Governor Francis Lovelace. By this deed the lands and islands held by Thomas Mayhew and Matthew Mayhew, his grandson, were erected into a manor called Tisbury Manor, according to the custom of East Greenwich in the county of Kent, England. A new grant and con-

[1] Ms. 7952.
[2] Ms. 7946/25.
[3] Ms. 7953/2, 3; Ms. 7952, 16 Jan. 1705.

firmation was made by Colonel Thomas Dongan on 25 April 1685, and less than three weeks later, on 12 May 1685, Matthew Mayhew and Mary his wife sold to Colonel Thomas Dongan, for £200 New York money, the lordship and manor of Martha's Vineyard with the exception of lands formerly granted by Thomas or Matthew Mayhew, the lordships of Edgartown and several other pieces of land.[1]

In July 1706 the Commissioners ordered Sewall, Edward Bromfield and Samuel Danforth to go to Martha's Vineyard and inquire into the state of the Indians inhabiting the Gay Head Neck who, it was reported, had lately been molested 'and Threatned to be Ousted.'[2] Writing to Sir William Ashurst on 9 March 1707/8 Sewall explained: 'The Gayhead Neck is the Westermost end of the Island: so called from a high Cliff, which by reason of its white, black, yellow colors makes a glistening shew to those that pass by. This Neck affords a convenient Recess for the Indians, that they may live confortably and inoffensively.' The land was used for grazing sheep and as there were no wolves, there were no shepherds: but this meant that when a sheep disappeared the Indians were blamed. Sewall suggested that if the Gay Head Neck were recovered for the Indians, it would promote peace between English and Indians, and that if the Company had the title now held by Lord Limerick, formerly Colonel Dongan, the Indians' right would be secure.[3] On 28 August 1708, he wrote to Jeremiah Dummer who, as Massachusetts' agent, was on his way to England: 'Be sure, doe your Uttermost to persuade my Lord Limerick to make a Release of the Gay Head Neck on Martha's Vinyard, to the Indian Inhabitants there; who are brought under a good Orderly Christian Regulation: and will be ruined, if turned off.'[4] Sewall took up the matter once more when he wrote to Sir William Ashurst on 22 March 1708/9 begging him to purchase the Gay Head Neck. He reported that there were fifty families living there: 'orderly settled, a school kept, and God's Word preached to them every Lord's Day.'[5]

On 5 April 1711 the Company's Court decided to offer the Earl of Limerick a sum not exceeding £600 for the title. It was agreed that this course was expedient as, if it were not followed, the Christian Indians

[1] Ms. 8003; Ms. 8004. [2] Ms. 7953/3. [3] Ms. 7955/1, no. 6.
[4] M.H.S. *Collections, 6th series*, I, 371–2. [5] Ms. 7955/1, no. 7.

might be dispossessed, be driven to the mainland and revert to their pagan ways. On 2 May 1711 Jeremiah Dummer reported to the Court that, on the orders of Governor Ashurst, he had negotiated with the Earl of Limerick who had agreed to sell the title for £550. In order to raise this sum the Court authorized loans from members and others under bond at 6 per cent interest for a term of six months. On 4 May 1711 bonds were signed and sealed under which the Company borrowed from Sir William Ashurst, Sir Thomas Abney, and Joseph Thompson £100 each, and £50 each from Samuel Powell, Mrs. Ann Partridge, Sir Edmund Harrison, Sir Edward Wills and Mrs. Ann Miller.[1]

The purchase was completed on 10 May 1711,[2] and it was with genuine satisfaction that Sir William Ashurst wrote to Sewall explaining: 'My Lord is a very good humoured Gentleman and always ready to do any thing for the benefit of New England . . . and he is pleased to complement me so far as to assure me That that Consideration and his personall respect for me was the only Inducement he had to part with his Interest at so low a rate.' If this chance of purchase had been missed, Ashurst continued, the property would have gone to the Earl's nephew, who 'being a Papist and a person of no great prudence' might have mistreated the Indians. In fairness Ashurst might have reminded Sewall that the Earl himself, however prudent, was also a Papist.[3] Two days later Ashurst wrote to the Earl expressing the Company's thanks for his co-operation and ready acceptance of the Company's terms. William Tailer, Lieutenant-Governor of Massachusetts, suggested that Limerick had parted with the title for less than half its true value and like several others recommended Dummer as deserving some reward for his part in the purchase. Sir William replied on 21 May 1711, promising that Dummer would be rewarded, and added: 'Tis probable my Lord might have parted with his Interest to Mr Dummer, If the Corporation had not offered themselves purchasers, but considering the

[1] Ms. 7952; Ms. 7949.

[2] Ms. 8003; Ms. 8004, bargain and sale by Thomas, Earl of Limerick to the Company for £550; Ms. 7911/3, f. 1; C. E. Banks, *The History of Martha's Vineyard*, II, 8–12.

[3] Letter book (Univ. of Va. Ms.), 104.

former pretentions of the Indians, and our Concerne and Charge to support them my Lord could not in honour have parted with it, unless we had refused it, to anybody else.'[1] Dummer, in fact, did not receive his reward until 28 January 1711/12; it amounted to only £25.[2] Sir William also wrote to Increase Mather expressing his pleasure at the Commissioners' approval of the purchase, and adding: 'I Hope it will be a means to make the Indians live comfortably upon it, and prevent their scattering abroad.'[3] He wrote to General Nicholson on 15 January 1711/12 in similar terms, explaining the Company's view that to anglicize the Indians was a good step towards Christianizing them: he pointed out that the Commissioners had insufficient funds to take legal proceedings against the English who encroached upon Indian lands, and accordingly asked Nicholson and the colonial government to do all they could to prevent these encroachments.[4]

Meanwhile on 15 October 1711 the Commissioners ordered the deed of purchase to be sent to Edgartown in Duke's County to be registered. The Company had also requested that several Commissioners should go to Martha's Vineyard in order to take livery and seizin, but this was 'deferred the days being short, and the weather growing Cold and Tempestuous.'[5] However, in the following year Colonel William Tailer, Colonel Penn Townsend, and Sewall's son, Joseph, afterwards a commissioner, did go to the Vineyard and took livery and seizin according to the Company's wish. Sewall himself was unable to go, as on the very night of departure he was 'arrested with an intermitting Fever.' He nevertheless reported: 'Tis accounted good Land; and in our Money, worth almost as many Thousands of Pounds, as the Company gave Hundreds in English Money. Yet I hope this will be no Temptation to the Company to part with one foot of it to English men upon any terms.' Tailer also remarked upon the value of the land in a letter to Sir William Ashurst, although his estimate of £3,000 or £4,000 was slightly more conservative than Sewall's.[6]

The title settled, the problem of what to do with the land remained. William Tailer had warned the Company: 'It will requier som skill &

[1] Ms. 8004; Ms. 7956, 12 and 21 May 1711.
[2] Ms. 7911/3, f. 1.
[3] Ms. 7936, f. 37.
[4] Ms. 7936, f. 36.
[5] Ms. 7953/7.
[6] Ms. 7955/1, nos. 19a, 18.

care to put things in such a proper method that the Indians, and the English upon the Iseland may be Easy.'[1] Sewall recommended that the Indians should pay 'some Acknowledgment; and 'tis hoped the consideration of their paying it to themselves in upholding their Schools; will Sweeten the Exercise, and make the yoke easy to them; being brought on gently and gradually.'[2] Cotton Mather on the other hand proposed having 'the Indian Lands lett out on such Leases, as may bring in Revenues for the Support of the evangelical Interests among the Indians.'[3]

In September 1713 Sewall and Penn Townsend were sent to Martha's Vineyard on orders drafted by Cotton Mather and approved by the Commissioners. 'Competent and Convenient Portions of this Land' were to be assigned to the Indians, while the remainder was to be leased at reasonable terms, the rents going towards the support of schools 'and other good Interests among the Indians of that Island.' The Commissioners also decided that the Indians should be informed of the revenue arising from this source and how it was applied.[4] Sewall reported the outcome of the visit in his annual letter to the Company in May of the following year: 'I judged it best to proceed gently, and could not find it convenient as yet, to Lett out any part to English-men; Wherein I had the Advice of Mr Thomas Mayhew who is our Pole-star, understanding the Language of the Indians well; and as a Justice, very laboriously seeking their Wellfare.'[5]

But the other Commissioners were not as willing as Sewall 'to proceed gently.' On 28 June 1714 they ordered that 600 acres should be leased to Ebenezer Allen for ten years at £50 per annum, the only stipulation being that he should choose an area close to the English settlements and that he should fence it off. In November the Commissioners found themselves in an ironical position, for it was discovered that several Indians lived upon the land to be leased to Ebenezer Allen. They decided to ask him whether another area would be acceptable to him. By February 1714/15, however, they seemed satisfied with the

[1] Ms. 8004.

[2] Ms. 7955/1, no. 20, letter to Sir W. Ashurst, 8 Jan. 1712/13.

[3] M.H.S. *Collections, 7th series*, VIII, 192.

[4] *Ibid., 5th series*, VI, 427–8. [5] Ms. 7955/1, no. 27a.

situation: the area of 600 acres was to be improved by Allen and 'If any Indians be aggrieved, the Commissioners will Consider them.' It was not until April 1716, however, that Allen actually received his lease.[1]

Thus the temptation to derive revenue from Martha's Vineyard proved too great for the Commissioners to resist, and in consequence they found themselves forced into depriving Indians of their land and so defeating the very purpose for which the purchase had been made. For the time being they were able to forget about this lease to Ebenezer Allen, but by May 1724 the matter was once more under discussion, as at that time Allen applied for a fourteen-year lease, offering £100 per annum for 1,000 acres. This offer the Commissioners approved, and duly authorized the bounds to be laid out, ordering the surveyor to report upon the number and value of Indian houses falling within the area — 'in order to the Indians having some way or other Satisfaction for them.' By November this second lease was drawn up and Allen was ordered to pay £16 compensation for two small Indian houses, while a larger house was 'to be compounded for the Commissioners on the best terms they can.'[2] The arrangement may have suited Allen and the Commissioners, but it did not suit the Indians, and so in March 1724, the Commissioners appointed Zaccheus Mayhew and John Chapman 'to make the Indians at the Gayhead easy about Mr Allen's last Lease and to induce them peaceably to go off from the said Land.' In July 1725 the Commissioners heard the Indians' objections to the lease, some Indians claiming that they had formerly been made grants involving this land. Thereupon a search was ordered to be made in the records at New York for anything bearing upon the Indians' title, but no trace of any such grants was found.

In March 1725/26 Allen reported to the Commissioners 'the violent opposition made by the Indians to his taking possession of the 1000 Acreas' which had been assigned to him, and as a result it was decided that he should only keep possession of the 600 acres originally assigned to him at an annual rent of £50. The Commissioners relieved their feelings by writing to their agents, John Chapman and Zaccheus Mayhew, signifying their resentment 'at the interruption given by the Indians.' But the Indians cared nothing for the Commissioners' resent-

[1] Ms. 7953/9, 10. [2] Ms. 7953/18.

ment, so that Allen was reported to complain that they 'resolutely hinder not only his taking possession of the . . . 600 acres . . . the Indians to his great damage did impound his cattle & pull down his fences, alledging that the Land is theirs.' The Commissioners ordered further search to be made at New York to prove the Indians' claim, but no deeds could be found,[1] and so they resorted to bringing actions of trespass against some of the Indians. This course was also unsuccessful as the Commissioners lost the case on technical grounds and had to pay costs.[2] In May 1727 the matter was finally settled by making a formal treaty with the Indians. Ten of them signed, or made their mark upon an instrument, resigning their rights to 800 acres of land. At the same time Paine Mayhew and Samuel Welles, the Company's attorneys, settled the whole of the Gay Head Neck upon the natives with the exception of the 800 acres to which the Indians had resigned their rights. A formal annual quitrent of one ear of Indian corn per family was to be paid to the Company.[3]

In July 1727 Allen reopened negotiations for the 800 acres and the Commissioners quickly effected a lease for twenty-one years. Adam Winthrop wrote to the Company informing them of the conclusion of the affair and referring to 'the Great Trouble Difficulty & Charge' which had been caused 'by the Obstinacy & perverseness of the Gay Head Indians in their hindering Mr Allen from taking possession of the land.' Allen's rent was to be £40 per annum for the first three years, £50 for the next four, £75 for the next seven and £100 for the final seven years. Winthrop saw fit to excuse the Commissioners for only letting 800 acres: 'It was taken for granted that the Honorable Company who are at so much expence for benefiting the Souls of those Indians would not be instrumentall of depriving them of outward Subsistence, and it was judged the Land left to the Indians after the 800 acres was set off would be no more than sufficient for accommodation of the families settled there.' The low rent he excused on the grounds that the Indians, having feared their land would be taken from them,

[1] Ms. 7953/19.

[2] Ms. 7953/20; Ms. 7955/2, no. 88, A. Winthrop to J. Williams, 10 June 1730.

[3] Ms. 7955/2, no. 79b, copy instrument of resignation; Ms. 7955/2, no. 79c, copy deed settling the remainder of Gay Head Neck upon the Indians.

had planted without manure thus impoverishing the soil. In any case, Allen had already lost £500 by being forced to surrender his earlier lease.[1] The Company in due course approved this settlement.

However, that things were not entirely as they should have been even at Gay Head Neck may be seen from two orders of the Commissioners: by the first, dated 10 July 1719, Paine Mayhew and Zaccheus Mayhew were to 'prevent the Inhabitants disordering themselves by excessive drinking Rum, and other Strong Liquors.' By the second order, dated 11 July 1727, the same two agents were to inspect the Gay Head Indians, see they improved their land, keep them sober and try to prevent the English from encroaching upon them.[2]

From almost every point of view the purchase of the title to Martha's Vineyard must be accounted a failure. Apart from the Gay Head Neck the purchase gave the Company title to a considerable amount of land, but in almost every case the title was uncertain. For instance, in 1714, Experience Mayhew asked for some allowance out of that part of the purchase 'on the North Shore to the Eastward of the Roaring Brook, extending to the Middle Line', because he had a deed granted his father by Tootoohe, the sachem, and confirmed by Thomas Mayhew in 1675. The Company and the Commissioners finally decided in 1718 to allow him half of what he claimed, lots being cast for which part he was to have, although another adjustment was made in 1720 at his request. Several Indians dwelt upon this land, and had, in Thomas Mayhew's phrase, 'a planting Right' to it. These were presumably allowed to remain. The Company also had crown rights to about 1,307 acres held by seven different people in the township of Edgartown, for which the quitrent was two pecks and fifteen quarts of flour. In Tisbury six people held about 2,180 acres at a quitrent of two bushels, three pecks, and six quarts of corn. In all about 3,817 acres of land to which the Company had crown rights, were held for purely nominal rents. Adam Winthrop, at the Commissioners' order, suggested that the Company should dispose of this land because the rents were so inconsiderable and the cost of collecting them so high.[3]

[1] Ms. 7953/21; Ms. 7955/2, no. 79.

[2] Ms. 7953/12, 21.

[3] Ms. 7953/9, 10, 13; Ms. 7955/1, no. 27a; Ms. 7955/2, nos. 79d, 79.

The Company's other landed property in New England was not extensive. The only other tract of any size was Hogg Island in Casco Bay, 1,346 acres in area, which William Stoughton had purchased from Vines Ellacot for £260 on 3 August 1688.[1] Sewall, writing to the Company in 1708, hoped that it would in time 'be a fair branch of the Company's estate, and that there will be no cause to repent its being left upon their hands.'[2] The Company also had a share in some land at Kingston in the Narragansett country held in common with John Nelson and others, which had been recovered from the estate of Richard Wharton of Rhode Island, who died owing the Commissioners £100. On the subject of this property Sewall excused himself as 'too great a Stranger' to give an account of it.[3]

In Boston the Commissioners held a house originally mortgaged by Edward Rawson which had fallen to the Company on Rawson's death. This was presumably the item referred to in an inventory of the Company's property, dated 25 February 1707/8, as: 'One Dwelling House and Land in the Ferry Street in Boston bounded in the rere with the Mill Pond as per the Plat John Farnham & Cornelius Bennington Tenants at Fifteen Pounds per annum.' They also held 'one wharf and land adjoining at Charlestown just below the Ferry Stairs with other parcels very near.'[4] But the select vestry of Charlestown had complained in October 1703 that the property had 'so far gon to decay that it is become dangerous to ye Inhabitants.' The Commissioners ordered it to be surveyed by 'a skillfull Carpenter or two' and these, in due course, condemned it. Sewall then advised the Company to sell both these properties and by January 1708/9 the Commissioners had been authorized to do so. Notice of their intention to sell was to be given in the *News-Letter*, and on 14 February 1708/9 it was decided the Boston house should be sold for not less than £250. In December the Charlestown land and wharf were sold for £350, and in March 1712/13 the 'Com-

[1] Ms. 7962, 25 Feb. 1707/8; Ms. 8010, copy patent of grant to Vines Ellacot, 23 July 1688.

[2] Ms. 7955/1, no. 6.

[3] Ms. 7962, 25 Feb. 1707/8; Ms. 7955/1, no. 6.

[4] Ms. 7962. A fragmentary plan dated 1707 shows the house to have had two stories (Ms. 8010).

pany's Chamber in Major Howard's Building in Fish-Street, Boston', was sold to Captain Thomas Thacher for the pitiful sum of £70. It was not until 2 June 1713 that Sewall wrote to Sir William Ashurst telling him of these sales. He had not reported them earlier, he said, as there was nothing specific to report; characteristically he added: 'Talk's but Talk: but Money buys Land.'[1]

Ultimately the work of the Commissioners for Indian Affairs must be judged on their efforts to find missionaries and schoolteachers for the natives. On this score, as the next chapter shows, they were often found wanting. But viewed against a background of colonial opinion generally apathetic, if not hostile, to the Indians' conversion, their efforts gain considerably in stature. Without them the New England Company could not have functioned at all.

[1] Ms. 7953/1, 5, 8; Ms. 7955/1, nos. 6, 22.

9

Missionaries and Indians, 1691–1776

'SINCE the death of Mr Eliot (that American Apostle) there has bin a signal blast of Heaven on ye Indian work, very many of the most pious Indians (both professors and preachers) being dead also; & others of equal worth not appearing to succeed them.'[1] In these words Increase Mather informed the Company in 1697 of the state of the Indian work. The problems, of course, remained the same as ever: how was the Indian to be taught Christianity and how were suitable missionaries to be found to teach him? The difference was that in the eighteenth century the Indians were a rapidly dying race and, as Increase Mather's letter mournfully acknowledged, there was no one of Eliot's stature to carry on the work.

Early in the eighteenth century it was decided that a third edition of the Bible in Indian would not be necessary, but the question of gospellizing in the Indian language or in English remained an open one. Cotton Mather was one of the main advocates of English as opposed to Indian, and championed it in his writings. In *India Christiana* (Boston, 1721), which was addressed to the Commissioners, he wrote: 'a Main Intention which you now have in your View, is, To bring the Rising Generation of the *Indians*, unto a more general Understanding of the *English Language*, and more into the *English Way of Living*.'[2] Sewall, on the other hand, was the last really effective advocate of the Indian language. In 1724 he wrote to Robert Ashurst agreeing with a plan

[1] Ms. 7936, f. 31. Increase Mather regarded this 'signal blast of Heaven' as being symptomatic of a general religious decline in New England. See *Ichabod, or, a Discourse shewing what cause there is to Fear That the Glory of the Lord is departing from New England* (Boston, Mass., 1702), 71–2.

[2] *Op. cit.*, 43.

of the Commissioners for training some Indians for the ministry: 'For they are very fond of their own Nation, and their own Language; Insomuch that Mr Joseph Bourn who succeeds Simon Papmonnit at Mashpaw, can't prevail with the Indians to assemble on the Lord's Day, unless he will preach to them in their own Language.'[1] This plan was so close to Sewall's views and so far from those of most of his fellow Commissioners that it is reasonable to suppose it his own. The Company responded with the proposal that two persons should be encouraged by the Commissioners to learn the Indian language, and suggested that, as Indian ministers might well be more successful than English ones, the Commissioners should also be on the look-out for likely candidates.[2] In May 1725 Sewall was no longer the Commissioners' Treasurer, and it was in very different terms that Adam Winthrop, his successor, wrote to the Company. He had laid the Company's plan before the Commissioners: 'Altho it seems to be pretty generally their Opinion, That it would be a very great Service to the Indians to be drawn off as far as may be from their own Language & to be more & more brought to the English Language which most of them do in a good measure understand.'[3]

An issue which swayed the Commissioners in favour of English rather than Indian was the cost of erecting meeting houses: if services were held in Indian there would be a stronger argument for separate meeting houses for English and Indians; on the other hand the English were often not willing to allow the natives the use of their meeting houses. The Commissioners therefore had to decide between the expense of building a separate meeting house for the Indians, or the expense of 'encouraging' the English minister and his congregation to allow the Indians 'convenient room' in the English meeting house. In 1718 Thomas Fitch, one of the Commissioners, wrote to Sir William Ashurst expressing what was by then a majority view. With the exception of those at Martha's Vineyard, the Indians generally lived near English towns: 'it would very much dispose them to more easie reception of knowledge,' he wrote, 'to Instruct their youth in reading and writing English, that so they might in some time be brot to attend on ye Public worship at the Neighbouring English Churches.' It was for

[1] Ms. 7955/2, no. 73.

[2] M.H.S. *Collections, 6th series*, II, 169.

[3] Ms. 7955/2, no. 75.

this reason that the Commissioners had ordered 'their being inducted in ye English tongue and appointed some English Schools.'[1]

By the 1730s the Commissioners had ceased to question this view: if the Indians lived near the English and understood English, it was better for them to use the English meeting house. Accordingly at Groton, Connecticut, it was agreed that one hundred or more Indians should have a place in the English meeting house provided the Commissioners allowed the minister £50 a year. But this, of course, did not mean that building could cease: in 1734, for example, small meeting houses were being built at Gay Head, Little Compton and Christian Town and a larger one at Westerly to serve both the English and the Indian population, at a cost of £100.[2]

The task of teaching the Indians English, indeed of teaching them anything, remained. In 1705 the Commissioners resolved to find more ministers prepared to take Indian youths into their homes. This system proved not altogether a failure, although it did not suit all Indian children; in 1734 John Robins, 'having a great love for Books', was placed with Peter Thacher, while John Mettawan lived with Samuel Whitman, minister at Farmington. But Benjamin Uncas, son of the Mohegan sachem, was 'tryed first at Mr. Adams & then at Mr. Peabody's & not having a Disposition to Learning, but rather choosing a trade' was bound apprentice for a short term.[3] Apprenticeship, however, still proved unsuitable as a means of educating the Indians: the Commissioners tried to improve it by ruling that justices should, when assenting to an apprenticeship indenture, ensure that 'the Master be Obliged to teach the Apprentices to Read, and learn the Catechisme.'[4] But the fact was that no one in New England believed any longer in the efficacy of Indian apprenticeship, though the Company still had hopes of this method: it was suggested in 1729 that more apprentices might be found, but the Commissioners answered that, if English children were meant, there were already more masters willing to take apprentices than children to be taught, but if Indian children were intended: 'Their Nature is so Volatile, they can few or none of them be brought to fix to a trade.'[5]

[1] Ms. 7955/1, no. 48.
[2] Ms. 7955/2, no. 104.
[3] *Ibid.*
[4] Ms. 7953/4, 5 July 1708.
[5] Ms. 7955/2, no. 86.

Apprenticeship bred few Indian ministers, and the very few Indians who attained to higher education seemed particularly prone to disease or 'the hand of God.' One of the most distinguished Indians academically during this period was Benjamin Larnell who had first been taught by Grindal Rawson. In 1710, at Rawson's suggestion, he was sent to school and two years later was admitted to Harvard College. Such was his progress there that Leverett described him as 'An Acute Grammarian, an Extraordinary Latin Poet, and a good Greek one.'[1] It was with obvious satisfaction that Sewall reported his success to the Company, but in July 1714 his brilliant career came to an end. During the vacation, as Sewall later related: 'he went into water, which prov'd cold, and put him into a Rigor.' In spite of medical attention his condition worsened: 'his apparent Delirium gave us an awfull Demonstration of a vehement Fever. . . . But it pleas'd God the Delirium went not off; and about Midnight after the 21 July; Wednesday night, he expired, to our great Sorrow. The Commissioners, and President and Fellows of the College were willing to be at some Cost for his Funeral and gave Scarves to Six Bearers; to one Senior Sophister, three of his own Standing, and two Sophimores. Because Larnell dwelt at my house, the President and I went next the Corpse following it to the Grave in the New Burying place.'[2] And so the Indians were once more denied a Harvard-trained minister of their own race.

But English ministers prepared to learn the Indian language were almost as difficult to find and, if found, their 'due encouragement' was costly. In 1702 the Commissioners ordered that any student having been so encouraged, who then failed to preach to the Indians, must repay the money spent on him.[3] Certainly the financial inducement to preach to the natives was not great. At the beginning of the eighteenth century the salary usually paid by the Commissioners was about £25. Yet from the Commissioners' point of view there was some concern as to whether those who received payment had really earned it. John Usher, a Boston merchant, expressed the view in 1692 that the Indians should be taught English, and that 'Sallarys be nott given for yearly Service, when perhaps nott 12 days in ye year any thing is done either

[1] Sibley, II, 202–3. [2] Ms. 7955/1, no. 29. [3] Ms. 7953/1, 21 Sept. 1702.

as to teaching or preaching among them.'[1] The proficiency of English ministers in the Indian language was also called into question from time to time and the Commissioners, on occasion, wished for some way of examining both their skill and 'their Diligence and Pains taken.'[2] At one time they even considered replacing salaries by payments of twenty shillings for each sermon preached, reckoning that this would be a saving. A year later they changed their minds but insisted that 'it be annually made appear unto the Commissioners, by due Accounts given in, That the English-Indian Preachers, either preach Five and Twenty Sermons a-year, at least: or, that on other Accounts their Merits are such as may deserve their Reward.'[3]

With the rapid depreciation of currency during the eighteenth century, these salaries became even less of an inducement than they had been formerly. In 1723 the Commissioners ordered that they should be increased in the proportion of fifteen to twenty 'because of the rising of the Exchange.'[4] In 1734 Experience Mayhew petitioned for an increase in the salaries of the Indian ministers and it was decided to raise them from £22 to £30 per annum and to raise other salaries in the same proportion. In November 1735 the Commissioners had second thoughts on the matter and, as their former decision had not been made public, they cancelled it, putting on record at the same time that it was the Company's oft-repeated wish that expenditure should not be increased.[5] It was not until 1743 that salaries were substantially increased, when Andrew Oliver, the Commissioners' Treasurer, wrote to the Company's Treasurer explaining that the salaries had been regulated: 'it is indeed a regulation & not an increase of them, for altho' the nominal sum rises higher in our depreciated currency, yet very few if any of those employed have so much sterling mony now, as when they were first settled.' In 1751 a further compensatory adjustment was attempted, when the Company ordered the Treasurer to provide each missionary with a suit of clothes.[6]

The Company was often very ill informed concerning the work of

[1] Ms. 7956. [2] Ms. 7953/6, 27 Dec. 1710.
[3] Ms. 7953/5–6, 10 Oct. 1709, 6 Nov. 1710.
[4] Ms. 7953/16, 24 Oct. 1723. [5] Ms. 7953/23–24.
[6] Ms. 7955/2, no. 145; Ms. 7952, 27 March 1751.

the missionaries and the size of their Indian congregations; the Commissioners themselves lacked adequate information. In order to remedy this, the Commissioners decided, at the turn of the century, to send to all the Indian settlements two itinerant preachers, who were to supply a full report on the progress of Christianity among the Indians. Their choice fell upon Grindal Rawson and Samuel Danforth.

Grindal Rawson, son of Edward Rawson, who had acted as the first Treasurer to the Commissioners of the United Colonies in their dealings with the Society, was a graduate of Harvard College, and in 1684 was ordained minister of Mendon. About three years later he began to study the Indian language and was apparently considered proficient by the Commissioners within the next two years, as in 1689 he revised and saw through the press Eliot's translation of *The Sincere Convert*. In 1700 he was described, albeit inaccurately, as the only minister employed by the Commissioners who could speak the Indian tongue, but there were certainly few other ministers equally well qualified to preach to the Indians in their own language. He was regularly paid £25 per annum for preaching to the Indians once or twice a month, and in 1708 spent the winter with the Indians at Nantucket.[1]

Samuel Danforth's father and namesake was one of John Eliot's colleagues in his ministry at Roxbury. Samuel Danforth junior may even have learned the Indian language from Eliot himself. He too was a Harvard graduate. Ordained minister of Taunton in 1687, he began preaching to the Indians about this time and received the same remuneration as Rawson. The Commissioners also made use of his knowledge of the Indian language by engaging him to prepare books for the Indians. In 1705, however, the Company 'being informed that he is very negligent and not fit to be employed in that work' asked the Commissioners to enquire into his behaviour. But Increase Mather vouched for his good conduct and assured the Company that he had been misrepresented. In 1726, a year before his death, the Commissioners were uncertain how well he was performing his duties and warned him that they expected him to preach at least twelve times a year.[2]

[1] Sibley, III, 159–68; Ms. 7953/4, 27 April 1708.

[2] Sibley, III, 243–9; Ms. 7952, 9 Aug. 1705, 16 Jan. 1705/6; Ms. 7953/20, 24 Nov. 1726.

Rawson and Danforth wrote an account of their visit to the Indians which had occupied them from 30 May until 24 June 1698, and were paid £46. 9s. od. by the Commissioners.[1] It was no doubt at the instigations of Increase Mather that this account was printed. The printer of Nicholas Noyes's election sermon for 1698, entitled *New Englands duty and interest* (Boston, 1698) found that he had insufficient copy to fill the last sheet and so the visitation was used as a stop-gap. The two missionaries had visited most of the Indian settlements in Massachusetts as well as Martha's Vineyard and the Islands. In most cases they gave an indication of the size of the communities they visited, but unfortunately, like all those who reported on the Christian Indians, they were not consistent — sometimes recording the number of individuals and sometimes the number of families in a particular settlement. In some instances, they merely mentioned the existence of a congregation and gave no further information of any kind. In other cases they named the pastor or schoolmaster employed by the Commissioners and occasionally noted that a particular community was in need of a pastor, or that a certain schoolmaster was unsatisfactory and should be replaced.

Yet the information they supplied was long to remain the most complete survey of the efforts being made to convert the Indians.[2] In 1705 Increase Mather, Cotton Mather and Nehemiah Walter signed a letter printed at Boston in that year which drew largely upon the visitation of 1698. On 5 March 1704/5 the Commissioners paid to 'Timothy Green for printing 198 Letters about Christianizing y[e] Indians & Stiching them 2 Doz and 4 in marble 50 In Coloured paper 34s. 6d.'[3] It was entitled: *A Letter, About the Present State of Christianity, amongst the Christianized Indians of New-England. Written to the Honourable, Sir William Ashurst . . .* (Boston, 1705). Ashurst was pleased with the copies he received and wrote to Sewall: 'we have presented some of them to y[e]

[1] Ms. 7946/24.

[2] Another survey was undertaken in July and August 1725 by Nathan Prince who received £20 as salary and £12 for expenses (Ms. 7953/19 *passim*; *C.S.M.*, XXXI, 452). The survey presented by Prince apparently needed revision before it was considered fit for the eyes of the Company's members who had asked for it (Ms. 7953/19–20, 22 March 1725/6, 28 March 1727). Unfortunately no copy has been discovered.

[3] Ms. 7946/27–8.

Bishops, which notices are convincing, that our ministers (tho' not Episcopal) are Capable of Doing Good.'[1] The *Letter* claimed that there were 'thirty several Congregations of Indians' in Massachusetts, and furthermore nearly all of these Indians were Christians. Thirty-seven Indian ministers or schoolmasters were employed to look after them, and seven or eight English ministers. The number of Indians was not what it had been fifty years earlier, the *Letter* explained: 'The Hand of God, has very strangely wasted them; and the *War* . . . [of] 1675, hastened a strange Desolation upon whole Nations of them.'[2]

One of the main causes of the Indians' decline was rum. All who observed them were agreed that few, if any, were able to resist the delights of strong drink, despite numerous laws to protect them from it and despite such effusions as Cotton Mather's *A monitory and hortatory letter, to those English, who debauch the Indians, by selling strong drink unto them* (Boston, Mass., 1700). Although both missionaries and Commissioners were well aware of the ruin caused by rum they were unable to prevent it. Sermons were preached, and sometimes printed, warning against the dangers of alcohol. An attempt was even made to found an Indian society of Rechabites, the Commissioners offering in March 1709/10 'some suitable Gratification' to foundation members, in the form of 'a Present of Indian Corn in these dear times.'[3] In November 1711 Cotton Mather proposed 'Presents to be made unto certain Indians, who are uncommon Examples of Temperance, and Abstemiousness, and Sobriety.' The Commissioners duly ordered that Joash Panu and Isaac Ompane should each be presented with a hat costing ten shillings which would, Cotton Mather hoped, 'be an encouragement unto others to follow the Pattern these have given them.'[4] But abstemiousness did not come easily to the Indians and the Rechabite society came to nothing.

Nowhere were the effects of disease and drink more marked than at Natick; its story after the death of Eliot is not a happy one. In 1698 Rawson and Danforth reported that the church had shrunk to 7 men and 3 women members, while non-members numbered 59 men, 51

[1] Letter book (Univ. of Va. Ms.), 71–2.
[2] *Op. cit.*, 5–6.
[3] Ms. 7953/6.
[4] M.H.S. *Collections, 7th series*, VIII, 133; Ms. 7953/7.

women and 70 children under the age of sixteen.[1] Fourteen years later the Rev. William Williams of Watertown received thirty shillings for reporting to the Commissioners on the state of the Indians at Natick. It can be assumed that his report was at least as pessimistic as the earlier one, for when the Commissioners had received it they decided to attempt a remedy by bringing several dwindling tribes together: the chiefs of the Indians at Ponkapog and other places round about were invited to meet Sir Charles Hobby, Samuel Sewall and Cotton Mather at Natick and discuss a plan for bringing them all 'unto a Cohabitation at Natick.'[2]

The Indians at Ponkapog were in no better state than those at Natick: in 1700 they had been allowed fifty shillings by the Commissioners 'to forward them in ploughing up their Ground: that so they may be Encouraged to a more Neighbourly, and fixed habitation.'[3] Peter Thacher, pastor of Milton, had long preached to them in their own language, receiving £25 per annum from the Commissioners. But by 1708, 'Upon Consideration of the Fewness of the Indian Familys now residing at Punkapaug', he was to be paid twenty shillings per sermon in lieu of his salary. As a result of this order payments to Thacher were reduced to £12 in 1709 and £13 in 1710.[4]

It seemed obvious, then, that if the Indians of Ponkapog and Natick could be united it would be a sensible economy; one minister could easily serve the combined congregations. The year after the meeting between chiefs and Commissioners, the Governor of Massachusetts and President Leverett were asked to help bring the plan into operation.[5] Yet Natick remained a problem. Daniel Gookin of Sherborn had continued since Eliot's day to preach to the Indians once a month in English with an interpreter, but by the year 1707 his health was failing.[6] In 1709 the Company asked the Commissioners to appoint a minister to visit

[1] Nicholas Noyes, *New Englands Duty* (Boston, Mass., 1698), 98.

[2] Ms. 7953/8, 3 July 1712.

[3] Ms. 7953/1.

[4] *D.A.B.*, XVIII, 389–90; Ms. 7953/4, 11 Oct. 1708; Ms. 7946/31–2. From 1711 onwards his salary was once more £25.

[5] Ms. 7953/8, 10 Feb. 1712/13.

[6] Sibley, II, 277–83.

all the converted Indians every month to administer the sacrament and talk with them: 'this being the Method that good Mr. Elliot took with them.'[1] However, Gookin continued to receive a salary until 1713; his assistant and later his successor at Sherborn was Daniel Baker, who was paid £10 a year for several years for preaching to the Indians at Natick once a month.[2]

One of the faults found by Rawson and Danforth in 1698 had been the lack of a schoolmaster: 'the want whereof has had a very evil influence into the non proficiency of their children, in those wayes of Education which formerly obtain'd amongst them, there being but one child that can read here.'[3] But at least this criticism was temporarily overcome by the appointment of an Indian minister, Daniel Takawombpait, who served at Natick until his death in 1716. 'Altho' he had his Errata,' wrote Sewall, 'yet the Commissioners will find it difficult to provide a man to succeed him in that Office of Teaching.'[4] Certainly in March 1716/17 the Commissioners had not succeeded in replacing him: John Neesnumun, whom they desired, was 'so entangled with Debts, that his coming to them is hitherto obstructed.' Sewall agreed to try to sort out Neesnumun's affairs when on circuit, and in due course he was installed as minister at Natick. But in 1719 Natick was entirely without a minister, and Sewall wrote in October of that year: 'John Neesnumun, the most accomplished person possibly, in the Province, for the understanding the English and Indian Languages, and Speaking them, died the last Moneth.'[5]

After this disappointment, the Commissioners sought an English minister to preach to the rapidly dwindling congregation at Natick. They chose Oliver Peabody, who, in his junior year at Harvard, had received £45 from Boyle's gift on the condition that: 'he continue his Intentions to doe & give proper Security to refund said money . . . in Case he should afterwards divert from the indian service.' In August 1721, he began to preach at Natick, much to the Commissioners' satisfaction. Encouraged

[1] Ms. 7952, 9 Nov. 1709.
[2] M.H.S. *Proceedings*, LXVII, 80, 89; Ms. 7953/9; Sibley, V, 307–9.
[3] Nicholas Noyes, *New Englands Duty*, 98.
[4] Ms. 7955/1, no. 41.
[5] Ms. 7955/1, nos. 43, 53.

by his zeal, they determined upon a new course: whereas formerly all ministers, even Eliot himself, had been part-time and had lived near, rather than among, the Indians, it was now decided that a minister should settle at Natick itself. Accordingly in June 1722 Thomas Fitch and Daniel Oliver were ordered to treat with Harvard's President and Fellows for arranging means of supporting Peabody at Natick. In November the Commissioners suggested a salary of £40, together with the sum of £50 to assist him in settling there; in February 1722/3 the President and Fellows of Harvard agreed to pay the same out of Boyle's gift, and Peabody was duly settled at Natick even before his ordination, though not before his marriage to the daughter of Joseph Baxter, another of the ministers who had been employed by the Commissioners.[1]

In April 1729, at a meeting of the President and Fellows of Harvard, it was agreed that a Committee of three should go with the Commissioners to Natick: 'to Inquire into ye State of Religion there, and whether it be proper to gather a Church.' The results of this visit were reported six months later: there were, it was understood, 29 or 30 families of Indians, but only 16 adults and 12 children had been baptized; the Indians were unable to read and did not send their children to school, nor did they catechize their children or send them to Peabody to be catechized; there were thirteen children bound apprentice in English families and these thirteen could read and write English; attendance at the services conducted by Peabody was restricted to eight families in Natick and thirteen other families in the neighbourhood. However, as both Indians and English wanted a church gathered, the Committee agreed to the proposal and ordered Peabody to get the assistance of the neighbouring minister to bring this about.[2] In December 1729 Peabody was ordained and, with the assistance of the Rev. Joseph Baxter, the church was gathered, consisting of three Indians and five whites. In fact this attempt to found a new church at Natick was a dismal failure: by 1740 it consisted of less than a dozen individuals. However, Peabody continued in office until his death, and the Commissioners

[1] Sibley, VI, 529–34; William Biglow, *History of the Town of Natick* (Boston, Mass., 1830), 53–7; Ms. 7953/15, June 1722, 9 Nov. 1722; *C.S.M.*, XVI, 483–4.

[2] *C.S.M.*, XVI, 572, 576.

proceeded to appoint a successor, Stephen Badger, and to have him ordained in 1753. He finally retired in 1799 when few Indians remained in the neighbourhood, and that was the end of the Indian church at Natick.[1]

Of all the communities of praying Indians by far the largest was that at Martha's Vineyard. In 1694 the total population of Martha's Vineyard and Nantucket was reckoned at 1,500 adults.[2] Ten years later Experience Mayhew reported that there were one hundred and eighty families on Martha's Vineyard and that only two people were still pagan.[3] The Mayhew family continued to identify itself with the Indians' welfare and continued to provide the Commissioners with some of their most successful missionaries: in fact the Company employed members of the family for nearly one hundred and thirty years. After the death of Thomas Mayhew senior in 1680, three of his grandsons continued his labours: Matthew had been educated at the Commissioners' charge and was later employed by them at a salary of £20 per annum until 1699, when he completely abandoned his work among the Indians. He did, however, write a tract publicizing the conversion of the Vineyard Indians entitled: *A Brief Narrative of the Success which the Gospel hath had among the Indians of Martha's-Vineyard* (Boston, 1694).[4] This also served to swell Cotton Mather's *Magnalia Christi Americana* where it appeared in full. Thomas, the second grandson, was not a minister but a ruler of the Indians and as such received a salary of £10 and later of £20. Sewall wrote of him after his death in 1714: 'He is very much Lamented by the English and especially by the Indians, of whom he was a most agreeable Ruler, understanding their language and waiting upon them with unparallel'd Patience.'[5] The third grandson John became pastor of Tisbury and Chilmark in 1673. He, more than his brothers Matthew and Thomas, was the true successor to his grandfather Thomas senior. At first he received a salary of only £10 per annum, but in 1686 this was increased to £30. He did not, however,

[1] William Biglow, *History of . . . Natick*, 59–60.

[2] Matthew Mayhew, *A Brief Narrative* (Boston, Mass., 1694), 28–9.

[3] Increase Mather and others, *A Letter About the . . . Christianized Indians*, 5.

[4] It was reprinted in London under the title: *The Conquests and Triumphs of Grace* (1695).

[5] Ms. 7955/1, no. 33.

have much time to enjoy this increase, since he died in February 1688/9[1]. He left behind him a son of sixteen who, only four years later, began to preach to the Indians and continued to do so for more than sixty years. This was Experience Mayhew.[2] No other missionary was so long in the Company's employ and none, except John Eliot, was more widely or more justly renowned.

Experience Mayhew was born in January 1672/3. He had the advantage over most of the other missionaries in having learnt the Indian language, as he himself said: 'by Rote, as I did my mother Tongue.'[3] He began preaching to five or six Indian congregations in March 1693/4, receiving from the Commissioners £35 a year for his first two years and then in 1700 £40 a year. By 1705 his salary was increased to £50, but thirteen years later it was only £15 more. This proved inadequate and Experience found it necessary to ask for help: in 1720 the Commissioners lent him £75 with which to pay a debt but three years later he petitioned them for assistance 'by reason of ye Largeness & chargeableness of his family.' They thereupon increased his salary to £100. In 1730 he petitioned the General Court of Massachusetts for a grant of land and six years later he once more begged the Commissioners' help in view of his 'numerous and sickly family' and the smallness of his salary. The Commissioners on this occasion allowed £30 for his relief, but did not increase his salary.[4]

Experience Mayhew had no single congregation of his own, but instead regularly visited all the Indian congregations on Martha's Vineyard. Early in his career the Commissioners were anxious that he should succeed Japheth, the Indian minister at Christian Town. Japheth had been one of the most distinguished Indian ministers employed by the Commissioners, and one of the first to be used as a missionary to unconverted tribes. In November 1705 he had been sent to visit the Narragansett, Pequot and Mohegan Indians 'and reside a convenient while among them.'[5] In November 1711 the Commissioners ordered that a

[1] C. E. Banks, *The History of Martha's Vineyard*, I, 247–9.
[2] *Ibid.*, I, 249–54; Sibley, VII, 632–9; *D.A.B.*, XII, 453–4.
[3] *N.E.H.G.R.*, XXXIX (1885), 13.
[4] Ms. 7953/11, 16, 25; Ms. 7955/1, no. 56.
[5] Ms. 7953/2.

letter be sent to the Indian church signifying their desire that, although Japheth was still living, Experience Mayhew should succeed him. But the Indians did not accept this advice and elected instead another Indian, Sonamog, who was duly ordained pastor of the Indian church. Less than three years later the church was once more looking for a pastor. The Commissioners received the news of Sonamog's death in January 1714/15 and wrote to the Indian church advising them to consult with Experience Mayhew, Josiah Torrey and Samuel Wiswall, and once more pointing out that the choice of Experience Mayhew would be not only pleasing to them but would be good in itself.[1] Once more their exhortation went unheeded: Sewall recounted the matter in a letter to Sir William Ashurst: 'Although the Indians at the Vinyard, their obstinacy in declining to chuse worthy Mr Experience Mayhew for their Pastor, causes some pain to the Commissioners; yet the unblamable conversation of their country-man Joash Panu, whom they have chosen and ordain'd, gives them Hope that he may become a Blessing in that Place.' The Commissioners allowed Joash Panu £8 per annum but on the recommendation of Experience Mayhew increased it to £12 in 1717.[2]

Thomas Fitch wrote to Sir William Ashurst in September 1718 praising Experience Mayhew who, in spite of 'Invitations given him per English Churches,' continued to preach to the Indians, hold lectures, inspect their schools and catechize their children. In 1720 the Commissioners had two of his sermons printed in order that 'the Company may have some Taste of the Gifts of one of your Preachers to the Indians. Partly to gratify the Bookseller that Prints it, he has annexed a Narrative of the Vinyard Indians.' Sewall hoped that the Governor and Company might be persuaded by it 'that GOD is, and will be present in this still small voice: and therefore you need not be discouraged, or put out of countenance by the great Noise of the Danish Missionaries.'[3]

It may have been this narrative which suggested to Mayhew the idea of producing a larger work advertising the progress in christianizing the Indians of Martha's Vineyard. Samuel Sewall, on 18 November

[1] Ms. 7953/7, 9. [2] Ms. 7955/1, no. 34; Ms. 7953/10.

[1] Ms. 7955/1, no. 48, 58. The book was entitled, *A Discourse shewing that God dealeth with Men as with Reasonable Creatures* (Boston, Mass., 1720).

1723, first referred to it in a letter to Robert Ashurst: 'Mr Mayhew is just come to Town from Martha's Vinyard and has shewed me the Lives of several Indians, Men, Women and Children drawn up by himself. I have enclosed one of them which was to me very entertaining.'[1] On the next day Sewall must have felt that one life would not be enough, for he added a note to a transcript of the lives of two Indian children: 'I have sent two Examples more of Early Piety: desiring to give a specimen of what Mr. Experience Mayhew, one of your Ministers, is preparing for the Press; by which it may be seen that out of the mouth of *Indian* Babes & Sucklings GOD is ordaining strength. The Articles are very well attested by Mr Mayhew, and may be credited.'[2]

Cotton Mather saw in these lives the need for his attentions and recorded in his diary: 'The Publication thereof may serve many good Purposes. I would therefore animate it, and employ my Cares about it, and prevail with several Ministers to join with me in Supervising of it.'[3] On 6 July 1724: 'An account of the Success of ye Gospell among the Indians at Martha's Vineyard in particular Examples having been collected & prepared by the Revd. Mr. Experience Mayhew was offered by him to the Commissioners in order to its being printed, Voted that the Revd. Dr. Mather, Mr Wadsworth, Mr. Colman & Mr Sewall be desired to peruse the same & to report what they judge proper for the Commissioners to do relating to the printing of it.'[4] At the same time Mayhew was voted £6 'to defray the charge of transcribing the said book,' and on the next day he was duly paid.[5] On 11 December the Committee reported, but the consideration of the matter was deferred to a later meeting. No record of this meeting has survived but it must have been decided not to take any further action on Mayhew's manuscript. In May 1727 a specimen sheet with proposals for printing the work was issued at Boston,[6] and a few months later the work was finally printed in London for Samuel Gerrish, the Boston bookseller. It

[1] Ms. 7955/1, no. 67. The letter, to which this postscript was added, was dated 28 Oct. 1723.

[2] Ms. 7955/2, no. 68.

[3] M.H.S. *Collections, 7th series*, VIII, 740.

[4] Ms. 7953/18.

[5] Ms. 7946/43.

[6] J. Sabin, *A Dictionary of Books relating to America*, XI (New York, 1879), 530. Sabin's reference to *Historical Magazine* appears to be mistaken.

was entitled: *Indian Converts: or some account of the Lives and Dying Speeches of a considerable Number of the Christianized Indians of Martha's Vineyard* (London, 1727). It was dedicated to the Governor and Company and had the imprimatur of the united ministers of Boston, whose signatures, headed by Cotton Mather's, were appended.

Although not regarded as belonging to the series of Indian tracts to which Eliot had so largely contributed, it was in fact a direct descendant, following much the same pattern of recounted conversions, and differing only in Thomas Prince's *Some Account of those English Ministers who have successively presided over the Work of Gospelizing the Indians on Martha's Vineyard and the adjacent Islands*, which was appended to the work. Although the Commissioners did not pay for its publication, they did welcome its appearance in print and, receiving a stock from England, ordered on 31 October 1727: 'That Each of the English ministers imployed by the Commissioners in the Instruction of the Indians be furnished with One of the Books of Indian Converts Published by Mr. Experience Mayhew, that they may animate those under their Care by the good examples therein recorded.'[1]

Experience Mayhew, like his grandfather, Thomas junior, was as modest as he was devoted to his labours. When Harvard College determined to honour him by conferring upon him the degree of M.A. he at first refused it. But in 1723 such pressure was brought to bear upon him that he was forced to accept the honour. He was conservative in his religious views and strongly opposed George Whitefield and the New-Lights. Above all he feared that simple Indian ministers might be infected with Anabaptist notions and come to believe that they were the recipients of God's direct and personal revelation.[2]

When Sewall visited Martha's Vineyard in 1714 he gained a very favourable impression of Experience Mayhew's labours. He visited the Gay Head Neck on Mayhew's lecture day, when there were present 'upward of an Hundred Men & Women besides Children: many of them well habited. The Women especially were attired with a very surprising Gravity and Decency, beyond what I have met with in other places.' But Sewall also found that only two young men could read

[1] Ms. 7953/21.

[2] Sibley, VII, 636.

English: he made one of them read 'in my Psalm-book with red Covers, and then gave it him.' To the other he promised an English New Testament which in due course he remembered to send.[1]

In 1709 the Commissioners had appointed an English schoolmaster, Benjamin Allen, at a salary of £35 per annum, to teach the Indians to read and write English, but the appointment seems to have come to nothing. Three years later in 1712 they ordered the Indians to nominate three schoolmasters from whom the justices and English ministers of the Island might choose one. They also ordered that the parents of the children who attended the school should either give a day's work or a bushel of corn to the schoolmaster in payment for their children's education. But it was difficult to make the children attend; in 1716 the Commissioners ordered that a cask of biscuits should be sent to Martha's Vineyard 'to Encourage youth in attending Sett times for their being Catechised.'[2] In 1718 Sewall reported that the Commissioners had 'ventured higher than ever before in setting a schoolmaster at Martha's Vineyard,' offering Jabez Athearn £40 per annum. Sewall spoke well of Jabez: 'He writes a very good Hand; and I hear the School prospers well under his management.'[3] Sewall was, however, misinformed, for by December 1718 the Commissioners ordered that the schoolmaster was to 'make up his year as profitably as may be, and then be dismissed forasmuch as the Indians neglect & refuse to send their children to be taught by him.' Experience Mayhew suggested in 1736 that an English school should be set up at Christian Town 'to ripen some Indian children & youths for officiating in due time in the places of the present Indian preachers who are most of them very aged & infirm & almost past service.' An Indian youth, John Robins, who had been living with an English minister, was suggested for this position by the Commissioners.[4]

Experience Mayhew's main assistant at Martha's Vineyard was Josiah Torrey, pastor of Tisbury. He was paid £20 in 1702 for learning the Indian language, Experience Mayhew having testified to his 'Capacity & Industry.' His salary was £25 per annum until 1716, when he received £30 per annum. In July 1724 the Commissioners paid to

[1] Ms. 7955/1, nos. 27a, 27b; M.H.S. *Collections, 5th series*, VI, 433–4.
[2] Ms. 7953/5, 8, 10. [3] Ms. 7955/1, no. 45. [4] Ms. 7953/11, 25.

his widow £15 'in full of his Salary & Gratuity.'[1] Another of Experience Mayhew's assistants was Thomas West. Appointed in about 1743, he only preached to the Indians of Martha's Vineyard for five years, moving to Rochester in 1748 to become minister of the Congregational church there.[2] Another member of the Mayhew family, Zaccheus, a great-grandson of Thomas senior, received a salary of £10 in October 1717 for 'governing the Indians for one year . . . as my Father Thomas Mayhew Esq. was wont to doe.'[3]

In 1727 Nathan, son of Experience Mayhew, was allowed £20 per annum by the Commissioners to support him at Harvard, his father signing a bond for £160 should he fail to teach the Indians when he left college. But Nathan was never put to the test as he died before qualifying, the bond being returned to his father in 1736.[4] Thus was Experience deprived of his first hope of a successor. Nor was his second son, Jonathan, to follow in his footsteps for in 1746 he accepted the call to the West Church, Boston, where he became even more famous than his father. And so, when Experience died, in 1758, he can have had little hope that his family would carry on the work which had occupied four generations of Mayhews. Yet nine years later Zachariah Mayhew, Experience's third surviving son, decided to preach to the Indians; at forty-nine years of age, in 1767, he entered into the Commissioners' service and became an ordained minister of the Gospel. The Indians under his care now numbered only about three hundred, of whom two thirds lived at Chilmark and Gay Head. So his task was not as exacting as had been his forebears', and he continued in it for nearly forty years.[5]

The Commissioners did not forget Nantucket during the eighteenth century although attempts to civilize the Indians there were far more haphazard than at Martha's Vineyard. In 1708 Grindal Rawson and Experience Mayhew visited the island and were entertained and lent horses by Jethro Coffin, whose help was acknowledged with a gift

[1] Ms. 7953/1; Ms. 7946/43; Sibley, IV, 419–21.

[2] Sibley, VIII, 793–7.

[3] M.H.S. *Proceedings*, LXVII, 96.

[4] Ms. 7953/21, 25.

[5] C. E. Banks, *History of Martha's Vineyard*, I, 254–6.

of £3 worth of books. As a result of this visit it was recommended that Samuel Wiswall, a young Harvard graduate, should be asked to learn the language and catechize the Indian youth once a week: but this he at first declined to do.[1] In the following year Peleg Wiswall, another Harvard graduate, was offered £20 for learning the language and the same amount for teaching school at Nantucket on the understanding that he live on the island; he was apparently no more tempted by the offer than Samuel had been.[2] But Samuel changed his mind when at a later date he was pastor of Edgartown, and in 1720 Experience Mayhew reported that he had 'almost learned the *Indian* tongue.'[3] He had been invited in 1717 to go as a missionary to the Eastern Indians, but to this suggestion he had given 'a possitive Denial'. In 1731 the Commissioners allowed Japhet Pannis, an Indian minister, £20 for his past services in ministering to a small Anabaptist congregation on Nantucket,[4] and in 1727 they promised Timothy White that they would subsidize him as minister of the church at Nantucket if the people would accept him. Accordingly in the following year he began to preach to the Indians, receiving at first only £10 but later £25. In 1749 his health failed and two years later he had to leave the island altogether.[5] By 1763 there were only 358 Indians living at Nantucket and in August of that year 'an uncommon mortal distempter' swept away 250 of them. By 1792 only twenty were still living.[6]

On the mainland, John Cotton continued his labours at Plymouth until his death in 1699. Six years earlier the Indians converted to Christianity in the Plymouth area totalled five hundred.[7] John Cotton's son Josiah, although not ordained, travelled all over the country preaching 'two Lords Days in every Moneth, except a Moneth or two in Winter.' Clerk of the county court and register of probate, he received £20 per annum from the Commissioners for preaching to the Indians. He was

[1] Ms. 7953/4, 5 July, 19 Oct. 1708; Sibley, V, 126–9.

[2] Ms. 7953/5, 14 Nov. 1709; Sibley, V, 176–9.

[3] Cotton Mather, *India Christiana*, 93.

[4] Ms. 7953/22.

[5] Sibley, VI, 417–21.

[6] M.H.S. *Collections, 1st series*, III, 158–9.

[7] Matthew Mayhew, *A Brief Narrative*, 53.

proficient in the Indian language and compiled a vocabulary which was not, however, printed during his lifetime. Like many of those who preached to the Indians, he believed that little or nothing was being achieved in spite of their exertions. In 1744, he wrote, the Commissioners 'gave me a dismission, because the Indians did not attend; a business I had been in about 39 years.'[1]

In 1693 Samuel Treat, minister of Eastham, reported that there were over 500 adult Indians on Cape Cod, all of whom attended service. They lived in four villages, each of which had an Indian schoolmaster who, as well as teaching the Indians, was taught by Treat. The Indians were friendly to the English, well behaved and, most extraordinary of all, 'serviceable by their labour.' Nearly twenty years earlier Treat had been encouraged to learn the Indian language by the Commissioners although it was not until 1679 that he received a regular salary of £25 a year. He continued in the Commissioners' pay until his death in 1717.[2] His place was then taken by Daniel Greenleaf, minister of Yarmouth, physician and apothecary, who had been interested in the natives for a number of years and had acted as their overseer. The Commissioners allowed him £20 a year for his services.

The Indians of the Sandwich area were tended by the Tupper family for over a century. Captain Thomas Tupper had first received a salary in about 1685 and less than ten years later he numbered his converts at one hundred and eighty souls.[3] He died in 1706, whereupon his son, Eldad, was chosen minister in his place. The Commissioners examined him 'as to his Orthodoxy skill in the Indian language, [and] Aptness to teach Conversation.'[4] They were apparently satisfied with his soundness as they paid him an annual allowance at first of £30 and then of £40. He was not actually ordained until 1719, and in April of the following year, according to Sewall, he had 'such a languishing Sickness, that . . . he has not once administered the Lord's Supper to his Church . . . since his Ordination.'[5] But from this sickness he recovered and by 1727 his salary had been increased to £80 a year. Eldad Tupper asked

[1] Ms. 7953/4, 19 Oct. 1708; Sibley, IV, 401.
[2] Matthew Mayhew, *A Brief Narrative*, 47–9; Sibley, II, 304–14.
[3] Matthew Mayhew, *A Brief Narrative*, 53.
[4] Ms. 7953/3.
[5] Ms. 7955/1, no. 56.

for permission to teach his flock English, which was readily granted. But in 1731, when his son Elisha was preparing to act as his assistant, it was still necessary for him to learn Indian and the Commissioners made him an allowance of £10 for this purpose. Three years later Elisha was examined by Dr. Colman and Dr. Joseph Sewall, who found him well qualified as a minister to the Indians and by 1736 he too was earning £80.[1] Elisha Tupper carried on his work amongst the Indians for more than fifty years.

The Mashpee Indians who lived in the hills behind Sandwich received a considerable amount of attention from the Commissioners during the eighteenth century. Roland Cotton, another son of John Cotton the missionary, preached to them and to other Indian settlements within easy reach of Sandwich and two years later claimed that there were more than two hundred converts in the region. Two years before his death in 1722 he had succeeded in gathering an Indian church with a native minister presiding over it.[2]

The Commissioners then approached Joseph Bourn, who had graduated at Harvard in 1722, asking him to tend the Mashpee Indians who lived near his home at Sandwich. He was an obvious choice as his great-grandfather, Richard Bourn, had formerly been their pastor, while both his grandfather and father had been interested in protecting Indian rights. In 1726 he was chosen pastor by the Indians although it was not until 1729 that he was ordained, the ceremony being performed by the Rev. Joseph Lord and two Indian pastors of Martha's Vineyard. At the end of his first year he wrote to the Commissioners reporting that there were 70 Indian families under his care and that there were 42 church members, five having been added during the year; the Lord's Supper was administered by a neighbouring Indian pastor, once every two months, and Bourn himself preached on the preceding Fridays a preparation sermon. On Sundays he preached twice and read passages from the Bible, with explanations. But the promise of this report was not ultimately to be fulfilled; in 1740 Bourn was convicted of selling liquor to the Indians, and was fined and sent to gaol for two months. He was

[1] Ms. 7953/22–4 *passim*.

[2] Matthew Mayhew, *A Brief Narrative*, 52; Ms. 7955/1, no. 60; Sibley, III, 323–6.

dismissed from the Commissioners' service although care was taken to see that any arrears of salary should be 'regulated according to equity'; he retired from his ministry in 1742.[1]

The Mashpee Indians were without an English minister until Gideon Hawley was appointed in 1758. Hawley, who had been employed as a schoolmaster at Stockbridge by the Commissioners from 1752 until 1754, went on a mission to the Six Nations in 1754, but was forced to retire on account of the war in 1756.[2] Jonathan Edwards, who knew him well at Stockbridge, described his character as 'that of a Person of Good Abilities, solid Piety, remarkable Prudence & Steadiness of Temper for one of his Years, a happy Talent in Teaching, Good Resolution & Spirit of Government, and has long had an Inclination to the Business of Instructing Indians.'[3] Once settled as minister of the Mashpee Indians he remained amongst them for the rest of his life.

The Commissioners also employed missionaries in Rhode Island. In 1698 Eliphalet Adams began preaching to the Indians at Little Compton. He was allowed £25 a year until October 1700; six months later he moved to New London without informing the Commissioners so that when he claimed the balance of his salary the Commissioners saw 'no Cause to make him any further allowance.'[4] His place at Little Compton was taken by Richard Billings who, from 1705, was paid £20 a year for preaching a monthly sermon to the natives. His salary was later increased to £25.[5] In October 1727 he claimed that of the three or four hundred Indians under his care, all the adults except three or four, 'were Capable of being preached to, in the English Language.'[6] In 1734 the inhabitants of Block Island, Rhode Island, had asked the Commissioners to send them a minister, in return for which they would allow the Indians the use of part of their meeting house. Joseph Mayhew was sent with a salary of £60 on the understanding that the inhabitants of Block

[1] Ms. 7955/2, no. 74a; Sibley, VII, 8–10; Ms. 7953/26.

[2] *D.A.B.*, VIII, 418.

[3] Lambeth Palace Library, Ms. 1123/1, no. 60, J. Edwards to Joseph Paice, 24 Feb. 1752 (copy).

[4] Ms. 7953/1; Sibley, IV, 189–98.

[5] Sibley, IV, 393–4; Ms. 7946/28–39 *passim*.

[6] Ms. 7953/21.

Island paid the rest, but after a year at Block Island he returned to Harvard where he became a tutor and eventually a Fellow.[1]

A slightly more successful appointment was Joseph Park who, in 1733, was sent to Westerly. In the earlier 1740s he succumbed to the revivalist preaching of James Davenport and by 1742 had organized a New Light Congregationalist church; a quarter of his congregation was drawn from the Indians, to whom the Great Awakening strongly appealed; the Commissioners were delighted with his success and paid him the exceptionally high salary of £120. However a few years later the Narragansetts withdrew to form a splinter church under the leadership of an Indian pastor, Samuel Niles. The Commissioners thereupon withdrew their support from Park, and so brought about the complete collapse of the first New Light Congregational Church in Westerly. As a result Joseph Park and some of his congregation appealed to the Commissioners in 1751 for some relief: and a little relief was in fact given.[2] A salary was also paid to Joseph Torrey, minister of South Kingston, in 1735. He was the centre of the controversy between Episcopalians and nonconformists over glebe lands, a controversy which lasted intermittently for more than twenty years. There is a suspicion that the Commissioners paid him in recognition of his part in the dispute, rather than for his services to the Indians.[3] In 1766 Joseph Fish was asked by the Commissioners to oversee a Narragansett school at Charlestown, Rhode Island, and to preach there once a month. Fish had more than twelve years' experience of teaching and preaching to the Indians at Stonington, Connecticut. He was also a correspondent of the Scottish Society for Propagating Christian Knowledge.[4]

It was not until the eighteenth century that Connecticut received the full attention of the Commissioners. During the previous century the efforts of William Leveritch and James Fitch had been met with nothing but failure. In 1706 the Commissioners wrote to John Winthrop, Governor of Connecticut: 'It is well known to you that you have a body of Indians within the very bowels of your Colony, who to this

[1] Ms. 7955/2, no. 104; Sibley, VIII, 731.

[2] Sibley, VII, 415–21; Ms. 7952, 25 March 1751, 24 March 1752, 3 April 1753.

[3] Sibley, VIII, 498–507; Ms. 7953/24.

[4] Sibley, VIII, 422.

day ly perishing in horrid ignorance and wickedness, devoted vassals of Satan, unhappy strangers to the only Saviour.' They had been preached to in the past without success but the Commissioners promised that if the ministers held a meeting to see what could be done, and if a suitable minister were chosen to preach to them, he would be given financial support.[1] This suggestion produced no missionaries: it was repeated in 1713 with slightly better result — the House of Representatives being prepared to make a grant in favour of the Pequots at Groton, near New London.[2]

Experience Mayhew visited the Pequot and Mohegan Indians of Connecticut in 1713 and again in 1714. After each visit he wrote brief journals, copies of which were sent first to the Commissioners and then to the Company. As these journals reveal the enormous practical difficulties to which missionaries were exposed in Connecticut and elsewhere, it is not surprising that neither the Commissioners nor the Company published them. In some places land disputes had made the Indians so hostile that they would not come to hear Mayhew, in others they refused on the pretext that their sachem was away hunting or that they could not come unless another tribe consented first. Even when the Indians did come to hear him their remarks show the kind of opposition the missionaries encountered. The natives asked why they should be good when there were so many bad English; they pointed out that many Indian converts were not converts at all and that the English themselves 'were divided, some keeping *Saturday*, and others *Sunday*, and others not keeping any day.' And finally they said that some had tried religion in Mr. Fitch's time, but had found it too difficult and had therefore abandoned it. Mayhew did his best to answer this barefaced cynicism but without success.[3]

The General Court of Connecticut determined to obtain a share of the funds distributed by the Commissioners. They therefore suggested that Jeremiah Dummer, their agent in London, should approach the Company to see what could be done. In February 1724/5 Dummer wrote to Timothy Woodbridge, pastor of the First Church, Hartford, informing him that Ashurst had promised that the money sent to New

[1] M.H.S. *Collections, 6th series*, III, 347–8.

[2] Ms. 7953/8–9, 25 Aug., 27 Oct. 1713.

[3] Ms. 7936, f. 38–9.

England would in future be equally divided between Massachusetts and Connecticut. But the Company needed a letter from the Governor of Connecticut — 'particularly setting forth that Your Colledge is founded upon principles agreeable to the Religion of the Countrey, for they have heard a foolish Story, as if you design'd it as a Nursery for the Church of England.'[1] Governor Talcott wrote to Robert Ashurst assuring him that Yale was not a nursery of the Church of England. He also recommended that three Commissioners for Connecticut should be appointed with power to act independently from the Commissioners at Boston.[2] The reply, written on 6 October 1726, which Talcott received more than a year later, was not from Robert Ashurst but from his successor, William Thompson, and it must have made unpleasant reading in Connecticut. Thompson stated that he had searched the records 'in relation to the expectation you seem to have had, that one moiety of what we remit abroad should be assign'd for the service of the Indians in your Colony', and that he had found nothing; in short Dummer had no authority for making such a statement and furthermore, although the Company was ready to help, it had insufficient income to do so. 'Our Commissioners there,' Thompson continued, 'are of opinion that your proposal is too chargeable. We pay a great regard to their opinion, and . . . it [is] impracticable to engage in what you propose without abridging very much the services we have already encouraged in the other Colony.'[3]

The General Assembly of Connecticut, prompted by the Commissioners, returned to the subject of gospellizing the Indians from time to time but with little result. In October 1723 Captain John Mason petitioned for permission to live amongst the Indians at New London, to protect them from encroachments upon their lands and to set up a school amongst them. His request was granted on condition that he first gain the Indians' consent.[4] This he obtained as well as the support

[1] *C.S.M.*, VI, 202.

[2] *Conn. H. S.*, V, 399–400. Gov. Talcott informed Dummer of his action in a letter, 30 Sept. 1725 (*Conn. H. S.*, IV, 61).

[3] *Conn. H. S.*, IV, 81.

[4] *The Public Records of . . . Connecticut, 1717–1725*, ed. by C. J. Hoadly (Hartford, 1872), 429.

and approval of Eliphalet Adams, who was a valuable ally. Even the Commissioners considered that Adams might be of use to them; when in July 1725 he claimed a year's salary owing to him for his stay at Little Compton a quarter of a century earlier, the Commissioners readily granted it 'in expectation of his future serviceableness to the Indians in Connecticutt Colony.'[1]

In August 1726 Mason appeared in person before the Commissioners with letters from Adams and Governor Talcott recommending him for the post of schoolmaster at New London. He came prepared with a careful estimate of his requirements, which were:

3 Stroud Blanketts for the Sachems of the 3 tribes Vizt the Mohegin Pequot & Nianticks	
27 Blanketts for the Councellours & other Chiefs or such as send their Children	
Cloathing for 20 children at 20/- each	20
Provisions for Corn &c to dine them for 1 year	20
The Boarding of 8 of 'em removed from their Parents for 1 year at 50/- Each	20
The hire of a House 1 year for the School	2

His personal remuneration he was ready to leave to the discretion of the Commissioners. His proposals were approved and it was decided that Connecticut should be asked to build a school-house and provide the Indians with a minister 'as soon as they shall be willing & Capable to receive his Instruction.'[2]

Six months later, in April 1727, Adams visited the school and reported upon it to the Commissioners: there were twelve boys who attended but Mason expected another eight to attend in the summer. 'Those that I heard yesterday', Adams wrote, 'could Spell very prettily in their primmers & some could read without Spelling, particularly those of them that were Elder & bigger than the rest & had been the Earliest at the School, They also rehearsed the Lord's Prayer, the Creed, & the ten Commandments in English very Expertly, and (as Capt. Mason assures me) They begin to take in the meaning of the Things . . . They seem to delight in their Learning & value themselves pretty considerably upon

[1] Ms. 7953/19. [2] Ms. 7953/20.

it.' Although Mason thought the Indians still unready for religious instruction, Adams hoped that they would accept Christianity 'when once their Children come (any Number of them) to be in some tolerable Degree Masters of the English tongue.'[1] The Commissioners were satisfied with Mason's efforts and in October allowed him £50 for his year's service. Mason, however, who was not retiring in character, at once informed them that he would be unable to carry on with such a salary, whereupon he was offered a further £30. But Mason remained unsatisfied and insisted 'that inasmuch as He must spend his whole time on the Affair, He could not without sensible Detriment to him, perform the service for less than One Hundred pounds per year.' In the face of this blunt demand, the Commissioners were forced to give way.[2]

In 1728 Adam Winthrop reported to the Company that the Connecticut General Assembly had agreed to pay for a school-house and might contribute to the annual charge; there were twenty scholars who attended and another ten were expected: 'The Females begin to think it hard that They are not taught, so that some girls are likely to be received in a Short time.' He further reported that the sachem was now sober and attended public worship 'and 10 or 12 of the Boys would do so if they may have shirts and hatts.' Finally, the Indians were now willing to have Eliphalet Adams preach to them from time to time.[3] Winthrop also wrote to Talcott expressing the Commissioners' pleasure at the action of the General Assembly in supporting the school and asking him to commend it further to the Assembly's attention. In May 1728 Adams wrote to Governor Talcott: 'Capt. Mason seems to me to have been faithful in his undertaking and to be worthy of encouragement.' Rev. Benjamin Lord, of Norwich, also wrote to Governor Talcott confirming Eliphalet Adams's report on Mason: the Indians 'are wonderfully suited with a Schoolmaster, who is truly a Gentleman.'[4] In 1733 Adam Winthrop reported that affairs were still proceeding satisfactorily and that the Indian children had 'been to a School of English children not far off to vie with them in their learning.' The Indians were now asking for a minister and the Commissioners intended to send Thomas Pegun of Natick, who was to be fitted out 'with some

[1] Ms. 7955/2, no. 79a. [2] Ms. 7953/21.
[3] Ms. 7955/2, no. 81. [4] *Conn. H. S.*, IV, 389–90, 107–8, 110.

decent cloathing, with travelling expence & a small matter to leave with his family.'[1] In the end, however, it was Jonathan Barber who in 1734 was sent to the Mohegans at New London, with a salary of £100 per annum, but he remained in the Commissioners' service for less than five years. Eliphalet Adams's son, William, was also allowed £20 in 1735 for preaching to the Indians at Groton. Two years later, however, the Commissioners refused him further payment.[2]

In 1735 the school run by Mason came to an end, as Mason entered upon a long dispute with the Connecticut government concerning Indian lands. He laid his case before the Commissioners, stating that the English had made encroachments upon Mohegan lands and that in spite of repeated applications to the General Court of Connecticut he was unable to obtain any redress. The Commissioners were not immediately ready to commit themselves and ordered a letter to be sent to Governor Talcott in order to hear his version of the story. Talcott was able to convince Governor Belcher and the Commissioners of the good intentions of his government, so that when Mason set forth for England to seek redress of his grievances, he went without the Commissioners' support. Talcott had assured them that the government of Connecticut would 'take effectual measures to do justice to the Indians with respect to their Lands, that so they may be in a capacity to live in compact manner, & in a better condition to receive instruction & the Christian religion.' Talcott asked the Commissioners to warn the Company that Mason was a man with a grievance, but although they were unwilling to lend Mason their support they were equally unwilling to prejudice the Company against him. However, in May 1736, they recorded that Mason was no longer in their service, and not long afterwards he died without having obtained a hearing in England.[3]

Two years before the dismissal of Mason, the Commissioners had employed Richard Treat, who during part of 1734 and 1735 taught and preached to the Indians between Middletown and Glastonbury.[4]

[1] Ms. 7955/2, no. 94.

[2] Ms. 7955/2, no. 101a, 104; Ms. 7953/24–5.

[3] Ms. 7953/24; *Conn. H. S.*, IV, 328–34, 338–43, 375; John W. de Forest, *History of the Indians of Connecticut* (Hartford, 1851), 319–24.

[4] *Conn. H. S.*, IV, 314–15; Ms. 7953/24.

Another Connecticut minister, Samuel Whitman, of Farmington, also tried to do something for the Indians; he ran a school for Indian and English children. The Commissioners undertook to pay for each Indian child attending the school at the same rate as the English children. The brightest of Whitman's Indian pupils was one John Mettawan, who lived with him; the Commissioners, on hearing of his progress, asked Governor Talcott to send for him: 'and if he inclines to be bro't up to Grammar, and even Colledge Learning, with a resolution to become a Minister to the Indians, the Commissioners will be at the charge of it, and in that case, if you will order him to be furnished with Homespun Coat, Jacket, and Breeches, two Shirts, Stockings, Shoes and Hat, after the English Fashion and send . . . a Bill of the cost, and it shall be answered.' A postscript clarified the Commissioners' intentions: 'If the Indian Youth does not desire to be bro't up to Learning and be a Minister, he is not then to be Clothed in the English Fashion, but only to have the largest Blanket.'[1] Two years later Samuel Whitman reported to the Commissioners that Mettawan was still making excellent progress: 'I take him to be a christian indeed. A letter written with his own hand is here inclosed; the writing is wholly his & affords you a specimen of his proficiency in that part of learning. It was first written in English, but I order'd him to turn it into Latin, which he has done, tho it past under some few corrections.'[2] Samuel Whitman built a school at his own expense where John Mettawan taught, although Whitman was still teaching him divinity. By January 1737/8 Whitman reported that his pupil had 'attain'd to a considerable knowledge and understanding of the principles of the Christian religion.'[3] But after this date his scholastic achievements are no longer on record and it is probable that, like so many before him, he succumbed to disease and died without fulfilling his early promise.

Jacob Johnson of Groton was one of Connecticut's more successful missionaries. He preached to the Indians once a month and taught them regularly; his congregation numbered from forty to seventy and, although he complained that 'Lay Exhorters' had at times stolen his

[1] *Conn. H. S.*, IV, 283–4; Sibley, IV, 315–17.

[2] Ms. 7955/2, no. 108.

[3] Ms. 7955/2, no. 128, extracts from Whitman's letters.

audience, he had managed to overcome them. In 1755 he sent to Andrew Oliver an account of the Indians at Groton and of his work there;[1] he made mention of an Indian schoolmaster, whose school numbered thirty pupils, half of whom could read. He concluded his account with a poem entitled 'The Indian Penitent', the substance of which had been dictated to him by one of his Indians and which he rendered in verse. One portion was, no doubt, particularly calculated to please:

> What shall Me speak to God, who is so good?
> O let me live to spread his Praise abroad;
> And to rejoyce England, both Old, & New;
> Society & ye Commiss'ners too;
> Society to Spread Free Gospel Grace
> Among Poor Indian Tribes, from Place to Place:
> Commissioners to see the Good work runs,
> By preaching Christ, and Scholling of our Sons.

Most of the ministers employed in Massachusetts and Connecticut only preached to the Indians in their own neighbourhood. To send the Gospel further afield was more difficult because it meant either full-time employment in the service of the Indians, which few were prepared to consider, or alternatively taking the minister from his congregation for long periods. It had always been Eliot's ambition to reach far-flung Indian settlements, and Boyle had encouraged him by sending a special gift for a mission to the Indians living 'further towards the East.' However, as funds were short and as there was so much to do nearer home, little was achieved during Eliot's lifetime.

In 1693 a number of ministers led by Increase Mather petitioned the Governor and Council of Massachusetts for sending missionaries to the eastern part of the province, 'That so we may answer our profession, in the first settlement of this country, as well as the direction of our present charter: And that the French essays to proselyte the heathen unto popish idolatry, may not exceed our endeavours to engage them unto the evangelical worship of our Lord Jesus Christ: And that we may the

[1] M.H.S. Ms. He was employed by Wheelock on a mission to the Six Nations in 1768. He left the parish in 1772. F. B. Dexter, *Biographical sketches of the graduates of Yale College* (New York, 1885), I, 649–51.

more comfortably hope for the blessing of God on our trade in those parts, when we seek first the interests of his kingdom there.'[1]

But it was long before any real attempt was made by the Commissioners to send missionaries to the Eastward Indians. In July 1715 Colonel George Vaughan, who had lately arrived from New England, proposed to the Company that it should send missionaries to Maine.[2] Unfortunately the precise nature of his proposals is unknown, but they were certainly unpalatable to the Commissioners, who were often suspicious of schemes not initiated by themselves; thus Sewall considered 'the aer of them was distastefull to all unprejudic'd persons that saw them.' He assured the Company that the Commissioners were extremely anxious to send the Gospel to the Eastern Indians but that it was extremely difficult to do so. Only recently Samuel Moody, pastor of York, Maine, had offered to Bombazeen, the Indian sachem, his only son to live with him and learn the Indian language on condition that Bombazeen would send his son to learn English in return. 'But,' Sewall concluded, 'Bombazeen could not find in his heart to agree to that Noble Offer.'[3]

The Commissioners were finally stirred into action by hearing of the success of the Jesuit, Sébastien Râle, among the Kennebec Indians, and their choice fell upon Joseph Baxter, minister of Medfield, because, as they pointed out to the General Assembly, he was the only minister prepared to go on this mission; he was further prepared to live there for six or twelve months, to learn the language and to preach to the Indians. The Commissioners recommended that the General Assembly should appoint him and at the same time give some assistance to Medfield which would be temporarily deprived of its minister. Baxter was offered £150 by the General Assembly and in August 1717 he accompanied Governor Samuel Shute and a group of Commissioners and others to meet a large number of Indians on Arrowsic Island, at the mouth of the Kennebec. Shute signed a treaty with the Indians on 9 August and at the same time introduced Baxter to them as their minister. But Baxter spent most of his time preaching to the white settlers at Georgetown, Brunswick, Augusta and Topsham, although he spoke with the Indians whenever he had the opportunity. He remained there, with one short

[1] M.H.S. *Collections, 3rd series*, I, 133–4.

[2] Ms. 7952.

[3] Ms. 7955/1, no. 37.

break, until May 1718, when he was reclaimed by his parishioners at Medfield, who were unwilling that he should undertake a further term in the mission field.[1]

While at Arrowsic, Baxter wrote a letter to Father Râle, to which the Jesuit replied with a dissertation of about one hundred pages in Latin proving the truth of Roman Catholic doctrines. Baxter replied to this in general terms and, to Râle's delight, left most of his arguments unanswered. Râle also found fault with Baxter's Latin. Governor Shute wrote to the Jesuit expressing amazement that he should not only oppose but also ridicule a mission which had the same aim as his own — he should have welcomed Baxter as a fellow-labourer; and to add force to his admonitions he enclosed a copy of an act relating to Jesuits in the King's dominions.[2]

James Woodside succeeded Baxter as missionary to the Eastward Indians. A Presbyterian minister of Dunbo, Londonderry, he had offered his resignation to the presbytery of Coleraine 'by reason of the wanting of his promiss'd Sallary or stipend': his resignation had been accepted, and the presbytery had furnished him with a testimonial.[3] He had arrived in New England in 1718 and had been chosen by the Commissioners to reside at Brunswick as 'he had in view the Instruction of the Eastern Salvages (which he should there have near him) in the primitive & reform'd Christianity.'[4] In June 1720 he was dismissed, according to Sewall, 'for several weighty Reasons'; in particular because there was no way of approaching the Indians who were 'in such a ferment about their Lands, lest the English should entirely engross them.'[5] Woodside left New England with his wife and, on arriving in the old country, wrote a memorial in which he explained that he had been forced to give up the mission on account of his own and his wife's health; he had been assured of assistance but in the event he had only

[1] *N.E.H.G.R.*, XXI (1867), 45–60.

[2] A full account of Baxter's exchanges with Râle is to be found in Sibley, IV, 146–53.

[3] Ms. 8010, 16 April 1718.

[4] Ms. 8010, copy testimonial letter from Increase and Cotton Mather, 14 June 1720; Ms. 7953/12, 19 March 1718/19.

[5] Ms. 7955/1, no. 59; Ms. 7953/13, 11 June 1720.

received £25 in New England currency; and this was the more unbearable as Baxter had been paid £150. Increase Mather and his son Cotton gave Woodside a testimonial which he duly presented to the Company in support of his claims: the Mathers stated that he had spent a considerable sum in going to Brunswick '& was at expence particularly in frequently entertaining the Indians at his house' and hiring an interpreter. 'But,' they concluded, 'he himself, & much more his wife upon finding their scituation there on many accounts disagreable to them, especialy in their want of Health . . . has been Inclin'd unto a return to Europe.' The Company decided to pay Woodside £25 in view of his circumstances and former service but noted that it was not to form a precedent, and that Commissioners must not in future give private letters of recommendation.[1] The subject of the Eastern Indians on the Kennebec was mentioned from time to time in the Commissioners' correspondence, but they did little more to foster missions there.

The Indians of New York had been almost entirely neglected by the Company during the seventeenth century. During the eighteenth the Commissioners were forced to review this field by the Lords of Trade and Plantations, who believed that Protestant missionaries could do much to foster British interests in the American colonies and make easier the path of the trader and merchant; they saw the Indians' conversion to the Protestant faith as 'one of the strongest bonds of union.' It was in the hope of obtaining missionaries to send amongst the Five Nations that the Lords of Trade approached the New England Company. In 1696, however, they reported that the Company would 'be very ready to apply their stock and Revenue when they shall be made to see, that the converting the Mohauqes . . . is of the greatest importance imaginable.'[2]

The Lords of Trade found a staunch ally in Richard Coote, Earl of Bellomont, who, on being appointed Governor of New England, was elected a member of the Company. Sir William Ashurst wrote to Stoughton in July 1697 expressing his approval of Bellomont whom he had known for many years: 'you will find him a Man of great bravery

[1] Ms. 8010; Ms. 7952, 22 Feb. 1720/21.

[2] E. B. O'Callaghan, ed., *Documents relative to . . . the State of New York*, IV,

and courage and of a most condescending meek and affable Temper, a Sober man that minds Religion.'[1] It was a judgment confirmed by Hutchinson who described him as 'far from high church' and as professing 'the most moderate principles in religion and government.'[2]

Before leaving England Lord Bellomont attended the Company's meetings and took a keen interest in its affairs. So much so that his delayed departure was a disappointment to the Company 'ffor we judged, he would be very assisting in this work having possessed him fully with our great inclinations to do all the good we can with this Charity.'[3] When, in 1698, he finally arrived in New York, he became, for his few remaining years, a dominating and often salutary influence in the Company's affairs. From America he wrote to the Lords of Trade suggesting that £300 of the Company's funds should be spent on employing Protestant missionaries: 'which will without question be effected on signification of your Lordships pleasure therein to the Members of that Corporation.' The Lords of Trade, following this advice, asked Sir Henry Ashurst whether any of the money belonging to the Company could be applied to the conversion of the Indians of New York, to which he replied that it was appropriated to New England and could not be used elsewhere. The Lords of Trade informed Bellomont of this rebuff, adding 'we intend to inquire further into that matter.'[4]

In the meantime Bellomont had written to the Company proposing that it should provide five itinerant ministers as missionaries to the Five Nations. On 17 February 1698 the Company read his letter and accepted the proposal. It was ordered that Daniel Bondet, who had been recommended by John Quick, should be one of the five ministers and that the other four should be chosen by the Commissioners from Harvard College — each to be paid £60. On the same day the clerk reported that he had taken a bond of security for £1,400 from Lord Bellomont 'condicioned for his answering and making good of several Bills of exchange for 700[ll] remitted to New England at 35[ll] per Cent

[1] Letter book (Univ. of Va. Ms.), 19.

[2] T. Hutchinson, *The History of the Colony and Province of Massachusetts-Bay*, II, 84.

[3] Letter book (Univ. of Va. Ms), 19.

[4] E. B. O'Callaghan, ed., *Documents relative to . . . New York*, IV, 334, 455.

exchange according to the Order of 26th August 1697.'[1] Bellomont pointed out to the Lords of Trade that they should have approached Sir William Ashurst and not Sir Henry Ashurst, and promised that he would do his utmost to encourage the Commissioners at Boston to promote missions to the Five Nations. The Lords of Trade for their part, on 21 August 1699 and again on 11 April 1700, simply repeated their request for Bellomont's assistance in securing part of the Company's funds.[2] On 11 June 1700 the Company, on Lord Bellomont's recommendation, increased the annual sum to be allowed to each of the itinerant ministers from £60 to £80 for the next three years. The Company's revenue, it was pointed out, would not allow of a greater expenditure. It was also decided that the choice of suitable ministers should be left to Bellomont.[3]

Before he had received news of this decision, Bellomont wrote to the Lords of Trade on 17 October 1700 assuring them that the Company's members 'are worthy gentlemen and I am confident will at your Lordships desire order the salaries of the Ministers out of the Corporation Stock.' He enclosed an account of those receiving salaries from the Company with the comment: 'I have often told Mr. Stoughton . . . that I thought that Province able enough to maintain their ministers, and that the giving that mony to ministers that did not preach to the Indians in their tongue, and were so lazy as not to learn it, that they might the better instruct them, was a misapplication of the Corporation mony.' He further reported: 'I am a member of the Corporation myself, and we had some meetings at Boston to settle that business but did little in it.'[4] Yet the Commissioners openly disapproved of any scheme which diverted the Company's funds from the hands of ministers within the province of Massachusetts.[5]

Bellomont wrote again to the Lords of Trade on 19 October 1700 with the news that the Company was willing to pay £80 each to five missionaries to the Five Nations for three years provided they were

[1] Ms. 7952.
[2] E. B. O'Callaghan, ed., *Documents relative to . . . New York*, IV, 521, 549, 631.
[3] Ms. 7952.
[4] E. B. O'Callaghan, ed., *Documents relative to . . . New York*, IV, 717–18.
[5] I. Mather, *Ichabod*, 71–2.

Harvard men. To this offer Bellomont had two objections: firstly, the allowance should not be temporary, as that would discourage ministers from undertaking the mission; secondly, he would prefer Church of England ministers 'for in New England the Ministers pray ex-tempore and mightily decry set forms of prayer; insomuch that they never use the Lord's prayer at any time.' Bellomont suggested: 'The best way in my humble opinion is for their Lordships to send to speake with Sir William Ashurst and the members of the Corporation, which is the way to come to a right understanding in that matter. Sir William is a right honest gentleman and will hearken to reason.' The Company, he concluded, should pay £300 per annum for two ministers, and a further £70 should be divided between two Dutch ministers. The Lords of Trade, with commendable realism, replied by suggesting that Bellomont should take advantage of Ashurst's offer until something better turned up.[1]

In 1693 the Commissioners had begun to pay a salary of £40 a year to Godfrey Dellius, a Dutch minister at Albany. Stoughton reported to the Company 'that a good beginning is there made to gospelise the Indians.'[2] Dellius himself reported that he had translated six or seven psalms and the Ten Commandments into the Indian language, but that a Jesuit called Milet was doing his best to frustrate his labours.[3] In 1698 Dellius was convicted by Lord Bellomont of fraudulently obtaining a grant of land from the Indians and his salary from the Commissioners was terminated.[4] The Bishop of London wrote to the Council of Trade and Plantations in November 1700 regretting Dellius's dismissal as he was the 'only man that understood how to converse with ye Mohocks.' At the same time he suggested that Bellomont might be given a commission to examine the Company's accounts 'from their first planting.'[5] Dellius returned to Halteren near Bergen op Zoom in Brabant where he was minister of the reformed church. Meanwhile the Society for the Propagation of the Gospel in Foreign Parts approached him with a view

[1] E. B. O'Callaghan, ed., *Documents relative to . . . New York*, IV, 766, 844.

[2] Ms. 7936, f. 30.

[3] Matthew Mayhew, *A Brief Narrative*, 54–5.

[4] *C.S.P. Col., 1697–1698*, 425, 435.

[5] *C.S.P. Col., 1700*, 631.

to sending him as its missionary to the Five Nations; not unnaturally it wanted to see him first, the more so as he demanded a substantial salary. And so he came to London at the S.P.G.'s expense.[1] While in London in February 1703/4 he took the opportunity of petitioning the Company for two years' pay which he claimed was still owing to him. In 1706 he came to England a second time and pressed his claim once again, this time with some success.[2]

In December 1700 Bellomont had written to the Commissioners recommending John Lydius of Albany and Bernard Freeman of Schenectady for salaries. In 1700 Freeman had been ordained pastor of the church at Albany by the classis of Lingen but this was irregular as Lydius had already been chosen for that position. Freeman was therefore given the post at Schenectady by Bellomont. The Commissioners ordered him a salary of £40 and Lydius a salary of £30, noting that 'The Stock was found much exhausted, and therfore came not up to his Lordships Proposals sent in Letters from New Yorke.'[3] Freeman became very proficient in the Mohawk language and Sewall sent him a number of books in Indian, asking him to try and discover whether 'there were any affinity between their Indians and ours in their language.'[4] By February 1705/6, however, Freeman gave up his life at Schenectady and went to Long Island.[5] Lydius seems to have been a more difficult employee: he apparently complained to Sir William Ashurst that the Commissioners were not paying him, but Sewall explained that 'he ordered no body to receive what was due to him: but spent much time in expostulating with the Commissioners about the doubling, or at least augmenting his Salary,' and this they had not been willing to do.[6] The Society for the Propagation of the Gospel in Foreign Parts kept a friendly eye upon them both. Freeman was reputed to be 'an extraordinary Man' and 'well affected to the Church of England, and has translated a great part of its Liturgy into the Indian Language.'[7]

[1] S.P.G. Journal, I, 49, 83, 111, 140, 154; Lambeth Palace Library, Fulham Papers, Box 2, no. 12, Dellius to the S.P.G., 11 Oct. 1703.

[2] Ms. 7952, 23 Feb. 1703/4; Ms. 8010, petition; Ms. 7953/3, 8 April 1706.

[3] Ms. 7953/1; *D.A.B.*, VII, 8–9.

[4] M.H.S. *Collections, 6th series*, I, 257.

[5] Ms. 7953/2.

[6] Ms. 7955/1, no. 6.

[7] S.P.G. Journal, I, 556–7.

Lydius had been given 'an honourable Gratuity' amounting to £10, for which he had made 'a civil and grateful Answer.' In February 1709/10 he applied to the S.P.G. for a regular salary, but on 1 March 1710 he died, and his widow petitioned the Commissioners for the remainder of his salary, which was still unpaid.[1]

At Oxford, N.Y., Daniel Bondet, a French minister, received a salary from the Commissioners until 1700. He then moved to New Rochelle, where he became an ordained minister of the Church of England and was employed by the Society for the Propagation of the Gospel in Foreign Parts from 1709 until his death in 1722. In 1700 Bellomont informed the Lords of Trade of developments at New Oxford: 'Mr Stoughton and I joyn'd in putting Mr Laborie into a Plantation where are some French and Indians, with a salarie of £30 a year.' But Jacques Laborie was hardly more successful than Bondet had been and by 1703 he had moved to Providence, his last payment being made in the following year.[2]

In 1701 Lord Bellomont died at New York and his brief but important association with the Company was at an end. Had he lived longer the character of the Company's work might have been radically changed, perhaps for the better; his wide vision was unbounded by the prejudices of the Boston Commissioners, and he was in favour of financing ministers who devoted their whole time to the Indians, rather than of subsidizing part-time workers.

It was with his criticism in mind that the Company's Court ordered that no salaries should be paid to any who could not speak the Indian language or 'at least discover God's mind and Will to them by Interpreters.' The Company also noticed that ministers had been paid in the past 'tho they have not bin particularly & zealously serviceable.' At the same meeting the Company heard that peace had been made with the New York Indians and it was hoped that the five ministers would now be sent forth. A letter from Sewall had been received doubting the

[1] *An Account of the Society for Propagating the Gospel in Foreign Parts* (1706), 45; S.P.G. Journal, I, 143, 145, 212, 455; Ms. 7953/6.

[2] Ms. 7953/1, 8 April 1700; Ms. 7952, 31 Oct. 1701; C. F. Pascoe, *Two Hundred Years of the S.P.G.* (1901), II, 855; E. B. O'Callaghan, ed., *Documents relative to . . . New York*, IV, 718.

wisdom of the venture, but the Company felt sure that its missionaries would be more successful than the Roman Catholics: 'seeing the Protestants have truth & the God of truth on their side, if the Commissioners of this Company can but have men fitly qualifyd with abilities & courage to go amongst them.'[1]

The question of sending itinerant ministers to the New York Indians was revived in the 1740s when the Company received the first fruits of Dr. Williams's bequest. Daniel Oliver had suggested to Colonel John Stoddard that two missionaries might be sent amongst the Six Nations. Stoddard wrote to John H. Lydius on 9 March 1746/7 and asked him to discover whether the Indians would receive two ministers. The remainder of the letter was devoted to explaining the bounty which the Massachusetts government would be prepared to pay for French or Indian scalps. Lydius reported that the Indians would accept two missionaries but predicted trouble with the Hudson River Indians.[2]

On the recommendation of David Brainerd, two young Yale graduates were chosen as the first itinerant missionaries under Dr. Williams's bequest — Elihu Spencer and Job Strong. The choice was endorsed by both the Company and the Trustees of Dr. Williams's charity.[3] They spent the winter of 1747 with John Brainerd, at Bethel, New York, learning the Indian language, and the following summer with Jonathan Edwards at Northampton studying theology. In July 1748 their salaries were fixed at £30 per annum and two months later Spencer was ordained at Boston as a missionary to the Oneidas. They proceeded on their mission but the difficulties of the work and an unfortunate choice of interpreter made them abandon the enterprise. They received £36. 8s. between them 'for their Attempt to Reside as Missionaries among the Indians.'[4]

Gideon Hawley went on a mission to the Six Nations on the Susquehanna in 1754, but was forced to retire on account of the war in

[1] Ms. 7952, 31 Oct. 1701.

[2] M.H.S. Ms. Lydius's reply was dated 26 March 1747.

[3] Ms. 7952, 15 July 1748; Dr. Williams's Library, Trustees' Minutes, 1742–8, No. 12, p. 84.

[4] *D.A.B.*, XVII, 447–8; F. B. Dexter, *Biographical sketches of the graduates of Yale College*, II, 132–3; Ms. 7912/1, f. 67.

1756. In 1761 the Commissioners employed him again to introduce two missionaries, Eli Forbes, minister of the second parish in Brookfield, Mass., and Amos Toppan, to the Onohoquaga (at Colesville, Broom county, New York). Here they found the Indians were civil and greatly improved both 'in morality and religion as well as husbandry.' At Jeningo, however, which they visited for several days, three quarters of the Indians were drunk and the missionaries had finally to fly in order to save their lives. The mission was not a success and was brought to an end because the interpreters deserted.[1] In the following year Elia Forbes, accompanied by Asaph Rice, afterwards pastor of Westminster, Mass., revisited Onohoquaga but the mission was soon abandoned because of war.

In 1764 Jasper Mauduit wrote to the Commissioners suggesting that, as peace had been reached with the Indians, it should be possible to send out two itinerant preachers again from the proceeds of Dr. Williams's charity. The Commissioners did not succeed in finding anyone willing to take on this work at a salary of £30 a year, but four years later Mauduit was able to inform Andrew Oliver that the Company could in future allow £45 per annum for each missionary.[2] The first missionary appointed on these terms was Ebenezer Moseley: graduating at Yale in 1763, he had then studied theology and was ordained four years later. He was accompanied to Onohoquaga by James Deane, then a boy of fifteen, to act as his interpreter. Moseley's salary was later increased to £102, a large part being paid by Harvard out of its share of Dr. Williams's charity.[3] He continued at Onohoquaga until 1773 when he left the Commissioners' service altogether, married and settled down as a country merchant at Windham, Connecticut.[4] Deane's place had been taken by T. Spencer in 1771 and 1772, and in 1774 Aaron Crosby, who had been educated at Dartmouth College, took over from Moseley. Crosby continued in the Commissioners' service until August 1777, when the mission was abandoned. Even then they were prepared to pay him a retainer in view of 'his Spirit for this Service, his Stediness &

[1] Ms. 7927, f. 3–4 & Ms. 7955/2, no. 149, report by Hawley and Toppan.
[2] Ms. 7927, f. 7, 16.
[3] Ms. 7920/1, p. 2.
[4] F. B. Dexter, *Biographical sketches*, III, 39–41.

diligence in it, his long experience and uncommon acquaintance with the Indians Language, and the great share he appears ever to have had in the affection and Esteem of his Charge.'[1]

The Company subsidized Samuel Kirkland, who was employed by the Scottish Society for Propagating Christian Knowledge as a missionary to the Oneida Indians. Kirkland had been prepared for college at Eleazar Wheelock's Indian School at Lebanon. He took his degree at New Jersey College in 1765, having already undertaken his first mission in the previous year under Wheelock's auspices. In 1770 his relations with Wheelock became so strained that he turned to the Commissioners for assistance; they were, of course, delighted and gave the Company glowing accounts of his work. The Company too was pleased and Mauduit wrote to Oliver: 'Mr Kirkland's character is very pleasing and we hope he will continue an useful Missionary.'[2] In 1771 the Commissioners voted their thanks to Sir William Johnson for encouraging him in his mission to the Oneida Indians, and in 1773 allowed him £105: but it is not clear whether this was an isolated payment, or whether the Company paid him regularly in addition to what he received from the Scottish Society.[3]

The Company occasionally received suggestions from visitors to England as to how it should spend its funds. In 1692 John Usher had expressed his thoughts on the subject in a letter to Joseph Thompson, an active member of the Company and afterwards its treasurer: 'I judge itt moste proper to infuse into them good morall principles before they [are] perswaded to greatter matters of religion, [and] doe judge in y[e] firstt place, itt nott be a miss to order presentts of Laced Coates Shooes stockins hatts & shirts with a Small Sword and beltt be given to the Sachems as from y[e] King & to lett them know justice Shall be done them as well as any of his Majestys subjects.' In fact the Commissioners did make gifts to Indian chiefs from time to time, usually on the Company's recommendation. Usher had also suggested that, as Indian wars had interrupted missions, the funds thus saved should be expended upon

[1] Ms. 7953/27.

[2] Ms. 7927, f. 26.

[3] *D.A.B.*, X, 432–4; E. B. O'Callaghan, *The Documentary History of the State of New-York*, IV (Albany, 1851), 460; Ms. 8009, abstract of Commissioners' accounts, 1773.

'some releife to ye poore distresed towns impoverished by ye enemy' which would not only be an act of charity but in 'noe ways injurious to ye design for which ye Stock was given.' But Usher's main concern was not so much with saving Indian souls as with winning them to the British cause.[1] A copy was sent to the Commissioners 'not as approving his method by pictures to promote Popery or by gifts to make hypocrites' but for their comments.[2]

More fruitful by far were the proposals made nearly forty years later by Governor Jonathan Belcher. He suggested in March 1729/30, that the Company should ask the Massachusetts government to grant it a tract of land for a township 'that shoud be sufficient to recieve a good Number of English & Indian inhabitants, & this Town to be settled at the Charge of the Company.'[3] The Company would employ a minister and 'a writing & grammar Schoolmaster both of them to be Masters of the Indian language.' He continued: 'Tradesmen of Sundry Sorts incouraged to Settle in the Town — they to take Indian Children as Apprentices & the Indians to have yearly some small presents. By these means they would soon be Civilized & more easily brought into the knowledge & Esteem of the true Christian Religion.' Then he got down to business. 'And the Charge of this Affair I suppose might be:

For building the Church & Schoolhouse	500
Incouragment to the first tradesmen to settle	350
Say *£850* N England or as the present Exchange is	
£250 sterling — & the yearly support	
To the minister	200
Schoolmaster	150
putting out 20 apprentices 20£^{aps}	400
Presents to the Indians	350
Say £1100 N. England or £350 Sterling per annum.	

The Company appointed a special committee to consider the proposals, consisting of the Governor and Treasurer of the Company, Samuel Ashurst, John Jacob, Thomas Stiles and Thomas Hollis. It met on 20 March and decided that the proposals should be accepted: Belcher should be asked to apply to the government in New England for a tract

[1] Ms. 7956. [2] Letter book (Univ. of Va. Ms.), 12. [3] Ms. 7956.

of land for a township, eight miles square; the Commissioners should be ordered to lay out £600, in New England currency, for building a church and a school; £300 for encouraging settlers, and a minister and schoolmaster should be allowed a salary. Five days later the committee's report was accepted by the Company's Court and it was ordered that a copy be given to Belcher.[1]

Although there was much which had a very familiar ring in these proposals, the idea of obtaining a tract of land from the Massachusetts government was to prove fruitful. But it was not until December 1734 that Belcher explained to the Commissioners the nature of the proposals he had made to the Company; meanwhile he had recommended the General Assembly to grant a tract of land for the Indians, and a committee had been set up accordingly to consider the matter.[2] Adam Winthrop, on the Commissioners' behalf, wrote to the Company asking for its help in obtaining grants for Indian townships and suggesting that two grants, one in the east and one in the west, might be easier to obtain than one. This, he suggested, would avoid a dispute over whether the grant was to be in the east or the west.[3]

At about this time Samuel Hopkins, pastor of Springfield, suggested that a missionary should be sent to the Housatonic Indians. In May 1734 the Commissioners asked Hopkins and Stephen Williams of Springfield to visit the Indians there, but when the time came Hopkins was ill and Nehemiah Bull of Westfield accompanied Stephen Williams instead. In August the Commissioners empowered Williams and Bull to search out a suitable missionary for the task; he was to be offered £100 per annum for his services. The post was promptly offered to John Sergeant, a graduate of Yale and a tutor there, who had already expressed his intention of preaching to the Indians. Williams recommended him to the Commissioners as 'a worthy, ingenious, learned & pious Gentleman.'[4] In fact, Sergeant was to become one of the most renowned missionaries to the North American Indian, and it was at Housatonic that Belcher's plan was to be realized.

The Commissioners agreed to Sergeant's appointment for three

[1] Ms. 7952. [2] Ms. 7953/23. [3] Ms. 7955/2, no. 102a.

[4] Ms. 7953/23. The following account of John Sergeant's career is largely based upon Samuel Hopkins, *Historical Memoirs* (Boston, Mass., 1753).

months, after which he was to return to Yale until the spring; he was then to settle permanently at Housatonic. Stephen Williams was also appointed to visit the Indians there. In October and November Sergeant duly visited Housatonic and, with the aid of an interpreter, preached to the Indians. The following year he settled there. In May 1735 he wrote to the Commissioners reporting that there were about forty Indians learning to read, and asking support for Timothy Woodbridge as a schoolmaster. 'The Indians,' he wrote, 'I find have a fondness for me, which I can impute to nothing but the overruling hand of providence; & if God is pleased to make me an instrument of serving their souls, it will be my greatest satisfaction.' He thought that he should be ordained as soon as possible in order to be fully effective.[1] The Commissioners decided that he should be paid an extra £50 per annum to compensate, as they put it, for the expense of living 'in such a new & wilderness place.' They agreed that he should be ordained and proposed 'that for the greater solemnity thereof, & in order to make a deeper impression on the minds of the Indians, that the ordination if possible be performed at Deerfield, in presence of his Excellency the Governor.'[2] On 31 August 1735 Sergeant was duly ordained before Governor Belcher and members of the General Court at Deerfield, the Housatonic Indians sitting by themselves at the service. The Rev. Nathaniel Appleton came from Cambridge to preach the ordination sermon. 'The Commissioners thought it expedient that the transactions at that time & the sermon preach'd on that occasion should be printed.'[3] It appeared under the title: *Gospel Ministers Must be fit for the Master's Use* (Boston, 1735). Winthrop sent some copies to the Company which were greatly appreciated; in 1736 he sent three dozen more and in July 1738 he informed Secretary Lane that he had bespoken all that were left and notified Treasurer Williams in August: 'According to directions for sending home what of Mr Appletons sermons were to be had, I got five dozen.'[4]

By November 1735 Sergeant had baptized four families, some

[1] Ms. 7955/2, no. 108, extracts made by Adam Winthrop and sent to the Company.

[2] Ms. 7953/24.

[3] Ms. 7955/2, no. 111, Adam Winthrop to Sir Robert Clarke, 2 July 1736.

[4] Ms. 7955/2, nos. 113, 112, 122, 124.

twenty-eight individuals in all; his conscience was not altogether easy about this — he feared that it might have been too soon, but pleaded that the Indians were set on it.[1] Then in January 1735/6 he received a letter from Governor Belcher bearing the good news that he had asked the General Assembly to make a grant of land to the Housatonic Indians. The General Assembly granted to the Indians in April 1736 an area six miles square, which subsequently became known as Stockbridge, and it was here that Sergeant laboured for the rest of his life.

Sergeant had suggested to Belcher that English families should be encouraged to settle at Stockbridge, an idea which Belcher himself had advocated a few years earlier. But it was not until September 1739 that Ephraim Williams and Josiah Jones moved there with their families, at the order of the General Assembly. They were soon joined by two other English families. From Sergeant's point of view this was particularly successful, for he married Abigail Williams, the daughter of Ephraim.

Life at Stockbridge was far from easy; Sergeant's salary by 1738 was £150. At this time the Commissioners allowed him £50 towards building his house and during the year Jacob Wendell came from London bringing with him a present of £100 from the Company. But in April 1741 Sergeant petitioned the Commissioners for an increase of salary on the grounds of currency depreciation, and he was granted an additional £50; the schoolmaster, Timothy Woodbridge, received the same increase. At the same time Sergeant warned the Commissioners: 'by reason of the Early frost last Fall the Indians crop of Corn was wholly destroyed, that they are now destitute of necessary food.' The need for relief was so acute that without it the Indians 'must certainly disperse.' £60 was therefore voted for their relief.[2] By 1747 Sergeant's salary was once more increased to £300 but this hardly did more than keep pace with depreciation.

The Stockbridge mission, it is true, did not depend entirely upon the Commissioners. Isaac Hollis, nephew of Thomas Hollis, the famous Harvard benefactor, supported twelve Indian boys who were fed, clothed and given lodging at his expense. Samuel Holden, a Director of

[1] Ms. 7955/2, no. 108. [2] Ms. 7953/26.

the Bank of England, gave £100 towards educating Indian children. Dr. Benjamin Colman, who had won the interest of Hollis and Holden, was a keen champion of Sergeant's cause. It was through his support that Sergeant made public his ideas on educating the Indians. They appeared in a small tract entitled: *A Letter from the Revd Mr. Sergeant of Stockbridge, to Dr. Colman of Boston; Containing Mr Sergeant's Proposal of a more effectual Method for the Education of Indian children; to raise 'em if possible into a civil and industrious People; by introducing the English language among them* (Boston, 1743). His plan was that ten or twenty children should be placed under the care of two masters: 'one to take the Oversight of them in their Hours of *Labour*, and the other in their Hours of *Study*.' The 'Fruit of their *Labour*' would provide the funds to maintain the school, but an initial sum would be necessary to start it, and if enough funds were raised it might be possible to take girls as well.[1] However, as in nearly all plans for the Indians' education, Sergeant gave no indication of what he meant by either the 'Labour' or the 'Study'. The Commissioners apparently considered the scheme themselves but decided that, as Sergeant was particularly favoured in London, it would be as well to send a copy of his scheme 'for the consideration of the Honourable Company', which course had the added advantage of postponing their decision.[2] The Company, however, resolved to consider the matter seriously only after some definite steps had been taken. Nevertheless, the Company's Treasurer informed Andrew Oliver, who in turn informed Sergeant, that the Company was favourably disposed towards the scheme. Thereupon Sergeant wrote to the Company explaining that the initial cost would amount to about £200 sterling. In July 1748 the Company voted Sergeant half that amount towards the school; a year later it voted that the money might be spent either in building the school or in maintaining it when built.[3]

But John Sergeant died at the age of thirty-nine, in 1749. At this time the Indian population at Stockbridge numbered 218 Indians, of whom 182 had been baptized and 42 were communicants. It is extremely difficult to judge Sergeant's success from these figures. He was certainly dedicated to his labours and had more to show for his work than many other missionaries employed by the Commissioners. Yet he

[1] *Op. cit.*, 4. [2] Ms. 7955/2, no. 146. [3] Ms. 7952.

was particularly fortunate in the additional support he received from both Dr. Colman and Governor Belcher. It must also be admitted that his posthumous reputation owes a good deal to Samuel Hopkins's *Historical Memoirs, Relating to the Housatunnuk Indians: or, An Account of the Methods used, and Pains taken, for the Propagation of the Gospel among that Heathenish-Tribe, and the Success thereof, under the Ministry of the late Reverend Mr. John Sergeant* (Boston, 1753).

Sergeant's position was first offered to Ezra Stiles, later President of Yale, who declined it,[1] and then to Jonathan Edwards, the distinguished Congregational theologian and philosopher who, as the result of the famous dispute with his parishioners at Northampton, was looking for another post. After two preliminary visits to Stockbridge, he settled there with his family in 1751. Apart from his fame as a theologian, he must have commended himself to the Commissioners as the author of David Brainerd's *Life* and the editor of his *Journals*. But his appointment was a good one from neither the Indians' nor his own point of view. He did not know enough of the Indian language to preach in it, which made him wholly dependent upon interpreters, although in addressing the Indians he took care to be, according to Gideon Hawley, 'a very plain and practical preacher: upon no occasion did he display any metaphysical knowledge in the pulpit.'[2] Personal disagreements with Ephraim Williams, one of the original English settlers, and with the whole Williams family, made his life at Stockbridge very difficult. Edwards did his best to obtain the Company's help but Mauduit, in writing to him on 19 April 1753, merely wished him 'wisdom for a right behaviour in ye difficult station providence has placed you.'[3]

In July 1751 the Company considered a memorandum drawn up by Elisha Williams; after describing the school at Stockbridge where '12 Boys were taught to read, Husbandry & other things', the memorandum proposed a school for Indian girls 'where they might be taught the Arts in use among ye English women (as well as reading &c.).'[4] Elisha Williams, himself a Commissioner, had been prompted by Ephraim Williams to whom the scheme was particularly attractive, the more so

[1] Ezra Stiles, *The Literary Diary*, I (New York, 1901), 209–11.
[2] M.H.S. *Collections, 1st series*, IV, 51.
[3] Letter book (Univ. of Va. Ms.), 274.
[4] Ms. 7952.

as his daughter, John Sergeant's widow, was the most likely candidate for the post of schoolmistress. Williams's plan also suggested that the school would fit the girls 'to become wives for ye young men educated in ye boys school', but the Company erased this part of the proposal. It was decided that a school for girls should be started, with not more than ten girls, and that Mrs. Sergeant should indeed be offered the post of schoolmistress at a salary of £30. A further £7. 10s. was to be allowed for board and clothing for each girl and £10 was to be allowed initially, so that Mrs. Sergeant could put her house in order. In 1755 the Company voted that the cost of erecting a tombstone to John Sergeant should be paid to Ephraim Williams and that £20 should be paid to his widow and £30 divided amongst his children.[1] Edwards himself envisaged an academy for the more advanced Indians at which it would be necessary 'to go out of the usual method of Scholastic & Academical Instruction, & particularly not to begin with Teaching the Boys the Learned Languages, but to begin with more Entertaining & Rational Studies, which will better suit the Genius of these People.'[2]

In 1757 Jonathan Edwards resigned his post at Stockbridge in order to become President of the College of New Jersey, a position to which he was far better suited, though he did not live long enough fully to enjoy the change, as he died in the following year.[3] The position at Stockbridge was filled by Stephen West who had graduated at Yale in 1755. In November 1758 he settled at Stockbridge and was ordained a few months later. His congregation consisted of eighteen English and forty-two Indian families. Fortunately perhaps, he married Elizabeth Williams, another daughter of Ephraim, and so at least did not suffer from that quarter as his predecessor had done. Although he at first taught the Indian children, he gave this up in about 1770.[4] His salary from the Commissioners was £80 sterling per annum. According to Ezra Stiles: 'He questioned whether it was honest for him to receive it when he could do so little good.' By this time there were fifty English families at Stockbridge who were comparatively well-to-do. Conse-

[1] *Conn. H. S.*, XV, 338–40; Ms. 7952, 3 July 1751, 4 March 1755.
[2] Lambeth Palace Library, Ms. 1123/1, no. 60.
[3] *D.A.B.*, VI, 30–7.
[4] F. B. Dexter, *Biographical sketches*, II, 388–94.

quently West and the Commissioners thought that these families should pay half his salary; but this they refused to do. West thereupon voluntarily gave up half his salary and after six months the English population relented and agreed to pay him £40 sterling per annum.[1]

In 1775 West gave over the whole Indian mission to John Sergeant's son. In March 1767 the Company had authorized the Commissioners to make him whatever allowance they should think fit.[2] He was, according to Stiles, 'Not of College Education, but an ingenious sensible and worthy Man'.[3] John Sergeant junior had been teaching the Indian children for several years and had been paid £10 and then £20 per annum; when he took over the whole mission, however, his salary was increased to £80 per annum.[4]

Stockbridge was certainly the most impressive Indian settlement in New England by the third quarter of the eighteenth century, ranking with Natick and Martha's Vineyard a century earlier. Eliot's plan of bringing the wandering Indian tribes into settled habitations had remained for more than one hundred and twenty years the most likely way of converting them. But it also remained supremely difficult to change a deeply rooted pattern of living. It is impossible, even if it were profitable, to estimate the total number of Indians converted by the Company's missionaries, but it cannot have been great.[5] The Indian population of New England was constantly dwindling, disease and rum continuing to take their toll. But if converts were few, so were those who attempted to make them: a few missionaries practising what so many propagandists had preached.

[1] E. Stiles, *The Literary Diary*, I, 209–10.
[2] Ms. 7952.
[3] E. Stiles, *The Literary Diary*, I, 210–11.
[4] Ms. 8009, abstract of Commissioners' votes, 1773.
[5] For some statistics, see *C.S.M.*, XXXVIII, 134–218.

10

Epilogue

THE beginning of the American War of Independence made no immediate impact upon the New England Company. In November 1775 it was resolved that, as the Commissioners were unable to meet on account of 'the Present disturb'd Scituation of Affairs in America', their treasurer was to make payments on his own authority.[1] This course had been suggested by Gideon Hawley who was apprehensive about his own salary as the Commissioners were 'dispersed over the country.'[2] But on 13 April 1779, the Company resolved: 'that the Governor do write to Mr Isaac Smith, the Company's Treasurer in New England, to desire he will Grant no further Certificates in Favour of any Missionaries or Schoolmasters for any Services perform'd after the Receipt of the said Letter, or at furthest after Midsummer 1779 until the State of Affairs in America shall admitt of the Meeting of the Company's Commissioners there.' Isaac Smith was, at the same time, to inform the missionaries of this decision. Little more than a month later, on 19 May, the Company resumed its consideration of the American situation. The charter was read and it was resolved: 'that this Court do not think themselves warranted by their Charter from the Crown in remitting Money to New England so long as that Country continues in Arms against his Majesty & their fellow Subjects & in Confederacy with the French King are levying War against Great Britain & their lawful Sovereign.' At the same meeting it was decided that the Company's Treasurer should accept no more bills of exchange 'drawn by any Persons in New England during the Continuance of the present Rebellion & until the

[1] Ms. 7920/1, p. 27.
[2] M.H.S. Ms., Alexander Champion to Isaac Smith, 23 Nov. 1775, copy 8 April 1777.

Resteration of Peace Order & Good Government.' But the Company's attitude was still lenient in April 1780 when the Treasurer reported that he had received several demands for payment which he had honoured; the Court even empowered him to discharge any further bills which he thought should be paid. But in November the Company considered that it had shown enough leniency and that no further bills should be paid, unless by special order of the Court. In fact, however, it did make a payment to John Sergeant as late as May 1783, in spite of its earlier resolutions.[1]

Isaac Smith, who had been appointed the Commissioners' Treasurer on the eve of the war, was confronted with a most difficult situation. Indeed he confessed to his son that he was sorry he had accepted the position as he found 'a good deal of Trouble in itt.'[2] It was not until the middle of 1777 that he received a copy of the Company's resolution of November 1775, ordering him to pay the missionaries and to draw bills of exchange upon the business house of Alexander Champion, the Company's Treasurer.[3] When some of these bills were no longer honoured, Smith had managed to get a few Commissioners together for a meeting on 18 January 1781. At this meeting the Commissioners approved a letter written by Smith to the Company's Governor, in which he pointed out that he had received no notice of the Company's intention to discontinue payments to the missionaries. It was only by chance that he had heard of the resolution of May 1779 and he supposed it genuine only because the Company had ceased to honour the bills of exchange. The Company's action was causing the missionaries great hardship, and he added: 'Thus are these Gentlemen depriv'd of their just dues of their living, who have been engaged by us, in the Name upon the Authority & Credit and by the Express order of the Company to promote the Common cause of Humanity and the Christian Religion.' Furthermore, as many of these missionaries had been in the Company's service for twenty years or more, they were now too old to find other employment.[4]

[1] Ms. 7920/1, pp. 43, 45–7, 51, 62.

[2] M.H.S. Ms., letter to I. Smith junior, 10 Feb. 1778.

[3] M.H.S. Ms., A. Champion to I. Smith, 8 April 1777.

[4] M.H.S. Ms., I. Smith to William Bowden, 18 Jan. 1781.

Isaac Smith wrote to the Company again on 30 September 1783, sending a copy of his letter of January 1781 and reporting that the missionaries were in great need of relief which, he hoped, would now be forthcoming.[1] In December 1784 he reported that three of the Commissioners had died, that James Bowdoin refused to serve any more and that Dr. Chauncy also refused 'having never Attended.' He therefore proceeded optimistically to nominate a new commission.[2] Others too hoped that, the war being over, the Company would return to its charges in New England. In July 1784 Nathaniel Gorham attended the Company's Court and proposed that it should advance money for building a place of worship at Charlestown. The inhabitants of Charlestown would, in return, clothe and educate one or more Indian children for a number of years.[3]

But both Isaac Smith and Nathaniel Gorham sadly misjudged the temper of the Company. At a meeting on 23 May 1785 the Court discussed 'the Legality of the Companys executing the several Trusts mention'd in their Charter,' and resolved to obtain legal advice.[4] Israel Mauduit, one of the most active and able of the Company's members, made a speech strongly opposing the continuance of the Company's activities. This he published under the title *The Substance of a Speech made at a General Court of the Company...* (1785).[5] 'Many respectable Members of the Company having been absent at the Court held the 23d of *May* last' he had had the speech printed 'for the use of such of my friends as may wish to see it.' Mauduit argued that the colonies comprising New England had revolted from the King's government and by express treaty had become foreign states: each 'more truly a different nation than *France* is: for the Crown of *England* has never renounced its title to *France*.' But the Company's charter was granted by the King for the benefit of his kingdom. Furthermore the Commissioners were no longer subjects of the crown and therefore could not execute the charter in the interests of Great Britain when they were bound by allegiance to their own governments. One of the motives in granting the charter was to increase commerce between England and the colonies, but these states

[1] Ms. 7956.
[2] Ms. 7953/28a.
[3] Ms. 7920/1, p. 65.
[4] Ms. 7920/1, p. 71.
[5] A copy of this scarce tract is bound with Ms. 7933.

were now rivals. The skin and fur trade depended entirely upon the good will of the Indians and now the new American government would force the Commissioners to employ the Company's money for the purpose of alienating the Indians from the English interest. In fact there would be no need to force the Commissioners as 'they were many of them among the prime leaders and first stirrers up of the rebellion.' As an instance of this perfidy, the Stockbridge Indians had been brought to Boston when British naval vessels were there 'on purpose to insult them, and were taught, by turning up their backsides, to express their defiance of them.' The missionaries were equally culpable, in particular Kirkland, who had led the Indians in Washington's army and had been employed by General Gates to negotiate a treaty with the Six Nations against the English: Mauduit concluded by arguing that 'the part of *America* which is next adjacent to the *Massachusetts* State, and is a part of ancient *New* England, is the King's colony of *New Brunswick*.' The Company should therefore transfer its activities to that colony.

The views expressed by Mauduit were readily accepted by his fellow members, and the Company was able to make use of its full title: 'the Company for Propagation of the Gospell in New England and the Parts adiacent in America' — as it was styled in its charter. Not only had 'New England' originally referred to a much greater area than the present term implied but it was argued that the phrase: 'Parts adiacent in America' practically exempted the Company from any territorial limitation. Although carefully qualified, two legal opinions seemed to confirm Mauduit's arguments.[1] On 25 April 1786 the motion 'that this Company cannot legally exercise the Trusts of its Charter in any part of America which is out of the Kings Dominions' was passed with the word 'legally' amended to 'safely' as was also the motion 'that this Company do transfer the Exercise of its Trusts to his Majesty's Province of New Brunswick which is the part next adjacent to that wherein we have hitherto exercis'd it & which in all the Charters of the Crown is consider'd as part of New England.'[2]

The rift was complete. Indeed, the Company did not even trouble to notify its American Treasurer, Isaac Smith, of these resolutions. Early

[1] Ms. 7964 & Ms. 7931, John Scott, 23 March 1786, and G. Hill, 6 April 1786.
[2] Ms. 7920/1, pp. 73–4.

in 1787 he wrote pointing out that he had received no reply to his letter of December 1784; to this William Lane, the Company's Secretary, replied assuring him that the failure to answer his letter 'did not proceed from any intended neglect.' He also informed Smith that the Company had agreed to pay his incidental expenses amounting to £22. 12s. 9d. and that the missionaries were being dealt with individually.[1]

Most of the missionaries in the Company's service before the war petitioned for assistance. A committee was set up in May 1786 to consider their petitions and to decide what allowances should be made. Thomas West of Rochester reminded the Company that he had helped Experience Mayhew for five years on the Vineyard before moving to Rochester and that he had been in the Company's service for about forty-three years. He asked for £100, and received £60 as 'Bounty & Compassion'. The Committee warned him that he was to 'consider this as his final dismission' and that he could expect nothing more.[2] Gideon Hawley was given £200 with the same warning. John Lane, a member of the Company visiting New England in 1788, asked that Hawley might be given further compensation as he had behaved during the war 'in a manner that was rather Examplary considering the Temper of the Times.' He would have been prepared to go to Nova Scotia as one of the Company's missionaries if he were not now too old.[3] But no further assistance was forthcoming. Even less fortunate was Elisha Tupper to whom the Committee allowed only £90.[4]

John Sergeant, who had followed in his father's footsteps at Stockbridge, was fortunate in having supporters for his claims. Stephen West, minister to the English at Stockbridge and previously in charge of the Indian mission there, wrote to Harrison Gray on Sergeant's behalf claiming that he was particularly deserving as the most successful of all the missionaries employed by the Company. He described Sergeant's financial position: 'He is the owner of a little plantation, which, with

[1] M.H.S. Ms., 5 June 1787.

[2] Ms. 7956, petition 28 Nov. 1786 and draft letter from William Lane to Thomas West, 5 June 1787; Ms. 7920/1, pp. 77, 80.

[3] Ms. 7956, John Lane to William Lane, 2 Jan. 1788.

[4] Ms. 7956, William Lane to Elisha Tupper (draft), 14 June 1786; Ms. 7920/1, p. 80.

proper cultivation, might afford a bare subsistence to himself and his increasing family. But, neglecting his temperal interest in order to promote the eternal good of the people of his charge, he is now so much involved in debt that, unless the Company will be pleased to assist and relieve him, he must soon be reduced to absolute poverty and want.'[1] Sergeant wrote to William Codner, his brother-in-law, who did what he could to promote his claims with the Treasurer, Alexander Champion, and with Richard Jackson, the Company's Governor.[2] These entreaties were successful and finally Sergeant was granted more than twice as much as any of the other missionaries — the lump sum of £450.[3] Two years later John Lane wrote to the Company from New England informing them that Sergeant had helped himself to further compensation by claiming the Company's property at Hubbardston.[4]

Zachariah Mayhew at Martha's Vineyard had had the use of a farm on Gay Head Neck as part of his salary since 1779. He now asked that he might be given a grant and continue in the Company's service; he also asked for grants on behalf of two Indian preachers, Silas Paul and Zachary Hoswit.[5] The Company decided that he should be left in possession of the farm but made no grant.[6] Mayhew wrote to the Company in 1787 asking further assistance and explaining that the Indians contested his title to the property. Two years later he reported that he had been forced to quit the farm altogether and asked the Company to compensate him for his loss. In 1790 he wrote once more and this time he was rewarded with a grant from the Company of £233. 6s. 3d. This he acknowledged in July 1793, at the same time suggesting that the farm at Gay Head should be placed in the hands of the Boston Society for Propagating the Gospel among the Indians and others in North America. This Society (which was a revival of the organization suppressed by the Privy Council in 1762) petitioned the New England Company in November 1793 concerning the Gay Head farm. The petition requested that the Boston Society should recover the land and that the income, reckoned to be £40 per annum, should be used for

[1] Ms. 7956, 20 Sept. 1785.
[2] Ms. 7956, letters from William Codner, 5 Feb., 29 March 1786.
[3] Ms. 7920/1, p. 80.
[4] Ms. 7956, 16 Feb. 1788.
[5] Ms. 7956, 26 Dec. 1786.
[6] Ms. 7920/1, p. 89.

educating Indian children and as an allowance for Zachariah Mayhew himself; if something were not done quickly those holding the farm would gain the title to it by possession. The Company promised the Boston Society that it would investigate the matter and this it did, although apparently no further action was taken.[1] Nevertheless the Boston Society took over the support, not only of Zachariah Mayhew, but also of Gideon Hawley and John Sergeant.

In September 1795 the Company heard that Stephen Badger, the minister at Natick, was taking legal proceedings against it. William Lane considered that a defence should be offered against 'such an impudent Fellow' as, if he were successful, he might well bring the Company into disrepute. In 1796 the case was carried by demurrer to the Supreme Court of Massachusetts but news reached London in October of the following year that the action was terminated: 'the attorney for Badger, upon opening our evidence to the court was by them compelled to become non-suit.'[2] This unhappy incident was the Company's last contact with its New England missionaries.

For more than one hundred and twenty years the Company had sent its small annual income to New England and during these years had done its best to ensure that the money was wisely spent. In many respects it was time that its funds should be spent elsewhere, for the Indians in New England were rapidly diminishing in numbers while there were wide mission fields in Canada which lay untilled. It is in these fields that the oldest extant Protestant missionary company is still at work today.[3]

[1] All the Mayhew letters, the Boston Society's petition, 30 Nov. 1793, together with letters reporting upon the state of the Company's property are contained in Ms. 7956. M.H.S. Ms., Benjamin Way to President of the Boston Society, 28 April 1794. C. E. Banks in *The History of Martha's Vineyard*, II, 13–14 says that no attempt was made to recover Gay Head after the Revolution and that it passed into the hands of the Commonwealth of Massachusetts.

[2] Ms. 7956, John Callender to William Lane, 21 Oct. 1797.

[3] Some information concerning the Company's later history may be found in *History of the New England Company from its incorporation . . . to the present* (Privately printed, 1871) and H. W. Busk's *A sketch of the origin and recent history of the New England Company* (1884).

LIST OF MANUSCRIPT SOURCES

(a) *Records of the New England Company*

BODLEIAN LIBRARY, OXFORD

Ms. Rawlinson C934. Letters and papers, 1649–56.

A considerable portion of this manuscript was published by G. D. Scull in *N.E.H.G.R.*, XXXVI (1882), 62–70, 157–60, 291–9, 371–6; XXXVII (1883), 392–6; XXXIX (1885), 179–182.

GUILDHALL LIBRARY

Ms. 7908. Charter, 7 February 1661/2.

Ms. 7911. Treasurers' general account books, 1660–1764. 3 vol.

Ms. 7912/1–2. Treasurers' ledgers, 1726–1801. 2 vol.

Ms. 7913/1. Treasurers' journal, 1764–1801.

Ms. 7914. Treasurers' rough ledger, 1748–65.

Ms. 7915. Treasurers' rough journal, 1765–1801.

Ms. 7918. Treasurers' pocket ledger, 1709–20.

Ms. 7919. Clerk's rough account book, 1763–87.

Ms. 7920/1. General court and committee minute book, 1770–1816.

Ms. 7927. Letter book, 1762–72.

For preceding vol., *see below*: University of Virginia.

Ms. 7930. Clerk's pocket note book (1692–1728), compiled *c.* 1721–8.

Ms. 7931. Copy opinions relating to the administration of Company trusts, 1786–7.

Ms. 7933. Printed pamphlets, including: *Rules and Orders respecting the Charity . . . of . . . Robert Boyle* and *The Substance of a Speech . . .* by Israel Mauduit, 1785.

Ms. 7936. Original correspondence, 1657–1711/12, and Experience Mayhew's journals for 1713 and 1714.

The contents of this collection were printed under the title: *Some Correspondence between the Governors and Treasurers of the New England Company in London and the Commissioners of the United Colonies in America* (1897).

Ms. 7942. Lists of governors, treasurers and members, 1668, 1741–1859.

Ms. 7943. Return of moneys received and disbursed, made to the Council of State, 11 January 1655/6.

This was printed by W. Kellaway in 'The Collection for the Indians of New England, 1649–1660', *Bulletin of the John Rylands Library*, **39**, 444–62.

Ms. 7944. Treasurers' general accounts, 1659–84. 4 pts.

Ms. 7945. Miscellaneous accounts, 1649–1728. 1 file.

Ms. 7946. Commissioners' accounts, 1657–1731. 2 files.

Ms. 7947. Bills of lading, 1651–2, 1708. 1 file.

Ms. 7948. Bills of exchange and receipts, 1682–1727. 1 file.

Ms. 7949. Bonds for payment of moneys borrowed by the Company, 1711.

Ms. 7950. Miscellaneous vouchers and receipts, 1664–1751. 1 file.

Ms. 7952. Loose court minutes, 1655–1816. 1 box.

Ms. 7953. Commissioners' minutes, 1699–1784. 1 file.

Ms. 7955. Correspondence from New England (mainly from the Commissioners), 1677–1761. 2 files.

Ms. 7956. General correspondence, 1664–1818. 1 box.

Ms. 7957. Papers relating to the Indians, 1669–1727. 1 file.

Ms. 7960. Catalogue of books in the library of Harvard College, *c.* 1764.

Ms. 7961. Vote of thanks from the Overseers of Harvard College for an additional grant towards the Library, 1 October 1765; with a list of books presented to the Library, *c.* 1770.

Ms. 7962. Inventories of the Company's property and effects in New England, 1707/8, 1714. 1 file.

Ms. 7964. Legal papers relating to the territorial limitations of the charter, 1786–1836. 1 file.

Ms. 7967. Papers relating to William Pennoyer's charity, 1670–1902. 1 file.

Ms. 8000. Muniments of title — documents relating to property at Aston, co. Hereford. 1669–91. 1 file.

Ms. 8002. Muniments of title — indenture tripartite relating to Boyle's charity, 30 Aug. 1695.

Ms. 8003 } Muniments of title — deeds, etc. relating to Martha's
Ms. 8004 } Vineyard, 1671–1730. 2 files.

Ms. 8009. Sundry accounts, *c.* 1700–1839. 1 file.

Ms. 8010. Miscellaneous papers, 1706–1806. 1 file.

MASSACHUSETTS HISTORICAL SOCIETY

Accounts, 1653–64.

Minutes, 1655/6 — 1685/6.

The Minutes were printed by G. P. Winship in *The New England Company of 1649 and John Eliot* (Boston, Mass., Prince Society, 1920). A photostat of the manuscript is available in the Guildhall Library.

Letters:

John Stoddard to John H. Lydius, 9 March 1746/7.

John H. Lydius to John Stoddard, 26 March and 5 May 1747.

Jasper Mauduit to Andrew Oliver, 28 April 1758.

Andrew Oliver to Eleazar Wheelock, 11 November 1767.

'A friend' to Jasper Mauduit, 30 November 1769.

Alexander Champion to Isaac Smith, 8 April 1777, with a copy of a letter of 23 November 1775.

Isaac Smith to Isaac Smith, junior, 10 February 1778.

Isaac Smith to William Bowden, 18 January 1781.

William Lane to Gideon Hawley, 1 June 1783.

William Lane to Isaac Smith, 5 June 1787.

Benjamin Way to Isaac Smith, 28 April 1794.

Jacob Johnson's account of the Indians at Groton, 20 June 1755 (addressed to Andrew Oliver).

Sundry Indian petitions.

Commission, 1764.

UNIVERSITY OF VIRGINIA, CHARLOTTESVILLE

Alderman Library (Tracy W. McGregor Library)

Letter book, 1688–1761.

(*b*) *Other manuscripts consulted*

DR. WILLIAMS'S LIBRARY, LONDON

Richard Baxter's Letters. 6 vol.

Baxter's correspondence with Woodbridge was published by R. P. Stearns in *New England Quarterly*, **10** (1937), 557–83. His correspondence with Eliot was published by F. J. Powicke in *Bulletin of the John Rylands Library*, **15** (1931), 138–76, 422–66.

Dr. Williams's Trustees; Minutes, 1716–86. 14 vol. Committee minutes, 1721–7. 3 vol.

H.M. GENERAL REGISTER HOUSE, EDINBURGH

Society in Scotland for Propagating Christian Knowledge:

Minutes, 1709–95. 5 vol.

Committee minutes, 1709–83. 9 vol.

General ledger, 1709–79.

ROYAL SOCIETY OF LONDON

Robert Boyle's Letters and Papers:

Letters, 7 vol.

Papers: Theology, vol. 4. Miscellaneous, vols. 35, 40.

The correspondence between Boyle and Eliot contained in this collection was printed in *The Works of . . . Robert Boyle* (1772), I, ccv–ccxiv; VI, 509–10.

SOCIETY FOR THE PROPAGATION OF THE GOSPEL IN FOREIGN PARTS

Journal, I–, 1701–

New England Letters (B22).

Occasional references were also found in: Bodleian Library, Ms. Clarendon 74; British Museum, Egerton Ms. 2395 and Add. Ms.4228; Corporation of London, Records Office, Repertories of the Court of Aldermen, **60–61**, 1649–51; Lambeth Palace Library, Fulham Palace MSS., American papers (Massachusetts) and Ms. 1123/1; Public Record Office, Proceedings in Chancery; Sion College, London Provincial Assembly Record Book, 1648–60; Society for Promoting Christian Knowledge, New England Letter book, 1721–3 (CN 3/1); Somerset House, Prerogative Court of Canterbury, Wills.

INDEX

The names of all members of the New England Company elected before 1776 and of all Commissioners appointed before that date have been included in this index whether they appear in the text or not. The following abbreviations precede the date of election or appointment:

SM Member of the Society
M Member of the Company
C Commissioner for Indian Affairs, appointed by the Company (Commissioners of the United Colonies have only been included when they appear in the text)
* Denotes the first mention of the name in the records when the date of election is unknown

Englishmen employed to preach to the Indians, even if only for a short period, are here described as missionaries. Individual Indians have usually been entered under their forenames.

Index